Wife SCHOOL Study Guide

Wife SCHOOL Study Guide

A 22 WEEK STUDY

Julie N. Gordon
MS, Marriage and Family Counseling

Copyright © 2021 Julie N. Gordon

All rights reserved. This book or any portion thereof may not be reproduced or used in any manner whatsoever without the express written permission of the publisher except for the use of brief quotations in a book review.

ISBN: 978-0-578-89580-2 (print)

Cover design by Lorie DeWorken. Illustration by Sonu Pawan.

Printed in the United States of America.

Dedication

To precious Elaina.
What a gift you are to Stephen and to us.
A wife of noble character who can find? She is worth far more than rubies.
—*Proverbs 31:10*

Other Books by Julie N. Gordon

Wife School, Where Women Learn the Secrets of Making Husbands Happy (2012)

Skinny School, Where Women Learn the Secrets to Finally Get Thin Forever (2015)

Skinny School Study Guide (2021)

Husband School, Where Men Learn the Secrets of Making Wives Happy (co-authored with David Gordon) (2017)

Happy School, Where Women Learn the Secrets to Overcome Discouragement and Worry (2020)

Happy School Study Guide (2021)

Table of Contents

A Note from the Author 1

WEEK 1   The Foundational Principles in *Wife School* 3
       DAY 1: A Longing of Women/Introduction
       DAY 2: Men Hate Emotional Turmoil
       DAY 3: What Exactly Is an Excellent Wife?
       DAY 4: It Isn't Fair That I Have to Do All This Work in the Marriage!
       DAY 5: This Program Is Hard to Do!

WEEK 2   First A: The Acceptance Lesson 15
       DAY 1: Changing Your Emotions
       DAY 2: But My Husband Is Very Difficult!
       DAY 3: A Hidden Expectation to Give Up
       DAY 4: I Don't Feel Loved by My Husband
       DAY 5: Getting Rid of the Resentment in Your Marriage

WEEK 3   Second A: The Admiration Lesson 27
       DAY 1: An Overview of Admiration
       DAY 2: Add Empathetic Listening to Your Admiration
       DAY 3, PART A: Drip Some Honey
       DAY 3, PART B: The Problem with Familiarity
       DAY 4: Praising Other Men
       DAY 5: How Do I Find the Time and Energy to Give a Daily Admiration Moment?

WEEK 4   Third A: The Appreciation Lesson and More… 37
       DAY 1: Good Managers of the Household
       DAY 2: She Can Laugh at the Days to Come, Part A
       DAY 3: She Can Laugh at the Days to Come, Part B
       DAY 4: Asking for What You Want (Just a Sneak Peek)
       DAY 5: A Few Random Tips

WEEK 5   Fourth A: The Attention Lesson 49
       DAY 1: Inattentiveness Sets in after the Wedding
       DAY 2: The Art of Being a Good Conversationalist with Your Husband
       DAY 3: An Effective Way to Show Your Husband Attention: Ask His Opinion!
       DAY 4: An Important Area in Which to Show Great Attention to Your Husband: His Food!
       DAY 5: If You Have a High-Maintenance Hubby

WEEK 6   Fifth A: The Activities Lesson and More… 57
       DAY 1: Thoughts about the A of Activities
       DAY 2: What If You Run Out of Energy to Pour into Your Husband?

DAY 3: Why Is Respecting Your Husband So Important?
DAY 4, PART A: Understanding Men's Tendency to be Inconsiderate
DAY 4, PART B: Beware of Not Feeling Appreciated
DAY 5, PART A: Thoughts about the Clothes of Christian Women
DAY 5, PART B: When Your Husband Wants You to Work Full Time outside the Home

WEEK 7   Sixth A: The Approval Lesson 67
DAY 1: Thoughts about the A of Approval
DAY 2: When Your Husband Is Selfish with His Time
DAY 3: Something Only a Man Can Give to Your Kids
DAY 4, PART A: Understanding Your Need to Release Emotional Tension
DAY 4, PART B: Tips for Traveling with Your Husband
DAY 5: Dealing with Difficult Parents/In-Laws

WEEK 8   Seventh A: The Affection Lesson. 79
DAY 1: More Thoughts about the A of Affection
DAY 2: Bump. It. Up.
DAY 3: When You and Your Husband Disagree about How to Handle Something
DAY 4: The Financial Pressure that Most Men Carry
DAY 5: Give Your Husband Time to Change the Way He Perceives the New You

WEEK 9   Eighth A: The Authority Lesson 89
DAY 1: More Thoughts about the A of Authority
DAY 2: Learning to Make Proper Appeals
DAY 3: The Beauty and Power of Empathy in Marriage
DAY 4: When Your Husband Doesn't Obey Scripture
DAY 5, PART A: If You Are Having Trouble Accepting Your Biblical Role
DAY 5, PART B: A Story to Encourage You to Persevere

WEEK 10   What to Do When Your Husband Fails or Has Adversity…and More 101
DAY 1: What to Do When Your Husband Fails or Has Adversity
DAY 2: Asking for What You Want in Your Marriage
DAY 3: Improving Your Mood
DAY 4, PART A: Another Important List to Start and Keep
DAY 4, PART B: A Fabulous Parenting Resource
DAY 5, PART A: Another Reminder about Expectations in Marriage
DAY 5, PART B: How One Wife Endeavored to Bump. It. Up.

WEEK 11   How to View Your Husband's Work from His Perspective …and More 113
DAY 1: Will My Husband Ever Reciprocate?
DAY 2: A Discussion about Charm, Beauty, and Fearing the Lord
DAY 3: Three Qualities that Predict Addiction
DAY 4: Learn Not to Be Offended
DAY 5, PART A: Another Quick Thought on When Others Fail
DAY 5, PART B: A Tirade on Health

WEEK 12 Regrets, Femininity, In-laws, Contentment… and More 125
    DAY 1: If You Struggle with Regrets
    DAY 2: Your Husband Wants a Womanly Woman
    DAY 3: Are You Causing Turmoil in Your Husband's Family?
    DAY 4: Helping Your Husband Grow Spiritually
    DAY 5, PART A: Beginning Thoughts on Acquiring Contentment
    DAY 5, PART B: When Husbands Let Down Their Guard

WEEK 13 If Your Husband Doesn't Celebrate Your Special Days Well, If You Don't Feel Loved by Your Husband….and More 137
    DAY 1: How Husbands Feel About Your Birthday, Anniversary, and Other Holidays
    DAY 2: Examining the Choices in Educating Your Children
    DAY 3: If You Don't Feel Loved By Your Husband
    DAY 4: Bump. It. Up. Story #2 (And a Word to You 20%-ers)
    DAY 5: A Superior Wife Skill

WEEK 14 Affairs, Feeling Misunderstood, Feeling Mistreated…and More 149
    DAY 1: Safeguarding Against Affairs
    DAY 2: When Your Husband Doesn't Understand You
    DAY 3: When You Have Been Mistreated
    DAY 4, PART A: Talking behind Your Husband's Back
    DAY 4, PART B: Throw Your Husband a Homerun Pitch
    DAY 5: What Makes Wives Happy in the Marriage

WEEK 15 Boredom in Marriage, Contentment, a Happy Heart….and More 161
    DAY 1: If You Are Bored with Your Marriage
    DAY 2: Learning Contentment in Hard Circumstances
    DAY 3: More on Learning to Have a Happy Heart
    DAY 4: The Awfulness of a Despondent Spirit
    DAY 5, PART A: The 2-Day Rule
    DAY 5, PART B: If Your Husband is Not Responding to the 8 A's

WEEK 16 In-laws, Incompatibility, Kids, Disappointment …and More 173
    DAY 1: More on Difficult In-Laws
    DAY 2, PART A: How to Discuss Conflict and Areas of Incompatibility in Your Marriage
    DAY 2, PART B: Yes, Kids Are a Lot of Work (Research That Documents Season 1 and Season 2)
    DAY 3, PART A: The Spiritual Leadership of Your Husband…Revisited
    DAY 3, PART B: Something Husbands Like
    DAY 4: Handling Your "Disappointing Thing"
    DAY 5, PART A: A Difficult but Necessary Discipline to Master
    DAY 5, PART B: Are You Having Difficulty with Your Faith and Subsequently, Your Role as a Woman?

WEEK 17 Flirting, Hospitality, Discouragement, Aging…and More 185
    DAY 1: Is a Little Flirting with Other Men Harmless?
    DAY 2: The Lost Art of Hospitality
    DAY 3: What Is A Life Well-Lived for a Woman?

  DAY 4: Conquering Discouraging Thinking
  DAY 5: Losses Accumulate with Age

WEEK 18 Giving Your Input, a Happy Heart, A Test…and More 199
  DAY 1: Two of the Most Important Wife Skills
  DAY 2, PART A: How to Give Your Husband Your Input
  DAY 2, PART B: When You Are Grieved by Your Husband's Lack of Spirituality
  DAY 3: The Advanced Wife Skill of Communicating Contentment
  DAY 4: More on a Happy Heart
  DAY 5: Are You a Marriage Champion Yet? A Test to See.

WEEK 19 Conflict, a Bossy Husband, Disappointment in Others…and More 209
  DAY 1: Celebrating Your Husband's Victories with Him
  DAY 2: Getting Hold of Your Emotions When You Have Conflict
  DAY 3: What to Do When Your Husband is Bossy and Inconsiderate of Your Opinion, Part 1
  DAY 4: What to Do When Your Husband is Bossy and Inconsiderate of Your Opinion, Part 2
  DAY 5: Cynicism and the Continual Disappointment in Others

WEEK 20 A Happy Heart, Alcohol, Parenting…and More 219
  DAY 1: A Relationship Skill that Grows a Happy Heart
  DAY 2: Drinking Alcohol
  DAY 3: Important Parenting Concept #1
  DAY 4: Important Parenting Concept #2
  DAY 5: Handling Your Husband's Sin Nature

WEEK 21 Ex-wives, Bad Circumstances, Discontentment…and More 229
  DAY 1: Thoughts on Ex-Wives and Stepchildren
  DAY 2: When Your Husband's Ideas are Not-So-Great
  DAY 3: When You Don't Like Your Circumstances
  DAY 4: For Those of You with a Non-Cinderella Disposition
  DAY 5: If You Are Still Often Getting Upset with Your Husband

WEEK 22 Loneliness, Church, Impact on Children…and More 239
  DAY 1: Struggling With Loneliness
  DAY 2: A Very Important Sentence to Frequently Say to Your Husband
  DAY 3: The Importance of Church in Your Family
  DAY 4: The Impact You Have on Your Children and Grandchildren
  DAY 5: Spend Time to Learn and Grow

Epilogue 249

TURQUOISE JOURNAL LISTS 251

LIST 1: Strengths, Gifts, and Qualities I Admire in My Husband
LIST 2: Things Other Husbands Do Wrong
LIST 3: Unmet Expectations I Have of My Husband
LIST 4: Nice Things My Husband Says or Does
LIST 5: Things My Husband Might Find Difficult to Accept in Me
LIST 6: 100 Things I Appreciate about My Husband
LIST 7: Activities My Husband and I Might Enjoy Together
LIST 8: My 8 Top Concerns/When to Use My Appeal Coupons

A Note from the Author

All athletic organizations know that one must *repeatedly* practice skills to acquire mastery. That is why there are twenty-two lessons in the *Wife School Study Guide,* so you can practice and become a Marriage Champion. There are few things in life you care more about than your marriage. Take the time to become an expert in this area.

Although many of these articles are not what our current culture believes, they work because they are based on Biblical principles. "The grass withers and the flowers fall, but the word of the Lord endures forever" (1 Peter 1: 24-25).

The best way to do this study is to meet with some friends after each week's lesson and discuss your answers to the group questions. Discussing the material with others *increases learning exponentially* (iron sharpens iron). After you have gone through the 22 weeks of lessons, consider taking a few other wives through the material. The best learning happens with repetition, and the very best way to learn anything is to *teach* it.

Just a reminder: If you are meeting with a group to discuss *Wife School,* please do not share anything negative about your husband. The rule is to pretend your husband is present, listening in. (That's how you would want him to treat you, right?) If you need to discuss a negative issue about your husband, please talk confidentially to a wise, older, godly woman or to a counselor.

Many of the lessons in the *Wife School Study Guide* were written during the few months after *Wife School* was first published in order to give further practical biblical advice to wives. Originally, many of these articles were online lessons and entitled *Wife School Online.* They have been revised and updated.

Prepare to master the art of being a wife!

Warmly and in Christ,
Julie Gordon
April 2021

WEEK 1

The Foundational Principles in *Wife School*

Contents

Day 1: A Longing of Women/Introduction
Day 2: Men Hate Emotional Turmoil
Day 3: What Exactly Is an Excellent Wife?
Day 4: It Isn't Fair I Have to Do All the Work in This Marriage!
Day 5: This Program Is Hard to Do!

Ever since Genesis 3, women have desired to rule over, boss, and change their husbands. When you ask a woman how she would like to change her husband, her answer is often, "Let me count the ways."

But as Christians, we are not to follow our natural fallen inclinations. We are to follow God's Word, as it was written for our benefit and happiness. Fools think they can figure out life on their own; wise people know that the Creator has written a handbook for living and then they study to learn the secrets.

Your marriage may be a mess now, but with months (and oh my, with years!) of living the *Wife School* principles, your marriage will sing. How happy to come to the end of life and to have enjoyed a happy, close, intimate marriage.

Men are the same as they were six thousand years ago. Learn how men think, what they want, and then, *give it to them*. That will turn them towards you and *then* they will be being willing to hear what it is *you think and want*. It's a slow system, but a *successful* one. It's the only system that I've ever discovered that wins and keeps the hearts of husbands, and I've been searching for marriage secrets for almost 40 years.

Please read chapter 1 in *Wife School, Where Women Learn the Secrets of Making Husbands Happy* before you read this week's lessons in the study guide.

*_Wife School_ was not written for couples struggling with alcoholism, drug abuse, infidelity, or physical abuse. Please get professional help if your husband has any of those issues.

DAY 1
A Longing of Women/Introduction

On page 8 in the first chapter of _Wife School_, Jessica says, "I only want a few things from this short time on Earth and one of them is a soulmate marriage." That's true for you, too, isn't it? It certainly is true of me.

Would you like to hear what a man, still captured by his wife's love, once said to her? In this very old love story, the husband is talking to his wife during their later years. He says to her, "Many (wives) have done nobly, but you excel them all." Do you know what that is equal to in today's language? That's as if your husband is saying to you, "There are a lot of awesome women out there, honey, but you are the best of the best." Can you imagine your husband being so _taken with you_ that although he acknowledges there are many fabulous wives, _you_ win first prize in the wife contest?

Now, I didn't make up this example. This comes right out of Scripture, Proverbs 31. This isn't some made-for-TV script to stir you up. This is the Word of God. God knows we women long for our husbands to adore us, and he gives us the secrets.

This carrot in Scripture is not dangled out there so we can be frustrated. God left that sentence in Proverbs 31 to show us that marriage _doesn't have to unzip_. Marriage can be incredible in your younger years and also can be a huge source of comfort and delight in your later years.

Marriage is not what you read in the magazines at the checkout lane in the grocery store. We will learn the skills and thoughts needed for a soul-stirring marriage. You will be a Marriage Champion when this course is over.

I'm so glad God didn't leave us in the dark as far as how to be an incredible wife. The Scripture pours out information on how to excel at this art. It loudly and clearly tells us what to do and how to think. We have access to the mind of God about being a wife! We don't have to hope we get this right. We _can_ get it right. We have the key to the Treasure Room with all the gems and jewels of knowledge and wisdom—the Bible!

What we will learn in _Wife School_ and in this study guide are the skills and mind-set needed to make a husband happy, the very oxygen he needs so he feels satisfied in his relationship with you. With consistent deposits of the 8 A's, your husband will develop affection for you and will turn and open toward your influence. When a woman begins to speak to her husband in a language that he can understand, the results are truly miraculous. Marriages flip-flop even when they were previously in trouble.

A wise wife looks at what she is _giving_, not at what she is _getting_. A wise wife looks at how she _is loving others_, _not at how she is being loved_. (1 Cor. 13:4–5: "Love is not self-seeking.") We women must look at the biblical standard of being a wife, not the culture's.

Many women come into the study of _Wife School_ thinking, "Something is wrong with my marriage because it is not naturally and easily a soulmate marriage." Friends, the norm is that marriage has tension. _The norm_! You must learn to be a wise wife and soothe the ruffled feathers of your marriage. You are the relational one (well, 80 percent of you are which we will discuss in another lesson). Take the time and energy to truly learn the art and skills of being an incredible wife. I've said before you have to study to master algebra. You take tennis lessons to get your backhand just right. But most women never invest the time to truly learn what men want and need in a marriage. Even if you are greatly disappointed with your marriage at this moment, try to put that disappointment on a shelf and give yourself to learning these principles. Marriage is a course to be learned and mastered, and that is what you are now doing.

One important word of caution. A farmer sows the seed in the spring. Then all summer in the blazing heat, he waters, weeds, and fertilizes. Months pass and there is no fruit. He sows the seed but doesn't expect to reap until fall, right? Please put on this mind-set. As you learn to love your husband in a language he can hear, the soil of his heart is being plowed. But it may take weeks or even months for him to respond. You are on the fifty-year plan. Many women who were disappointed (or even disgusted) with their marriages now have marriages overflowing with affection, friendship, and closeness. Lay down your expectations to have the marriage turn around quickly.

I detest exercise/weight loss programs that lie and say, "Do this, and in no time, you will be skinny and hard." Ridiculous. It is weeks/months of eating clean and exercising. Please get a long-road perspective on your marriage. Your marriage can turn around, but you must persevere for the long haul.

A study in a magazine recently polled men and found out what they think about 90 percent of the time. Here is the breakdown: 30 percent work, 30 percent money, and 30 percent sex. Where are relationships in that mixture? They are not there. Women are the ones thinking about relationships. Your husband is not a woman. Do not beat him up because he is not geared to care about emotional intimacy. You have to meet his needs and get him to *want* to listen to you and *want* to hear what you want and need. Women beat men up all the time because men do not give them enough relationship, care, and love. The poor guy doesn't even know what his wife is talking about. *That's not what he wants.* Let's give hubby a pass while we learn to love him and meet his needs. *In time,* he will turn to you. But not today. And not tomorrow.

DAY 2
Men Hate Emotional Turmoil

The emphasis today will be the emotional turmoil that we women bring into the marriage. On page 7, Jessica unloads the artillery on Matthew. "It's sad, that's all I can say, Matthew. It's really sad and pathetic." And she slams the door.

The truth is that men *hate* emotional turmoil. It *is one of the few things that husbands cannot tolerate for long.* Somehow, we were fed this lie that we need to say *whatever* we're genuinely thinking in marriage, and if we are unhappy with him, then let it rip! We think our husbands owe it to us to put up with our moods. That's so wrong! When we bring emotional turmoil into their lives, they lose affection for us.

Do you want your husband to want to escape from you? Do you want your husband not to like being around you? Solomon gives an exact prescription on how to drain the affection of a husband and make him want to escape. He says, "Better to live on a corner of the roof than share a house with a quarrelsome wife" (Prov. 25:24). Men hate emotional turmoil.

Women express emotional turmoil in marriage in different ways. Some women get angry and slam doors (Jessica). Some women use a sarcastic tone and quietly slice with their tongues. Some women give men the silent treatment, hoping the husband will shape up because mama ain't happy.

If you are creating emotional turmoil in your house, you are sucking the affection right out of your husband. Yes, he may shape up to make you happier at the moment, but you have lost in the long run because *his true affection for you just diminished.*

"Death and life are in the power of the tongue" (Prov. 18:21). Did you read that? Death and life? That's some pretty serious stuff, death and life. So we had better get control of our tongues and the emotional turmoil that we bring into the marriage. I have said this many times before, but most men are satisfied in the marriage if they get enough sex and there is *not* too much emotional turmoil. He hates your PMS-ing. He hates your emotional, hysterical, and sarcastic escalation. Honestly, your husband is more vulnerable to other women when you act like this. Give up feeling that you have the right to emotional escalation if you're upset. (We will discuss in detail how to communicate wisely when you are upset as we progress, but know for now to get hold of your tongue.)

We all have some skeletons in our closets from moments of which we are ashamed. Don't waste time with regrets. Pull the curtain down, and leave your mistakes in the past. One of my favorite verses in Scripture is when Paul says, "Forgetting what is behind and straining toward what is ahead" (Phil. 3:13). We all have regrets, but they are helpful only if they help us change. The enemy wants us to brood over the past. Draw a line in the sand. It is the past. We will now move on.

An opposite example of the woman whose husband wants to escape because of his wife's emotional turmoil is a character in *Toilers of the Sea* by Victor Hugo. Hugo writes, "Her presence lights the home; her approach is like a cheerful warmth; she passes by, and we are content; she stays awhile and we are happy." We all know these women who light up the room just by entering it. My hope is that each of you becomes this woman.

You can't buy this disposition on Amazon or in T. J. Maxx. You must pay the price by soaking your heart in Scripture and in prayer.

One thing you can count on for the rest of your marriage is that your husband will do things that you don't necessarily agree with (or like). Did you hear that? *You should expect* that he won't handle you, the kids, your finances, your friends, the church, his business, etc., *exactly the way you want him to.* It's coming. When you realize that *all* marriages are like this, *that spouses do things that disappoint,* you realize the importance of learning how to react wisely instead of unloading your emotional turmoil.

Remember the verse in Proverbs 14 that says, "The wise woman builds her house?" This is exactly what that verse is talking about. The wise woman builds her house by having self-control with her tongue and learning how to react/respond well (future lessons). The norm in marriages is that when the husband messes up, the wife, not having been trained, has a meltdown (or she chooses one of her other go-to responses, such as criticism, sulking, or the cold shoulder.) We are going to learn many great responses to when your husband gives you a *pie in the face,* but unloading the artillery is not one of them. Paul lists *self-control* in the short Titus 2 list for wives. Yes, you have the freedom to act and say exactly how you feel, but if it results in emotional turmoil in your home, you will pay the price of losing your husband's affection.

DAY 3
What Exactly Is an Excellent Wife?

There are many aspects to being an excellent wife that Proverbs 31:10–31 addresses. But today, we will discuss only the beginning sentences of this passage.

To begin with, King Lemuel's mother, from whom Proverbs 31 is derived, talks about how *difficult* it is even to *find* an excellent woman. The king's mother is certainly not talking about an *average* wife. No, this excellent wife is *rare*. She is in a small category of superior wives, rated very high, far above expensive jewelry. You can't find these uncommon wives easily.

Here's the first thing King Lemuel's mother says about the excellent wife. Ready? "Her husband has full confidence in her and lacks nothing of value. She brings him good, not harm, all the days of her life." Those little sentences are loaded with insight for us. In fact, those two sentences say more about an excellent wife than any other two sentences on marriage I've ever seen.

Read them slowly, and comb through them. The husband has full confidence in his wife to do what? To do him good! To choose the thing that would benefit him! Why, in 1 Corinthians 11:9, we are told the woman was created for the man. Dad gum, we hate that verse. Because if that verse is true, then we have to realize that maybe we seriously need to think about how to make our husbands happy and successful.

Can you say your husband has full confidence in you in every situation? Does he know that you are going to choose wisely for his benefit? Does he feel he lacks nothing because of you? One translation says, "he will have no lack of gain." Why? Because he has a wife who is in his corner, always looking out for his comfort, success, and happiness. See why she's rare? See why her worth is far above gems and jewels? This is not your average little cutie-pie in yoga tights. No, this is a woman who is hard to find. Scarce. Extraordinary.

Can you imagine how a husband would feel toward a wife who had his back like this or who was always thinking about his benefit? No wonder he exclaims later in life (as the husband did in Proverbs 31), "Baby, you are the most unbelievable woman on the face of the earth!" (Uh, sorry, maybe I took a few liberties in that translation. But then again, maybe not.)

An excellent wife buoys up a husband. She fills in where necessary and helps make him successful and happy, no matter what. Men have car accidents and lose their legs. Men have health issues and can't work. Men lose their jobs and get depressed. This is life and, obviously, not the pretty side. When your husband has hard times (and he will), that is the time you rise. That is the time you find your strength in prayer, and you get full at the Well so you can pour refreshing water on his wounds. No woman wants these trials. But an excellent wife, a wife of noble character, *does him good all the days of his life,* not just the days when there's health, wealth, and happiness.

Don't fall prey to self-pity and start stomping your foot, saying how much you give and that no one is taking care of you. This is the path of blessing to you. When you treat your husband like this, his affections grow and quadruple for you. God created woman so that nothing on Earth is more satisfying to her than a husband who delights in her. Not her children. Not a size 2 figure. Not a big bank account. There is nothing on earth that replaces or equals a husband's true devotion and affection toward you.

But we don't want to do the work to win a husband's devotion. The truth is, we want to be beautiful and alluring and have him want to serve us—without us serving him. That is only in the movies, friends. Women who have their husbands' love after twenty/thirty/forty years of marriage have earned their love by *doing them good all the days of their life.*

This is so like God. He tells us to lose our lives so that we find them (Luke 17:33). This same principle works in marriage. When you start to treat your husband like the Proverbs 31 woman did—the rare, uncommon, extraordinary woman who seeks to make her husband happy regardless of how he is treating her at the moment—you eventually reap your husband's affection and entry into his heart.

Wives say to me all the time, "I don't want to love him like that." Since when is that how we live our lives? If your baby cries and you're tired, do you still get up and take care of the baby? We choose to do the right thing because that is *who we choose to be.* We choose to be virtuous. We choose to keep our vows. We choose to return good for evil, because that's the kind of Christ follower we want to be. Not a whiny, lukewarm, self-pitying small clot of dirt. We do our husbands good, not harm, all the days of their lives, because that's the kind of woman we know we are to be. It's a choice to be valuable, rare, and uncommon.

I can tell within a few minutes of talking to a woman if she is a *self-pitying, woe-is-me, life-is-hard, life-is-unfair, they-treat-me-wrong* kind of person. These women wear you out. They suck the life out of you. Decide you will *not* be this woman. Rise. Pull on the Lord and rise. You can't always choose your circumstances, but you can always choose *how you respond.* You can respond with humility, love, support, kindness, self-control, meekness, and goodness. That's what an excellent wife does. That's what a wife of noble character does. She is different. She is not the weak, whiny norm. Do you see diamonds, rubies, or emeralds loosely lying around? No, they are valuable and rare. They are desired and adored. You get to choose whether this is the kind of woman you are going to be. Or instead, are you going to be the norm—a self-pitying, complaining wad of estrogen?

This is not about *if* your husband deserves this treatment. No husband deserves this treatment. This is about you being the kind of wife who God wants you to be. This is about who *you* are, not about your husband. Husbands get in messes. When women can give and love (and get their own needs met in the Lord), the husband's knots are often untangled. I know you want your husband to be perfect and to take care of you. But husbands fall in ditches and need help. When you can rise with an inner beauty and an inner strength and love this man, accept this man, and build up this man when he is low, he will never forget it.

I love the story of a man who lost his job and had to move his family to a little house, leaving a big, beautiful house behind. The man felt very guilty and upset with himself, feeling like a total failure. He came home, discouraged from another unsuccessful day of trying to secure a job, and the wife met him on the driveway. Instead of demanding, "Well, buddy, did you find a job?" she met him with a full, happy heart. "Honey, the wild flowers are beautiful in the woods behind this house. I picked some for our dinner table. Come in, and let me give you a massage and get you some hot tea and a bath. Then, you can tell me about your day." The man said he wanted to cry. How could this woman love him and have such a happy heart when he was such a failure? Women, we have a call to buoy up our men. That's one way a wise woman builds her house (Prov. 14:1). It is our call to do what it takes to fill their tanks. We were created for them, not them for us. You are a gift from God to your husband, to do him good all the days of his life. Especially you are called to fill his tank when he's down, when life is kicking him. You have to rise and deposit the 8 A's. You have to accept that his trial is God's invitation to you to step up to love and give to him without anyone loving or giving to you. If you are empty, then as I said, drink at the Well, eat at the banquet table of the Lord, and take responsibility to find God's peace and filling for yourself with Him. Psalm 23:5 says, "You prepare a table before me in the presence of my enemies."

It's easy to love when there's money, health, vitality, and well-being. But you show your true colors when the bottom falls out. That's when we see who is an excellent wife, a woman of worth, a woman of virtue. This woman buoys up her husband in whatever way she can to help him be successful. She takes responsibility for her own needs, not blaming her husband. If he gives her love or benefits, she sees that as extras, as a bonus. Living *without expectations* from your husband is the most freeing thing you can do. Because then, all his many gifts are appreciated. Since you have no expectations, you are delighted with *what he gives you.*

How different this is from having a list of unmet expectations and being angry all the time. Yes, maybe he's got some huge issues that eventually need to be dealt with (and we will deal with them in these 22 lessons). But with months and years of this kind of devotion from you, you will see incredible healing in your husband.

DAY 4
It Isn't Fair That I Have to Do All This Work in the Marriage!

I cannot tell you how often I hear this lamentation from women: "Why do I have to go first? Shouldn't we both work on the marriage simultaneously?" or "Why do I have to learn all these skills and pour into him? When are my needs going to be met?"

I will repeat myself on this issue over and over again because as we come out of wandering in the desert, we have to be reminded and re-reminded of truth. That truth is that our husbands have no idea that we want a lot of emotional intimacy, conversation, and deep sharing. Husbands think about money, work, and sex. The pressure they feel to support the family is gigantic, and relationships are barely on their radar. They think they are loving you by bringing home their paycheck and by being sexually faithful. You are beating your husband up for not admiring you, not listening to you, and not *having enough deep conversation* with you. But he has no idea what you want or how to give it to you. Yes, you tell him, and he still doesn't have a clue. You tell him again, he still doesn't get it, and then you cry. He proceeds to think, "Oh my, what have I done, getting myself in this marriage with this temperamental woman? How can I escape?" (He might be nice while you're crying, but this is what he's thinking.)

Women cry mainly to manipulate their husbands. They are trying to say, "You don't love me well, and I am sad about that. I will cry so you will pay more attention to me." Women, this works in marriage for a few months or maybe a couple of years. But guess what? He gets used to you crying, and it becomes like any other background noise, and he can ignore you and your tears. David said I cried every Saturday the first year we were married. (Although I had a master's degree in marriage and family counseling, I was still a numbskull about men and loving them.) Why did I cry every Saturday? I wanted him to love me more, build me up more, and romance me more. In my small mind, my personal Disney movie was not supposed to be over yet. But after marriage, men begin to seriously think about supporting a wife, about paying taxes, about insurance, and so on. They are not schooled in how to *love you in a language you can hear* and they certainly don't understand what you want or need. After the wedding, men see little need for romance and deep conversation. Instead, *what they enjoy is doing activities together and sex.*

This is the norm in marriage, but *you are no longer the norm.* You are finding a way to express love to your husband in a language he can hear (the 8 A's). Then, you are going to learn to teach him a new language—one that he doesn't understand right now, the language of *how you feel as a woman.* But again, not yet! Can you imagine going to work at a new office and telling the boss the first week that you want the corner office? No, you work there a while, show the boss what an amazing employee you are, and then you ask for what you want and need after he sees *how indispensable you are.* Love your husband to the moon, and then we'll soon discuss asking for what you want.

You and I can stomp our feet. We can throw mud balls at heaven. We can yell and scream and have a hissy fit. But we won't change the fact that men don't get us and that we have to win them and win their hearts, making them turn toward us and open to us, *wanting* to learn to love *us* in a language *we* can hear. You can't take the stripes off a tiger, and you can't change the way men are created. You decide to say you will accept *what is.*

At some point, wisdom enters our heart, and we say, "OK, I will play by these rules." If I had written the rules, I would not have written them like this. But I wasn't in on the Holy Trinity huddle when these rules were written. I realize that if I jump out of a nine story window, the rule of gravity will win. Likewise, these rules of filling my husband with the 8 A's to turn his heart to me are not negotiable. Demanding he love me in the way I want doesn't work any better than jumping out of a building and flapping my arms. I will quit complaining about the rules and start filling his tank.

I know some of you have some difficult and unreasonable husbands. But remember, they are *annoying, not evil.* Granted, they have some wrong thinking and some wrong priorities. But again, when you fill them with the 8 A's, over time, they open to your influence. If your husband has some really selfish, wrong priorities, tell yourself that you are going to give this a full year. A year is ridiculous by most standards (women want results by next weekend). But give it a full year of living *Wife School* principles and learning the advanced skills in this study guide. Give your marriage a year of pouring and pouring into him. Eventually, gently ask him to move toward a better use of time/resources. No head bashing. No meltdowns. Just sweet requests and more filling with the 8 A's. A man has no choice but to move toward his wife when she is consistently loving him by pouring in the 8 A's.

DAY 5
This Program Is Hard to Do!

Repeatedly, I hear from women, "Giving my husband the 8 A's is so *hard.*"

No, what is *hard* is not living like this. Let me explain.

I recently went on a six-hour car trip by myself. I listened to a CD series by Robert Rohm on the book of Proverbs. He talks for thirty minutes on each Proverb. For six steady hours, I listened to about ten or eleven of the talks. At the end of my trip, do you know what stood out from those six hours of being immersed in Proverbs thinking? It is simple but profound. Over and over again, the Proverbs teach (in different words and different examples) this thought: *the way of the righteous has one set of consequences, and the way of the wicked has another.* That's the theme of Proverbs. One path in life produces certain consequences. Live another way, and end up with another set of circumstances (for example, read Prov. 13:15). The choices we make largely determine our circumstances.

If you watch a foolish woman, you will see that she tries to live exactly as she wants, choose what feels good at the moment, and *still* get good results. That is so ludicrous. That's as if saying, "I am going to eat a diet of sweets and starches and be thin." Ridiculous. To get the *prize* we want (a great marriage), we pay the *price* of living a certain way. At some point, wisdom teaches us that if we want to reap certain consequences (a great marriage), *we are going to have to make some choices that might be difficult or uncomfortable in the moment.* When wisdom enters our hearts, we realize giving our husbands the 8 A's is *not* hard. What's hard is being in a marriage where there is *not* kindness, thoughtfulness, or closeness. What's hard is having your husband's heart somewhere besides being turned and open to you. That's what's hard, *not giving* the 8 A's. Yes, the enemy tries to tell us we can live as we want in the moment (Gen. 3 is the first example of this), but wisdom and experience tell us otherwise.

Closing Comments

Women are not given the sole responsibility for growing the marriage in Scripture, and neither are men. But what is true is that the only person you can change is yourself. (In *Husband School, Where Men Learn the Secrets of Making Wives Happy,* David and I tell husbands that they are the only person they can change.) Hitting men over the head with their inadequacy of being a proper leader, husband, or father has never changed men but temporarily. Men can learn from sermons, from other men, and from Scripture. But few men will take instruction by their browbeating wives. They usually return to their prior behavior. The only thing that changes men is when they *want* to change, and the 8 A's make men *want* to change.

Even later when we learn to ask for what we want, we still *lay down the expectations that they will do it.* We ask but don't demand. It's tricky stuff, for sure. But isn't that how we are to approach God? We ask but don't demand? We will spend time dissecting this issue in the future.

Prayer

Lord,

You know how disappointed I've been in my marriage. I'm going to have to hold onto You while I learn the principles in the 8 A's. It all sounds a little much, to be honest.

I pray as the psalmist in Psalm 63: "You, God, are my God, earnestly I seek you; I thirst for you, my whole being longs for you, *in a dry and parched land where there is no water.*" It's certainly a dry and parched land in my marriage, Lord. You know that. I know that. I'd like you to change that, please.

I confess that I have brought *emotional turmoil* into my home. I ask you to forgive me for that, and show me if I need to ask my husband to forgive me.

Also, I know I need to get hold of my tongue, Lord. James 3:8 says the tongue is "a restless evil, it is full of deadly poison." Guard my words, for they are often ugly. My heart is a true piece of work, and I am ready to start that journey of letting You work on it.

I confess the way I want my husband to give to me, to meet my needs, *instead of* focusing on *me meeting his needs*. Help me give up my expectations for now and focus on giving him the 8 A's.

In Jesus's powerful and merciful name,

Amen

Assignments and Group Discussion Questions

(Remember to not share anything negative about your husband with your group.)

1. Have you been waiting for your husband to meet your needs? Are you willing now to learn how to meet his needs instead? What stands in your way?

2. What emotional turmoil do you bring to your house? Anger? Sarcasm? A demanding spirit? A sulking spirit?

3. Don't ask him, but what do you think your husband would say is the emotional turmoil you bring to your home?

4. In day three, *Being an Excellent Wife*, how do you react to the phrase, *She does him good all the days of his life*?

5. Do you cry to manipulate your husband?

6. Day five says, *To get the prize we want (a great marriage), we pay the price of living a certain way.* What are your thoughts about doing that?

WEEK 2

First A: The Acceptance Lesson

Contents

Day 1: Changing Your Emotions
Day 2: But My Husband Is Very Difficult!
Day 3: A Hidden Expectation to Give Up
Day 4: I Don't Feel Loved by My Husband
Day 5: Getting Rid of the Resentment in Your Marriage

Day 1 of this week is one of the most important lessons in all of *Wife School*. Please read and reread until you completely embrace the concept.

Please read chapter 2, "First A: The Acceptance Lesson," in *Wife School: Where Women Learn the Secrets of Making Husbands Happy* before you read the articles in this study guide.

DAY 1
Changing Your Emotions

A lot of women resist filling out the Turquoise Journal lists that the Genie gives Jessica in *Wife School*. Please digress with me and follow these two examples to understand why filling out these lists is ridiculously important to your marriage success.

Imagine you are in an alley, it is midnight, and you are in the worst part of town. You are alone, and you hear garbage cans tip over and see shadows move across your path. What is your emotion? Fear, right? What if I told you that *the truth is* that you are perfectly safe, that there is no danger anywhere in the vicinity? Do you see that your previous emotion of fear followed *your thoughts* instead of following *reality*? It is of utmost importance that you understand that your emotion of fear followed your *thoughts*.

Let's take another example. Imagine you are at a park with your four-year-old and your two-year-old (either children or grandchildren). The day is sunny and warm, and the children are delighted that they are floating their sailboats on the pond. The four-year-old brings you flowers and tells you how pretty you are. Then, the two-year-old runs to you and kisses you on the cheek. What are your emotions? Joy and happiness, right? What if I then told you that *the truth is* that there was a kidnapper hiding behind the tree, waiting to grab one child while you were occupied with another? Do you see that your previous emotion of happiness followed your *thoughts* and not *reality*? Emotions follow thoughts, not reality!

Do you see the gigantic implications of this? If we can learn that our *emotions flow from our thoughts*, then we can take responsibility for and choose to have *good thoughts*. The concept of thinking good thoughts is not my idea. Paul tells us in Philippians 4:8 what to think about (whatever is true, noble, right, pure, lovely, and admirable).

There is a term in psychology called *cognitive restructuring* which simply means "learning to think different thoughts." Paul tells us the same thing in Romans 12, to "be transformed by the renewing of your mind." That's what we are going to do with the Turquoise Journal lists. *We are going to transform your emotions for your husband by the renewing of your mind.*

When you consistently and continually bathe your mind with your husband's virtues and gifts, you begin to have different thoughts about him, which then produces different emotions toward him. I cannot adequately express to you how important this is. Many women have completely changed the affection they feel for their husbands because they consistently wash their brains with what their husbands bring to the marriage (benefits) versus focusing on what is missing. Our natural tendencies are to focus on *what is missing and disappointing*. You must change this normal tendency if your marriage is to see a quantum improvement. These Turquoise Journal lists are nonnegotiable.

I have lists from years ago, and I think my overflowing affection for my sweet husband is from bathing my mind for years with his virtues. As you focus your thoughts on what your husband does right (and overlook his weaknesses, which we will learn to do), your emotions for him escalate.

Collect your husband's sweet words, kind acts, and virtues as if they were valuable stocks or bonds. *Your thoughts will then begin to produce affectionate emotions,* just as your thoughts in the alley example produced fear and your thoughts in the park example produced happiness. Thoughts produce emotions! You can learn to *choose* your thoughts and therefore change the emotional climate you live in. Astounding!

We humans read each other's spirits. Your husband will sense your positive affection for him (versus your previous disappointment), and it will propel a new cycle in your marriage. If women do *not* do this step in *Wife School*, I cannot guarantee all the results that I have mentioned about your marriage having a quantum transformation. This step is absolutely critical to the success of *Wife School*.

Remember, your brain hates new ideas. It likes what it is used to and what is familiar. Even if you fill out your lists and change your emotions for your husband for a season, it will be temporary if you don't repeatedly immerse yourself in your new thinking. Our brain grooves are deep, and we return to prior thoughts if we don't bathe and rebathe our minds. The newest psychology books on how to evoke change in a human repeatedly say *find a way to change one's thinking*. That is why I am so insistent on filling out the Turquoise Journal lists. This is the means by which we override our prior cemented grooves of thinking.

At the very end of this study guide, you will find the Turquoise Journal lists that the Genie assigns to Jessica. Begin to fill them out wholeheartedly, and add regularly to them. What a delight it will be in five years to read your accumulated lists.

DAY 2
But My Husband Is Very Difficult!

I recently talked with a woman who had *disdain* for her husband. He definitely didn't meet her needs, he flirted with other women, he bragged, and he wasn't really interested in their children. She said *she was sick of it*. I felt sorry for her pain. In her opinion, she had poured and poured into this man, and he was still, in her words, *a jerk*. Hearing this initial description, I thought her husband certainly did not appear to be blue ribbon material.

"What do you do when your husband is such a *huge* disappointment?" she asked.

All husbands have a dark side, and this one certainly did. However, when we pulled apart her marriage, we both realized that her husband did bring a lot of good into her life, and we decided to focus on that. (She was able to list that he provided a decent income; he listened to her, sometimes; occasionally, he was calming to her; occasionally, he gave good advice to the children; etc.) This woman had many beautiful gifts and blessings in her life, but having a five-star husband was not one of them. By continuing to deposit the 8 A's into her husband (especially the A of Acceptance), she was growing her garden the best she could. Actually, she later said that her husband was *decently* nice most of the time. Also he did take the family to church (although she didn't think he spiritually led the family).

I assured her that many women experience this deep disappointment in marriage. She didn't actually want to leave the marriage; she just wanted more from her husband. In truth, this was a decent man, and when she *dug around to look for his virtues*, many surfaced. Granted, it's hard to see a man's virtues when he isn't meeting your needs or reflecting your beauty as a woman.

The best way to help a man like this grow is for you to develop your ability to influence him, and that is done by meeting his 8 A's and by striving toward high character. As we repeatedly say, we become like the people we hang around. Being around a godly, meek, humble, serving, grateful wife is the best way in the world for your husband to develop these qualities. I know you don't want to hear that. You want *him* to be the godly, serving person. But that's not the man you were given. This one is. And this is all about your heart. Only *the very wise* woman knows how to forgive, overlook, and focus on the strengths of the man, believing that depositing the 8 A's over years is truly life and marriage transforming.

Work on the one person you can change, you. After you change, you will influence him to grow, too. I wish there were an easier way. (I promise, I have looked for an easier way to help women in their marriages, and I cannot find one.) Hard work, laying down your rights, giving in the face of not getting…*this* is how wise women build their homes. Foolish women want pampering and ease. Take the hand you were dealt and play it. Miracles can occur when godly women live out biblical principles. In this life, you will have tribulation and trials. Demanding that we have heaven while we are still on earth is lunacy.

Being a woman of joy and strength requires a lot of practice. Proverbs 31:25 says that the Proverbs 31 woman "is clothed with strength and dignity." We don't want to have strength and dignity. We want to be mushy and needy and for our husbands to fill us. Another translation for dignity is honor. We are to be clothed with honor. That's not whininess, neediness, or self-pity. *It's a regal emotional nature that is calm, composed, and respectful.* Get rid of the idea that your PMS craziness gives you a license to let it rip. You are to be a woman of strength and honor. I know there is a learning curve, but decide you will attain this character. Decide you will find other women who want this, and become close friends with them. Immerse yourself in good reading and prayer. There is no easy path to acquire a life of strength and honor, but it is a life that **calls others up**.

So your husband has a few issues, does he? Welcome to the human race, where we all have concerns and problems. I understand that you have a difficult husband. But this is the man you were given to love. Bow down before the Lord, get full of Him, and then rise and go forth to serve. This is how wise women with difficult husbands build their homes. For decades I have noticed that wise women who adopt these principles can work miracles in their marriages. Your marriage is no different from millions of others. Hopefully, what will soon be different is *you*! After years, your husband will see your *strength and honor* and will move in that direction himself.

DAY 3
A Hidden Expectation to Give Up

In our Christian culture, we women repeatedly hear that our husbands are to be our spiritual leaders. Yes, that is a beautiful thing (chapter 22 in *Wife School* is "How to Help Your Husband Be a Spiritual Leader").

However, what is *not* beautiful and is downright offensive to husbands is when we think they *owe us* spiritual leadership. It's as if it is OK to badger them to be more in this area because it is *spiritual*. Women! Peter wrote to women with advice on how to act if their husbands are disobedient to the teachings of the Word. In 1 Peter 3:1, he wrote the following:

> In the same way, you wives, be submissive to your own husbands so that even if any of them are disobedient to the word, they may be won without a word by the behavior of their wives, as they observe your chaste and respectful behavior.

The Greek word for *disobedient* is this verse is ἀπειθέω. Strong's Greek lexicon number *G544* means to "refuse compliance; to disbelieve (willfully and perversely)." If your husband is not acting as he should (or is not a believer), he is not to be whipped into shape with your words. When your husband sees your purity (sincere motives to love him) and reverence (deep respect) for him, he opens to your influence. That's what *Wife School* is all about. You learn to fill this man with the 8 A's, operating out of a pure heart (not manipulation) and a reverent respect for him (not because he deserves it but because he holds the office and position of *husband*). The great long-term benefit is that you gain the ability to influence him. Not by beating him up with a sermon do you win him, but by your behavior, your life, and your pure motives to make him happy.

I cringe when women say to their husbands, "I need more spiritual leadership from you." Those are simply manipulative words women use to tell husbands that their needs are not met and that the husbands are (again) a disappointment. Accept this man. Quit doing all your little tricks to change him. Yes, eventually, *you will learn to ask him for what you need*, but you have some major makeover to do in your heart and mind first.

Ruth Bell Graham, wife of Billy Graham, said, "God called you *not* to make your husband good, but to make him happy." 1 Peter 3 confirms this. You are not the Holy Spirit in your husband's life.

We all know deep down inside that we are all losers. When someone accepts us as we are, we have a deep appreciation for that. Accept your husband. Maybe he doesn't accept you and criticizes you. Again, we will deal with that in another lesson. But for now, know that your acceptance for him is healing to him, and that's the first step in him eventually someday accepting you.

DAY 4
I Don't Feel Loved by My Husband

The phrase I hear most often by women when discussing marriage is "I don't feel loved by my husband." That sentence is quickly followed by "I feel empty and sad as well as unloved." Interestingly, I hear this from *spiritually mature* women! I will address this issue in detail in the future. But because it is so prevalent, I want to give you an outline of where we are going when we solve this problem. I will discuss the solution below in outline form with four points.

One. Remove expectations from your husband that he must make you feel emotionally loved for now. Free him. We women have read the romantic Jane Austen novels and watched many romantic comedies/dramas. We naturally feel unloved at our core anyhow, and then those novels/movies don't help. We think that when we get married, a husband will change that. What is very helpful to know is that he has *no idea* what you want or need. What love means to him is *sex and sharing activities together*. Can you see how dumbfounded he is when you tell him you want emotional closeness, a lot of deep sharing, and lots of verbal affirmation?! He thinks you're a mental case! Give up this expectation for now.

Two. Instead of looking at how empty you are, focus on filling and filling the guy with the 8 A's. That's right. Don't look at how empty your tank is; instead, focus on giving the 8 A's. In fact, when you have a thought about feeling unloved, use it as a springboard/alarm clock to ask yourself, "What A can I deposit into my husband's tank to make him happy?"

Three. At this point, you have no expectations and are filling and filling. You are also writing down in your Turquoise Journal all the benefits your husband brings to your life. You are recording his strengths and virtues. You are bathing your mind daily with these thoughts. Yes, I know things are lopsided for now. Please bear with me.

Four. We have barely begun the 8 A's. But after you fill him with them, he will say or do something nice. *Record it.* Then, thank him once after he does it, and (importantly!) *thank him again*, hours or days later. The second thank-you is the important one. This is the meaningful thank-you that begins to burn a thought in his brain that if he does such and such, *you like it.* For example, one woman told me that her husband never told her she looked nice. One time, he did. She thanked him. Hours later, she said, "Honey, I keep thinking about when you told me this morning that I looked nice. I can't explain why, but it is very important to me that you think I look nice. I keep thinking about that compliment. I want to thank you again for saying that to me." *That* is when he realized how important the compliment was to her, not the first thank you. You train him with thanking him *twice* when he gets it right.

Do you see the whole progression? You have reduced/eliminated expectations, you have filled his tank, and now he is more inclined to do or say nice things. You catch him doing the right thing, and then he gets rewarded (twice) for that behavior. Again, we will discuss this in detail in another lesson. But for now, put down that feeling that "I don't feel loved by my husband." The poor guy has no idea at this moment how to do that. You will eventually teach him. That's why this is a fifty-year plan. This takes a while. But remember, what on earth means more to you than your marriage? That's right, nothing.

DAY 5
Getting Rid of the Resentment in Your Marriage

Resentment. I don't think there's a woman alive who doesn't understand this word. Resentment comes when others hurt us or treat us poorly. Resentment is ill feeling (anger, blame) toward another. We will address the resentment wives have toward their husbands in this section, but these principles are also applicable to other people in your life whom you resent

I have received many emails with stories about husbands who are selfish with their time, energy, and money. I have also had multiple conversations with women about husbands who are insensitive, inconsiderate, and unkind. When husbands are repeatedly selfish and immature, it is very common to resent them. We can forgive them once or twice, but the repetitiveness of their selfishness is what builds the resentment.

Before I address the necessity of forgiving our husbands, I want to remind you that for centuries, husbands have often been selfish and immature. Wise women have the strength and dignity to forgive repeatedly. 1 Corinthians 13:5 says that *love keeps no record of wrongs*, and 1 Corinthians 13:7 says that *love bears all things*. This is how godly women have **called men up** for ages. They do not insist on a two-week cure. I will address the qualities needed to influence others soon. But for now, know that for you to influence others, you need self-mastery, integrity, and to be unselfish. Focus on *who you are,* not on *who your husband isn't.* As you grow in goodness and kindness, your example will call him up. Continue to focus on the 8 A's, and soon we will learn how to ask for one or two things at a time. Steel yourself. This is a five-year program. That is not for the weak to hear. It is for the wise and the noble. Men change astronomically in the presence of a wise, honest, kind, and unselfish wife. But you have to go first.

Now, let's address Scripture's call to forgive. We really do not have a choice whether we forgive or not.

In Matthew 6:14–15, Jesus says, "For if you forgive other people when they sin against you, your heavenly

Father will also forgive you. But if you do not forgive others their sins, your Father will not forgive your sins."

You can read commentaries on those verses and get different opinions on what authors think about them. But the bottom line is that no matter how you try to spin it, *we must forgive others*. It is not optional. I hate this and so do you. We don't want to release people who have hurt us, ignored us, or hurt people we love. You have heard the cliché "To err is human; to forgive, divine." Forgiving others is ridiculously hard.

Your job right now is to take that person who has offended/harmed you—your husband? your mother-in-law? your old best friend who dumped you? the woman who excluded your child?—and let him or her off the hook. Offer that person release and forgiveness.

There are two huge reasons you must do this. First, the verse above says your Father will not forgive your sins if you don't forgive others. That's reason enough. Second, resentment is the poison you want the person who hurt you to drink, but instead, the poison eats you up from the inside. No woman can be beautiful in spirit when she hangs on to resentment. We've got to let it go. We have to. We must.

I am with you. I get how hard this is. But we are cornered and have no other choice.

Let's say that you have forgiven the perpetrator. Now what? The standards are different, according to who offended us.

If our enemies offend us, we must forgive and then return *good for evil* (*agape* means to love them, which is choosing to do them good). If our parents/in-laws offend us, we must forgive them and still honor them (Eph. 6:2; more on this in another lesson). But if our husbands offend us, we are to forgive them and *then* learn how to *phileo*-love them. Let me explain.

When our enemies offend us, we are first commanded to forgive them and then commanded to love them (Matt. 5:44). The good thing is that we have only to agape-love them, not phileo-love them. There are four kinds of love in the Bible. *Agape* love means "to do good to others," whereas *phileo* implies a higher standard to do good *and* to have affection toward them. Thankfully, we are not commanded to have *affection* toward our enemies but only to do good toward them.

But guess what? You *are* commanded to phileo-love your husband. In Titus 2, it is in plain sight, right there, in your Greek Interlinear Bible. (Plain sight in Greek 😀.) Young women are to phileo-love their husbands. That's love with affection. So, if you have resentment toward your husband, you have to first, forgive him; second, do him good (agape); and third, develop phileo-love affection for him.

The Turquoise Journal lists were specifically created to help you do this. As you wash your mind with his strengths, virtues, and benefits to your life, you grow your phileo love. But again, this is third, *after* forgiving and *after* choosing *to do him good all the days of his life.*

Do you think you have a lot to forgive? Is your situation unusual? Do you think that maybe you should have different rules about forgiving that *mean* person because your situation is so extreme? While the Jews were *stoning* Stephen (Act 7:60), Stephen said, "Lord, do not hold this sin against them." And when Jesus was *hanging on the cross* (Luke 23:34), Jesus said, "Father, forgive them, for they do not know what they are doing." If your situation is worse than being stoned or crucified, then I understand your complaint. But most of us have normal resentment for unmet expectations of how others should treat us, and *our call and duty* is to forgive.

The parable of the unmerciful servant (Matt. 8:21–35) is incredibly powerful to help you understand forgiveness. The servant was forgiven a multi-million-dollar debt and then wouldn't forgive a fellow servant who owed him a very small debt. Getting in touch with how self-absorbed and self-focused you and I really are (sorry, but Scripture says we are all like this) and then seeing *how much we are forgiven* for all our selfish, wrong, idiotic, stupid, rebellious, and mean choices, *we can therefore begin to extend this forgiveness* to others, even though they have hurt us countless times.

Are you going to dig deep and find the strength in prayer to forgive this man (or other person), even though his actions seem very selfish to you? Please believe me when I say how much another human being can change when confronted with the Spirit of God in another person. When you are *remaining on the Vine* (John 15) and the Sap is flowing through you, your husband will be repeatedly confronted with the fruit of the Spirit in your life. Women, God changes others through your godliness! He changes others using your unselfishness. Don't demand that others change on your timetable. I cannot tell you the times I have seen husbands wisely respond to godly wives. In reverse, I have witnessed marriages when the woman won't go first and demands that the husband change. This often leads to a divorce. Persevere. Be willing to be the giver and *not get credit for it*. You are getting credit, just not here on earth (see Matt. 6). Forgive lavishly and extravagantly, and remember that a woman with a gentle and quiet spirit is of great worth in God's sight (1 Pet. 3).

Healthy marriages must have vast storehouses of forgiveness. For many wives, the resentment in a marriage is toward her husband because he does not *understand her*. She feels unloved and is therefore disrespectful to him. Then, he develops resentment toward her for her disrespect. As I've said repeatedly, most men are satisfied in the marriage if there is not too much emotional turmoil and there is enough sex. We women are usually the stir sticks! We want x and y and z and more. These poor guys are trying to make a living, figure out how to protect us financially for the long haul, and wrestle with their daily/hourly struggle against sexual sin. Then we come in with, "You don't love me well" (as well as "You don't do life well, either").

Over and over again, a woman resents her husband because the husband doesn't understand her. But you, the wise Proverbs 14:1 woman, now know he has no idea what loving you well even looks like! He says to himself, "I show her I love her when I bring home my paycheck. I show her I love her when I am sexually faithful. What is her deal?" I say the same things over and over in *Wife School* because we all fall right back into the same patterns in marriage. Once we begin to cut our husbands some slack in this area of not loving us well (and begin to treat them with respect, demonstrated by filling their tanks with the 8 A's), then the lightheartedness returns to the marriage.

David and I were playing cards the other night, and we began laughing at this ridiculous inside joke we share. As I sat and watched this man belly laugh, I thought about the goodwill I have toward him. Women don't laugh when there is resentment. Don't forget our girlfriend, the Proverbs 31 woman, who laughed at the days to come. Wrestle down your resentment in prayer. Get back your girlish spirit that can laugh and forgive. I know you've been hurt. We all have. But now, who are you going to be? Are you going to be an old, cold, resentful, judging, easily offended, critical, contentious woman? Or are you going to keep your girlish heart until you are ninety—the one that is open, free, and loving? God heals broken hearts when they are offered to him. Isn't it time you let go of all that dirt and smut that you are keeping in your heart toward your husband (or someone else)? Haven't you wasted enough time holding onto that bitterness? Friend, you are harming only yourself (well, your children, too, because they lose when Mom has a hard heart).

Forgiveness is not for the wimpy. You are a Proverbs 31 woman of strength and dignity. She forgives. She releases others from their sin against her. And honestly, women who hold grudges and who are easily offended are *downright unpleasant*. Wouldn't you agree? Is this who you want to be? A drama queen who is always obsessing about how others don't treat her right? Of course not! You are the excellent wife of Proverbs 31!

An Important Disclaimer

I heard of a husband who wouldn't let his wife leave the house. Another husband wouldn't let anyone speak to him unless he spoke first. That is not normal; it is mentally unhealthy, and you are *not* to accept this. Instead, seek help. Please get professional help if there is any kind of physical abuse, drug abuse, alcohol abuse, adultery, or serious emotional degradation. *Wife School* does not address mentally unstable or abusive situations. Please contact a Christian counselor and get help if you think your marriage may be in this category. *Wife School* addresses annoying habits but not evil or seriously mentally unhealthy habits.

Prayer

Lord,

I bring to you a cold heart today, a heart that doesn't want to give and love my husband. Instead, I admit I want to be *given to and loved* by him. I feel helpless to change this mindset that I have.

Remind me of how you want me to live. Remind my soul that I am not to follow my natural inclinations but instead that "whoever wants to save their life will lose it, but whoever loses their life for me will find it" (Matt. 16:25).

How I forget that "your yoke is easy and your burden is light" (Matt. 11:30). My constant downward stream is away from your ways. Help me remember. "For my thoughts are not your thoughts, neither are your ways my ways" (Is. 55:8).

Help me find the time, energy, and desire to fill out these Turquoise Journal lists. They look like a lot of work to me. But, Lord, you designed the brain so that it has to be bathed with the correct thought to be renewed. Therefore, I accept this work, knowing that you created the brain to change by being renewed with *thought*. Help me choose to bathe my mind with good thoughts about my husband.

This is only the first A, Lord, and I already want to quit. The work seems too hard. I keep wanting to ask, "What about me?" Please fill me with "the peace of God, which passes all understanding" (Phil. 4:7) and remind me that "they that wait upon the Lord shall renew their strength" (Is. 40:31).

God, I do want a great marriage. Please teach me how to acquire that.

In Jesus's name,

Amen

WEEK 2

Assignments and Group Discussion Questions

(Remember to not share anything negative about your husband with your group.)

1. Begin to earnestly fill out the five Turquoise Journal lists that are at the end of this study guide. Add regularly to the lists.

2. Did you have expectations for a Prince Charming, only to find you married an average Joe? Did you sign up for rose petals and lace and realize your husband is average and thinks about work, money, and sex? Are you ready to free your husband from this impossible standard you have set for him and ready to accept that he is half strengths/half weaknesses? Are you willing to begin to accept and overlook his set of weaknesses for now? No husband has it all. Do you believe that? What thoughts do you have in this area?

3. Women want their husbands to change, and instead of giving them the best environment to grow and change (the 8 A's), they have chosen the opposite situation, such as whining and being critical. Do you correct, advise, hint, and suggest? How has your critical nature contributed to the tension in the marriage?

4. Do you have a very difficult husband? If so, are you willing to grow your heart and character to such a high level that your life (not your words) calls him up (1 Pet. 3)? Have you settled in for the long haul (years) of waiting while God plows his heart to grow him? Do you believe that "love never fails" (1 Cor. 13:8)?

5. Did you enroll your husband in a husband-improvement course after you got married? Do you feel he is *yours* to coach and maneuver?

6. Do you understand that in your marriage, your husband wants to relax, be comfortable, and *not* work on the relationship but simply wants to enjoy your companionship? What do you think about this?

7. Can you begin to understand that emotional intimacy is not even on his radar? Not only does he not care about it, he doesn't realize you have these needs. Like the Genie says, you have to teach a four-year-old to read. Are you willing to meet his 8 A's before you ask for what you need in this area? Can you give up your self-pity? What are your thoughts about this situation?

8. All our naturally wrong inclinations in our marriages are discussed in the Bible. Our proclivity to be prideful, fearful, lazy, demanding, unforgiving, selfish, and inconsiderate is repeatedly addressed in the Scripture. You know that in your Christian life, your natural downward pull is away from God and doing as you want. That is why Matthew 4:4 says, "Man shall not live on bread alone, but on every word that comes from the mouth of God." Just like we need food every day, we need the Word every day, or we cannot override our natural downward tendencies. Discuss what your intake of Scripture looks like, and comment on your struggle (or victory) in this area.

WEEK 3

Second A: The Admiration Lesson

Contents

Day 1: An Overview of Admiration
Day 2: Add Empathetic Listening to Your Admiration
Day 3, Part A: Drip Some Honey
Day 3, Part B: The Problem with Familiarity
Day 4: Praising Other Men
Day 5: How Do I Find the Time and Energy to Give a Daily Admiration Moment?

Please read chapter 3, "Second A: The Admiration Lesson," in *Wife School* before you read the articles in the study guide.

This is one of my favorite A's. If there ever was an A that pulled a husband's heart to his wife, it would be the A of Admiration (well, this one and the seventh A).

DAY 1
An Overview of Admiration

Recently, a friend told me she had made the coffee at their church the previous week. Because there were so many compliments on the coffee, a staff member asked my friend to make the coffee every week. This friend said jokingly, "I am now the official coffee manager."

We laughed together at how starved we all are for compliments. Even someone telling us that we make good coffee makes us feel good about ourselves.

Human beings are ravenous and famished for admiration. You are, and your husband is. Humans all naturally crave and love admiration. Now of course you and I both know that laying down this desire for the praise of man—and instead being humble—is what God wants from us. But we are to have two different standards. We have one for ourselves, which is to forgo rights and get our approval/admiration from the Lord. Then we have another standard for others, *which is to love them and meet their needs.* (To a husband, filling his tank with the 8 A's is how he feels loved by you.) This situation of having one standard for you (humility) while having a higher, giving standard for others is one of the major tenets that define mature people. How rare to find someone who takes personal responsibility for his or her own needs yet passionately attempts to fill others. The Few. The Proud. The Godly.

Getting rid of emotional turmoil (week 1) *and* getting off your husband's back (week 2 on Acceptance) are both to precede giving the A of Admiration. Your husband will think you are deranged if you are still having meltdowns and barking orders but then turn around and give him the A of Admiration. Put the brakes on those negative behaviors, and then begin to fill his tank with the A of Admiration.

Admiration has the polar opposite effect of emotional turmoil and trying to correct/fix your husband. Admiration draws your husband's heart to you. Men lo-v-v-e admiration! We all know the simple truth that we like being around people who make us feel good and don't like to be around people who don't. Somehow, we forget to apply that to husbands.

I read business books all the time to help my husband with his business, and one of the three pillars of building a good business is to develop *raving fans*. The method to develop raving fans is to *delight* your clients/customers. Why? Besides the obvious reason that you have a good product/service, it's because people shop where they are *treated well.* People do business with people they like. A man recently told me he quit going to an excellent dentist because he didn't like the receptionist. No surprise there. So why would husbands be any different? They want to be where they are treated well, too. The idea that we can be our natural ratty selves around our husbands is wrong. The idea of saving and exclusively using your best china for company is wrong. Our husbands should get our best—and especially our best words.

Proverbs 16:21 says that "sweetness of speech increases persuasiveness." Give your husband some sweetness of speech if you want to increase your persuasiveness. Admiration is the *sweetest* of speech. Even the most talented, brilliant, and gifted of men need and desire admiration.

Recently, I was talking to a group of women, and this question was posed to me: "What do you say to women who are not getting anything emotionally from their husbands but are still instructed to give them the A of Admiration?" My answer was that we give our husbands the A of Admiration by pulling first on the Lord to meet our needs. Then, because we are commanded to love our husbands, we simply give admiration to them because admiration feels like love to husbands. Even if there is still much resentment in the marriage, this will begin to break down those boulders.

One woman whose marriage was still very full of resentment tried to admire her husband. (We will discuss resentment soon.) Obviously, the husband wasn't used to this. He said, "What? What junk is that?" She felt so discouraged that she gave up. Of course, one little Admiration Moment is not going to turn around this giant ocean liner of resentment in her marriage. Why, she needs to realize her marriage may take months to turn around. (Honestly, most marriages don't even take weeks, but some do). Be prepared to persevere.

Why do the 8 A's work? They work because of something God said, not me. 1 Corinthians 13:8 says, "Love never fails." Isn't that incredible? That's why we are to love our enemies, because humans have no shield on their heart that can resist love. We soften to love. And the 8 A's are how men feel loved. Even if your husband doesn't respond and soften quickly, remember that the soil of his heart is being plowed. So fill, fill, and persevere! Galatians 6:9 says, "Let us not become weary in doing good, for at the proper time we will reap a harvest if we do not give up."

DAY 2
Add Empathetic Listening to Your Admiration

If I had written the 9 A's instead of the 8 A's, I would have added Empathetic Listening as the ninth A. Admiration builds up a man and makes him want to spread his peacock feathers. But empathetic listening is a very necessary gift also. It is in *deep listening* to a man's struggles that a wife is then able to give him understanding and compassion for the stress and hardships that he faces. Empathetic listening is another cry of the human soul, and learning to give your husband this gift is almost unmatched for pulling his heart to you.

When a husband complains or shares how hard his situation is, it is common for a wife to feel as if she should help him get over his sadness with her great advice. She is inclined to tell him, "All men have it rough. So buck up, buddy, and get over it. Also, here's what you should do." That is an incredibly harmful strategy.

As tough as men appear, they need compassion and pity at this moment, not advice. They love it (just as you love it) when others say, "Wow, that sounds really hard. That sounds difficult to me." We women forget that men have a fragile side that they hide from the world but allow you, the sweet wife, to see. *You must be trustworthy with their hardships, not giving direction and orders but giving tenderness, understanding, and compassion.*

Recently, one woman's husband was overlooked for a promotion. A coworker got the job that her husband wanted. In the privacy of their bedroom, he slumped in a chair and told her how utterly disappointed he was that he didn't get the promotion. Women, hear this. When your husband has disappointment and failure, *it is a golden opportunity* for you to win a crown in his opinion. Men want to share their hardships with their wives and want to receive compassion and understanding, not a three-point lecture how they could have done it better. This wise wife sat quietly in a chair, listening until he was finished. Softly, she said, "I'm so sorry. I know how disappointed you are because you wanted that job." Then he went off again about how unfair it was, how overlooked he felt, yada yada. She wanted to tell him *his blind spots and why he was probably overlooked.* But this was *not* the time. This was the time *to step forward with compassion and empathy.*

This next advice is for you A+ students out there. Are you ready? After the compassion has been given and he has thoroughly dissected his sorrows and disappointments, it is helpful to him at this moment for you to bring up some positive quality he has that relates to the conversation (drumroll…admiration). After you let him talk and get it all out (and you express the appropriate sincere empathy), now is the time to pour a little concrete into the man's veins with some admiration. Maybe you say, "Although you didn't get the promotion this time, your creative idea of how to increase the department's sales won't go unnoticed for too long. That was brilliant how you devised that plan! Maybe Joe got the promotion this time, but I think it's just a matter of time until they realize how valuable you are. Remember the way you devised that program for reducing expenses? That was very smart of you. I was incredibly impressed with your insight in that project."

He needs the one-two punch when he feels as if he's failed. One, empathetic listening. Two, a heavy dose of admiration. This one-two-punch approach buoys up a man as few things can (again, the seventh A is huge, but I must demonstrate patience here and wait until week eight to discuss that A).

Wise wives build their houses. They learn the secrets that build their men. They practice the art of being an exceptional wife. What affection men grow for this rare, beautiful gem of a wife. We give our husbands empathetic listening and admiration because we genuinely try to love them by giving them what they want and need.

Don't be a know-it-all around your husband. There may be an opportunity for you to softly fingertip drop your ideas later, but we will learn that the best way to give a man some advice is to make him think it's his idea. (This takes a lot of humility not to insist on getting the credit for your brilliant ideas. But remember, in life, humility is exalted, and pride is abased. This is *your* husband, and his success is yours because you are one. Never bemoan not getting credit from your husband for your ideas.)

More on this in another lesson.

DAY 3, PART A
Drip Some Honey

Today, we are going to let adulteresses teach us this lesson. That's right, women who seduce other women's husbands. People never change, and women seduced other women's husbands 4000 years ago the same way they do today. They dripped some honey. Proverbs 5:3 says, "For the lips of an adulteress drip honey, and her speech is smoother than oil."

Why do adulteress' lips drip honey? Because men love the honey of admiration! Men have always been drawn to women who admire them. We have wives barking orders and adulteresses dripping honey. Christian wife! Drip some honey! This man of yours is drawn to it, taken by it, and attracted to it. Honey is sweet and alluring. Fill your husband's mind and heart with the sweet honey of admiration.

DAY 3, PART B
The Problem with Familiarity

You've heard the cliché, "Familiarity breeds contempt." If there were ever familiarity, and if it ever bred contempt, it is in marriage. But we don't allow what is normal to rule in our homes. We are Proverbs 14:1 women, and we intentionally build our homes.

Often when we don't know people, they can appear to have it altogether. We can even find ourselves idolizing them. I think of how common this is with actors or even prominent Christians. But once you live with anyone and get to know that person, the shine comes off, and what you have (as we discussed last week) is a set of half strengths and half weaknesses. Admiration is often a feeling we have when we know only the *half strengths*. That is why in dating, we are infatuated (well, we have hormone support for this, too). But after the honeymoon, the rose-colored glasses come off. Familiarity makes admiration difficult. A man recently told me, "Don't get to know your heroes too well." What he meant was that once you get to know someone, you will see his or her humanness, and then that person will cease to be your hero.

Familiarity makes admiration difficult because you are very familiar with your husband's weaknesses. However, your husband needs admiration from you during the entire life of your marriage. After you get to know him well and his subsequent weakness package arises, you don't feel admiration. This very normal situation is why you hear many couples start to pick at each other. The man is starved for admiration, but because of familiarity, the wife no longer fills that need.

Wise women don't let natural inclinations rule. Wise women reverse the downward pull of marriage. We talked extensively last week about the Turquoise Journal lists. There are two skills needed to keep your admiration high. Number one is overlooking his weaknesses. (Remember how the Genie tells Jessica to turn Matthew so she's looking at his strengths, hiding his weaknesses, like an eclipse?) And number two is bathing your mind with his strengths, virtues, nice actions, kind words, etc., which of course is done by adding to and rereading your Turquoise Journal lists.

After you turn thirty, you begin to lose muscle mass. Unless you work out, you will lose more and more each year. This causes your metabolism to drop and that causes weight gain. *This is the norm.* These are the *natural inclinations* of the body. Energy (working out) is needed to override this natural phenomenon. In the same way, energy is needed (overlooking and reading the Turquoise Journal lists) to overcome the natural downhill phenomena of the marriage's familiarity (that keeps you from admiring your husband and giving him the oxygen that he will need until he dies). Decide you will give him an Admiration Moment daily until death do you part. Again, this is not because he deserves it but because that's what he needs, and genuine love gives others what they truly need. This is how wise wives build their houses. They do what works, what is right, and what is good, not what feels easy and comfortable.

DAY 4
Praising Other Men

Let's begin this section with an example about how you feel if your husband praises another woman. Pretend you and your husband are out getting a nice lunch. On the way home, your husband says, "Did you see that woman in front of the flower box outside the restaurant? I don't know who she was, but man, was she beautiful! She had that movie star glow. Did you notice? She walked with the ultimate confidence and grace, too. I can't get over how stunning she was."

If you are like most women, your heart drops if your husband raves about another woman's beauty. But likewise, *he does not enjoy you raving about other men's success*!

"Joe was just offered the vice president position of his company. I heard he's getting a lot more than six figures." Your husband is feeling pretty crummy at this moment, considering he's only an average breadwinner.

Don't do this, women. Don't brag on other men. It makes your husband feel bad, just as you felt bad when the husband earlier was bragging on the beautiful woman. We can be so dense.

If your husband is a doctor, and you see another younger doctor who is amazing, please tell your husband about the younger doctor's virtue in a way that doesn't make it seem as if you admire the younger guy more than you admire your husband. If you say to your doctor husband "I went to see Dr. X today. I can't believe what incredible bedside manners he had, as well as seeming very brilliant. I just loved him," I promise that if your husband is like most husbands, he is thinking, "Is he better than me?" Men are roosters, and roosters want to be the best rooster in the chicken yard. Always protect your husband's fragile ego. Foolish women think this is ridiculous. Wise women are always thoughtful of their husbands' fragile ego constitution. He wants to be your hero, not anyone else. You can talk about another man's skills, but always do it with a mindset of "My rooster husband is listening to me talk about another rooster, so I must be careful with my words."

DAY 5
How Do I Find the Time and Energy to Give a Daily Admiration Moment?

You can't have it all. That's just life. One reason some of us are exhausted is because we are trying to have a great marriage, be great parents, have wonderful businesses, serve at the church for hours, work out for hours, have a great social network, grow a hobby/interest, and achieve four other goals. Seth Godin has taken Zig Ziglar's goal system from the 1970s and has basically boiled it down to this: determine only four goals (Ziglar said to have six goals). If you try to do more than that, you'll end up doing nothing because you'll be scattered. *Focus is the key to productivity.* So pick a few things in life that you know God has called you to do, and let other things go. (If you are young, read Titus 2:4–5 for your assignment from God for now.) You can't have it all or do it all.

Faye Hardy, a Sunday School teacher I had twenty years ago, said, "I barely know what God is telling me to do. How would I know what he is telling you?" I am not trying to give you too many specifics. When I was a young mother and repeatedly got overwhelmed with all there was to do, I'd camp out in Titus 2:4–5. Often, I would (stupidly and pridefully) demand of God, "What *great* work do you want me to do?" The still, small, quiet Voice (humorously) would say, "Clean up your house." ☒ God was always directing me back to the Titus 2 list for the young woman. (I have always loathed housework, but God says that the Proverbs 31 woman "looks well to the ways of her household." Honestly, for years, this verse was a continual battle for me with homeschooling six small children. God's Word is beautiful in its ability to give guidance and direction.)

Now all six of our six children are grown, and I have freedom to use my gifts in a way that I couldn't for years. However, you young women have to choose exceedingly wisely how you spend your time because *there is not very much of it.* Being soaked in the Titus 2 mindset will help you figure out the few things you should be about. Grow in your walk with God, love your husband to the moon and back, pour into your precious children, be good managers of your household, etc. When your children are young, add one or two more goals. That's it. You can't do it all *or you'll not do the main things well.* Have some margins. If you're exhausted, you will have trouble giving your husband the 8 A's.

(While I'm on this subject, women love to blame their husbands for how exhausted they are. If there were only three things I could teach you, *one of them would be quit blaming your husband* and start taking responsibility for your own needs!)

One More Thought: Admiration Is a Picture of a Biblical Concept

You have heard that marriage is an analogy of Christ and his bride, the Church. The husband is the picture of Christ, and the wife is the picture of the Church. If we meditate on those roles, much wisdom opens up to us (Eph. 5:22–32). One recurring theme in Scripture is for believers (the Church) to praise the Lord. This is analogous to women praising and admiring our husbands.

Prayer

Lord,

The first thing I think of when I study admiration is how empty I am and how I would like to be admired by my husband. My emptiness again brings me before You for a filling. I often want this filling from my husband, but now I know I am to get it from You.

The familiarity of knowing my husband so well—his weaknesses!—makes me reluctant to give him the A of Admiration. This man is obviously a cracked clay pot. But I know that's not the way wise women live. We live by Your standards and principles. I know this, but it's easy to forget. I salute the position and office of *husband* because you want me to, not because he deserves it. This man is starved for admiration, and I am the designated person to fill the man's tank. I accept my assignment.

Focusing on *giving* when I want to focus on *getting* is going to be a huge switch for me. That's because my favorite trinity is me, myself, and I. Forgive me, Lord, for my self-consuming ways. The coldness and harshness of my heart continue to surprise me. What a tendency I have to criticize others! When I look inside myself, I realize that I don't even want to love the man you gave me to love; instead, I want to focus on his weaknesses.

God, when I look deep into my soul, I see how I mainly care about myself (well, and my children, but that's not surprising because I view them as an extension of me). I see how selfish and self-focused I am. I want comfort, I want praise, and I want to be noticed. I don't like it when others get treated better than me (or better than my children). My heart is full of wretchedness and self-preoccupation like this, Lord, and you see the ugliness in full. Right now, I repent and receive your forgiveness. With that great ocean of forgiveness that you extend to me, I now extend a bathtub portion to my husband. (Reader: See the parable of the unmerciful servant, Matt. 18:21–35.) I forgive him for all his weaknesses, disappointments, and failures. This is very difficult to do, because I wanted to marry a Savior, someone who would love and adore me and fill me to the brim. But You are the only Savior.

How prone I am to falling away from You all the time. Keep my heart on the narrow path.

In the name above all names, Jesus,

Amen.

Assignments and Group Discussion Questions

1. Do you understand the cry of the soul for Admiration? Do you see that your husband depends primarily on you to meet this need (although most husbands would never tell you this)? Describe your attitude toward giving your husband the A of Admiration.

2. Empathetic Listening is as valuable as Admiration. What kind of listener are you? Are you a stern army general? Or are you able to communicate understanding and compassion to your husband?

3. Can you relate to *dripping the honey of admiration* on your husband? What do you plan to do?

4. How has *familiarity* kept you from praising your husband?

5. Have you previously had a habit of praising other men in front of your husband? How do you feel about that now? What do you intend to do differently?

WEEK 4

Third A: The Appreciation Lesson and More...

Contents

Day 1: Good Managers of the Household
Day 2: She Can Laugh at the Days to Come, Part A
Day 3: She Can Laugh at the Days to Come, Part B
Day 4: Asking for What You Want
Day 5: A Few Random Tips

Please carefully guard what you say about your husband when you are with others as what you say shapes how they feel about your husband. His reputation is *yours* (the two of you are one). Remember the rule: only say things that he would want you to say if he was there listening. (If you need to discuss a negative issue in your marriage, please find an older, trustworthy, godly woman, or see a godly counselor.)

The Genie says on page 42, "I'm trying to teach you relationship skills that will endear you to your husband, skills that will arouse affection in him for you." And in *Wife School*, we address the skills to do that. But we are also going to address important heart issues for wives. Because the A of Appreciation is very similar to the A of Admiration (and is pretty self-explanatory), I will take this week to address some weighty issues of our inner person that relate to being a wife of noble character (Prov. 31:10).

Please read chapter 4, "Third A: The Appreciation Lesson," in *Wife School*.

DAY 1
Good Managers of the Household

(This section is primarily for the younger woman. Younger women and older women have different callings in different seasons of life. Titus 2 is phenomenal in describing the difference.)

Let's face it, men have a fantasy that their homes will be kingdoms where they rule as kings. It is the cliché picture of the 1950s husband whereby he comes home and relaxes in his chair with his newspaper, pipe, and slippers. His fantasy continues with a pretty, happy wife gloating over him with a beautiful meal and well-behaved and scrubbed-clean children—a meticulously well-ordered household. Rest assured, I realize I used the word *fantasy*, not *reality*.

I bring up this fantasy to remind you that husbands like to come home to *order*. They are slaying dragons all day at work, and to come home to a total mess is not their choice. Titus 2's advice to be "a good manager of the household" and Proverbs 31's advice to "look well to the ways of her household" are very important instructions for women to heed. We must pay attention to this important advice of the Scripture.

Women get all kinds of ideas, and one of them is that managing the home is not *that* important. Let's pull apart what Scripture says about women and the management of their homes.

The Titus 2 passage to young women continues to amaze me, especially now that I am on the other side of this passage and have slipped into the older woman's role. I have torn this passage apart in my interlinear Greek New Testament for years. (If you go to Scripture4all.org, you can do this, too.) The New Revised Standard Version translation reads that young women are to be *good managers of the household*. What does that mean?

The Greek word for "good managers of the household" is οἰκουρός, which means "watching the house." This phrase has the same meaning as Proverbs 31:27 which says, "She looks well to the ways of her household, and does not eat the bread of idleness." In other words, she is the one who makes sure *all is right* in her home: the food, the cleaning, the laundry, the clothes, the children's needs, all of it. She can have household help, but the responsibility was given to her to be sure it was done well. (The Proverbs 31 woman had household help and you can, too, if your budget allows it.) You are in charge of being a good *manager* of your household. You are to *watch the house.*

If I may say this with all respect, I personally don't like the King James translation that translates this Greek word as "keepers at home." For years, I mistakenly thought that the King James meant "*stayers* at home" but that's not what the King James translators meant. They meant, "house*keeping* of the home." Also I don't love the NIV translation that says "busy at home" because I think that misses the meaning, too, as the Greek word means "watching the house." I don't even like the translation, "domestically minded" because I think it insinuates a woman has her mind on housework and cooking, when the actual Greek word means "watching the house." I think the New Revised Standard Version *best* captures the original Greek word that says young women are to be *good managers of the household*. In my opinion, this better fits the Greek phrase "watching the house." We know the Proverbs 31 woman had multiple financial endeavors in her life, as well as many of the New Testament women also did. Dorcas made coats and garments (Acts 9), Lydia was a business woman (Acts 16), etc. Women are not obligated to always be at home.

Back to the thrust of the article: If your husband is coming home to chaos and disorder, then you may need to reevaluate some things. I know that sometimes women have to work full time outside the home. However, when I was in my thirties, I remember a godly friend who had little children. She said, "Working full time outside the home was one step above putting food on the table." She wisely understood the truth that women need to be at home *a lot* in order to look well to the ways of their household. Maybe your kids are in school. Maybe you have only one or two children, and your mother helps you. Maybe you are in a terrible financial situation and truly are looking at putting food on the table. (If so, my compassion and sympathies are with you.) But so often, women work outside the home and neglect *watching the home* so that they can have big houses, nice furniture, good vacations, new cars, designer purses, and the option to eat out often.

In my opinion, I think families are better off living in smaller houses, having older furniture, camping (instead of going on fantasy vacations), driving older cars, and eating at home, as well as having the mother at home *much* of the time who *manages the household*. I know that's hard to hear. It is very difficult to be a good manager of the household and be gone most of the time.

A few women with little children can do it all, but this is extremely rare. Maybe you are one of those who can be a good manager of your household, hold a full-time job, and still be a happy camper who pours into her priorities (her husband and her children). But if you are exhausted, angry, and not being a good manager of your household, then please consider reprioritizing. The difference in many households when they downsize and let mom be home more is gigantic. From years of experience, I can promise you it is much better to live a simple life and have mom at home most of the time than to keep up with an expensive social circle.

These are guidelines, not rules. If your mother is available and helps you a lot, you have more freedom. If you can afford household help and some great babysitters, you have more freedom. If all your kids are in school, of course, you have more freedom. The exceptions go on and on. However, if you are living in an environment without order and are not managing your household well, you must heed this centuries-old wisdom to correct it.

One more word to you wealthy chickadees. Some of you have time and money, and you are scooting around town, lunching, playing tennis, and even doing *something very valuable* such as ministry, helping a charity, etc. Much of that is good and fine, of course. But what I'm saying is that if you are young, then your responsibility is to be a good manager of your household, and *it comes before those activities.* Don't say that your volunteer work is more important than the order in your home. It's not, according to Titus 2. There is coming a day when you will have the time to volunteer and give away your gorgeous gifts. And it's fine if you can do it all now. But few women can do it all, and the priority is a well-ordered household that includes healthy meals, clean clothes, a clean house, and order.

As a new believer, I once heard a lady say, "If your home is not in order, you should not have a ministry." I agree. Your home is your major assignment/ministry *for this season of life.* The older-lady season will be here before you can blink an eye, and then you can accomplish all of those God-given dreams. But for now, make adjustments so your family is your top priority, and a home in order supports that goal. I am not trying to stop anyone from using her gifts to serve the Lord (heaven forbid). I am only trying to illustrate the *priority* and *importance* of reminding young women to take care of their homes and what goes on inside them.

Believe me, this Titus 2 verse has slapped me around for years. My husband was working for a nonprofit Christian organization for years, and money was tight. The work of running a large, busy household (homeschooling with six kids) was beyond difficult for me. The battle raged to take consistent excellent care of my household. Some women struggle more with household duties than others, but the call to be an excellent manager of your home remains. It is a calling we have from the Lord to look *well* to the ways of our households, not just barely getting it done. If you comb through Proverbs 31, the woman had excellent meals, beautiful clothes, and provisions of all kinds for her home. No one is coming to make sure that your household runs well. It is *your* responsibility to make sure it's done well.

Godly women throughout the centuries have struggled with this monotony and burden as you do. But they don't neglect this important work that God gave us to do. I know it's hard. I know it's tedious. I understand completely. But I tell you, just as I would tell my daughter, *it still must be done*. And you must find a way to do it *cheerfully*. This again is all about your heart and your entitlement. ("I have such-and-such breeding" or "I have such-and-such degrees, so I shouldn't have to wrestle with such minutia!") Friend, it is a command from God, and there is no way out of this responsibility. Embrace it. Figure out a way to conquer it with a happy heart.

If you can hire help, then you are free to do so. (We used to say that we paid the housekeeper and then the electrical bill.) Often, a little household help is invaluable. Many couples find a little money to hire help by driving old cars, infrequently going out to eat, etc. Even having some help come in for a couple of hours every other week to clean helps many young moms stay sane. But again, I know many of you can't afford that (or would rather spend the money on something else). These are suggestions and ideas only, not rules.

I remember listening to a sermon by John MacArthur twenty years ago on the Proverbs 31 woman. I was in the midst of work up to my neck (six kids under eleven) and felt quite a bit of self-pity, to be honest. I remember how he said that the young woman was in the sowing season of life and that if she sowed well, *she would later reap*. At that time, I really didn't have any older Christian role models, so I doubted that. What I wanted was relief! But now that I'm on the other side of the fence as far as age, I can attest that what John MacArthur said was true. This is my happiest season of life so far. My marriage is my favorite earthly possession, our children bring us great joy, and God allows me to have time to use my gifts. The young years are sowing; the older years are reaping. Sow well, young woman, even though it's difficult. The reaping years are coming.

The call is for you to obey God in this season and do His will for you, so there's no way around the Titus 2 list. Many young women learn that working full time outside the home is absolutely exhausting and detrimental to the welfare of their priority, their family. You and your husband will have to work on this. But over and over again, the wise choice seems to often be to work from home if at all possible (or to work part time). This is a very difficult subject, and again, these are *guidelines, not rules.*

To conclude this section, I remind you that the Greek word οἰκουρός means "watching the house." Many young women greatly enjoy their work outside the home and are savvy enough to figure out great childcare, great domestic support, etc. If you can do that, congrats. If your work outside the home is important to you, then work hard to find a balance for this busy season of life. But don't sacrifice the well-being of your children or your relationship with your husband. I realize how difficult and unpleasant this section is. Ask God to show you His mind as you pray through Titus 2 and your season as a young wife.

DAY 2
She Can Laugh at the Days to Come, Part A

Proverbs 31 has so much wisdom packed in it that we must give ourselves to combing through it slowly. (I have never seen an essay on womanhood that can touch Proverbs 31.) Today we will talk about verse 25b that says *she can laugh at the days to come*. Notice the writer didn't say *smile*. Nor did the writer say *she can handle*. The writer said she can *laugh*.

I want you to sit and soak with me in that verse. What is it about this woman that she can *laugh* at the days to come? Isn't that a remarkable sentence? A remarkable *word*? The following is all my opinion. I am going to give you several reasons I think she could *laugh at the days to come*. It is from meditating and thinking about this verse for years that I write the following.

Do you know a woman with a *happy heart* that can *laugh at the days to come*? Isn't she just delightful? Even her hello and voice lift your spirit. We all love these women and we must learn how to become one of them.

This Proverbs 31 woman is very busy and productive, yet she is not stressed. Instead, she laughs. *Being able to laugh is a measuring stick of your stress.* No one is laughing when they are getting ready to hit the wall. I love how God cares about our stress and tells us that the wise woman learns to laugh at the days to come.

The first reason the Proverbs 31 woman was able, in my opinion, to laugh at the days to come was because she understood that you can't be ultra-stressed and laugh at the same time. Therefore, *she kept margins in her life.* You can't be scheduled to the brim and still laugh at the days to come. Sometimes we have to say *no* to *good things* in order to say *yes* to the *best things*. That is a difficult thing to do because we want people to like and respect us.

In Virginia, when our six children were ten and under (I had a newborn and I was homeschooling), a gentleman from church called and asked if I would "take over the nursery and preschool department." Now that is an important job, I admit, but *the need is not the call*. When I declined, he was unpleasant and accusatory. Sometimes we think that these people in authority are the same as God. The church nursery work was important but I was barely getting through my day and I knew (loudly confirmed by my husband) that I was *not* to take on that responsibility. After I declined, his wife then proceeded to tell me that I "needed to be more balanced" (although she was empty-nesting, only had two children, and both kids had gone to school.) Well, to be *balanced* and to handle my family at that season of life, I would have needed a 54-hour day. *Don't let others pressure you into something that is not of the Lord, however holy it seems.*

I say this carefully, with fear and trembling, because I want you to hear from God and do His will. But Jesus says in Matthew 11 that His yoke (His will) is a *light and easy yoke*. When we are prayer-led, Scripture-led, and husband-led, we will better be able to know what to allow and *what to reject*. Just be warned that others will try to press you and tell you that their agenda is God's will (at school, at church, at the charity, in the neighborhood, in your extended family, and in your social circles). Get clear on your calling and learn to graciously say, "That does sound like a worthwhile project, but I'm so sorry I can't right now. Maybe in the future." *Your stress depends a lot on your ability to say no.* Stressed women don't laugh at the days to come. Don't blame anyone else, either. It's your job to learn to say no.

Secondly, I believe the Proverbs 31 woman could laugh at the days to come because she understood that whatever hardship would come, God would match it with His comfort to get her through the trial. My husband was recently diagnosed with an autoimmune disease and there was a time he could barely walk to the bathtub. (At one point, the doctor said his illness was life-threatening. But God has miraculously restored him.) I still don't remember how, but the peace that flowed into our lives during those weeks was remarkable. In fact, our lives grew richer after that experience. *The grace showed up when we needed it.* Our children were wonderful during this time. Friends showed up for visits. People brought food. Christians showed up to anoint David with oil for healing. It was an amazing time, in hindsight.

I remember being downcast one day, sitting in front of Charlie's Meat Market, talking on the phone with one of my best friends, Kendall. She said, "People can live happy lives with chronic illness." I remember my shock at this statement. Why, my whole paradigm shifted. I went home and told David what she said. It was at this point that we changed how we viewed the illness and realized we could still have happy lives in the midst of it. God used that friend at our moment of need *to give us grace.*

God uses different strategies to bring comfort to our lives when we face difficult trials. But knowing that *the grace will come when difficult circumstances arise* helps us rest today and laugh at the days to come. 2 Corinthians 12:9 says, "My grace is sufficient for you." However, God doesn't give this grace *until the very hour we need it.* That's why we fear hard things now, because the grace isn't there yet. I used to tell my husband how much fear I had about the possibility of losing a child. He would tell me, over and over again, that if it happened, *the grace to handle it would show up.* I believe the Proverbs 31 woman understood this principle that *the grace will show up* and this trust calmed her deepest fears and anxieties. Therefore she could deeply rest and laugh at the days to come.

I think of Amanda, a sweet girl in one of my prior groups. Amanda was given a precious baby with Down's syndrome. At first, she was devastated. Later she said, "What we thought was the worst that could happen turned out to not be that bad." What happened? *Grace showed up.* Grace will show up for you, too, when you need it. We must *all learn* to trust that *the grace will show up.*

Tomorrow we will discuss the rest of the reasons.

DAY 3
She Can Laugh at the Days to Come, Part B

To continue from yesterday…

Thirdly, I believe the Proverbs 31 woman knew how to take her problems to God in prayer and *leave them on the shelf in heaven* while He worked on them. It's one thing to pray and leave our anxieties with God; it's another to pray over them and then continue to stomp around in their little mud puddles.

Early in my Christian life, I did a Bible study on having a quiet time called 29:59 by Peter Lord. I remember a striking thing he said that has always stayed with me. He said his first job every day was to get his *heart happy in the Lord.* What a way to live! We are to get our hearts *happy in the Lord.* That means learning to leave our burdens on the shelf in heaven.

We have to quarantine our negative thoughts. Once when David and I were dating, he broke up with me (actually, he broke up with me twice as I was quite the head case). I was devastated. I told God that I would *not* think about it, though, unless I was with Him in prayer. I quarantined the pain. Yes, God changed me in other ways and brought David back, but I learned early to pray and put it in God's hands, and *leave it there.* We have to learn to *leave our problems on a shelf in heaven,* knowing that Somebody has plans to prosper us and not to harm us and that Someone has plans to give us a hope and a future (Jeremiah 29:11). Believing the Jeremiah 29:11 concept—that there is a glad surprise around the river bend—is a great perspective to help grow happy hearts. (If you repeatedly struggle with discouragement, this is especially a huge concept for you. I recommend *Jesus Calling* to you as well as the book, *Happy School* and its accompanying study guide.)

To balance the third concept just presented, I now want to discuss the fourth reason the Proverbs 31 woman could laugh at the days to come. In my opinion, it was because she knew that she was very proactive. After David broke up with me, I got a new plan for my life. I was going to get a PhD in Marriage and Family Counseling. Obviously, God brought David back and we got married, but the point is, I didn't sit around and sulk. I proactively made plans during the heartache *to move on*. I often wonder if the Proverbs 31 woman's husband needed help with finances and that's why she had so many home-based businesses. Maybe she *proactively* assisted her husband in business because he was having problems. Look at how the Proverbs 31 woman proactively made sure her home was well-provided for. Look at how she proactively took care of her beautiful clothes. This woman saw what needed to be done and by golly, she did it. No blaming. No self-pity, but a good work ethic to get things done. She knew she could bring this work ethic mindset to whatever future trial she should encounter. As Dr. Adrian Rogers used to say, "Pray like it all depended on God and work like it all depended on you."

Fifthly, I think this fab woman could laugh at the days to come because she wasn't struggling with *insecurity or grandiosity*, those twin beasts which make us struggle with addictions (I warned you this was my opinion). I think our Proverbs 31 girl had figured out two things. One was how valuable she was to God (remember how a gentle and quiet spirit is of great worth in God's sight?) And two, this woman had given up trying to be a big shot in the world (there is such a clamoring in our hearts to be important instead of wanting to serve). This woman accepted herself, her lot, and her life. She wasn't eaten up with feeling insignificant, with feeling overlooked, or eaten up with self-pity. She had figured out how to *get emotional freedom*. She had given up regrets. She had given up addictions (no woman can laugh at the days to come if she's battling an addiction such as alcohol, spending, prescription drugs, or Trash Food). This smart woman had battled her pesky insecurities and her demanding entitlement issues *in prayer*, and she had won. Therefore, she could live each day with emotional freedom and joy.

The sixth reason I think this woman could laugh at the days to come is because she was free of her guilt. She had found forgiveness for all of her stupid, willful, mean, idiotic, dumb mistakes and actions. Then, she lived a virtuous life, daily surrendered to God's will. Remember, when you lose your life, you truly find it (Matthew 10:39). The freedom of walking daily in the Spirit and living by the priorities that God has set out in His Word is equal to the *size of the Pacific Ocean*. There is no freedom like this. Despair and depression come from thoughts that are different from those God would have you think. No woman can be a happy song if she is making wrong choices or *even if she is thinking wrong thoughts*. Give up those foxes, "the little foxes that ruin the vineyards" (Song of Solomon 2:15). Those pesky foxes are the sins that so easily entangle (Hebrews 12:1). You know what your sin issue is. Let it go.

The seventh (and final, ha) principle I think this woman understood was that she could choose to use her one-of-a-kind, genius, strength set to bless others. I believe she found her zone, that area where she buzzed and fired on all cylinders. I believe each of us has a genius, a gift zone, an area of brilliance, and we are to fan it into flame. 2 Tim.1:6 says, "For this reason I remind you to fan into flame the gift of God." Much of our boredom is because we are not in touch with our gifts. When we are not operating in our area of gifts, we are frustrated, bored, and critical of others. You have a gift. Discover it, fan it into flame, and give it away to bless others and receive great joy yourself. Learning how to enjoy giving away your genius will change your daily enjoyment and will help you laugh at the days to come. (If you have little children, you will have to be very careful about fanning into flame your gift during this season of life. But even pursuing and growing your gift for thirty minutes during naptime can mean a lot to promoting your emotional health.)

You simply can't put a price tag on being able to laugh at the days to come. The best things in life are truly free.

DAY 4
Asking for What You Want (Just a Sneak Peek)

Here is a teeny-weeny teaser peek at asking your husband for what you want. We will discuss this subject in detail later.

As a first reminder, it should be obvious you can't badger your husband with *many* requests simultaneously. Yes, yes, I know you want *many* things, but you are wiser if you figure out the top one or two things you want *most* and then ask exclusively for those things. Asking for many things dilutes your request for the one or two things you care most about.

Sometimes it is wise not to spend too much energy on *why* you want or need something. (You already went through all your reasons, right?) Now, just ask for it.

One woman wanted some household help. Her husband told her that "cleaning the house was her job, and she couldn't have household help" (even though they could easily afford it and that same husband hired a man to mow the yard). This woman put *household help* on the top of her list of things she wanted to ask her husband for. This wise woman said to him (*after* she was rocking all the 8 A's), "I know you don't think I should have household help, but I want you to consider giving it to me, just because you love me and I want it."

When you ask your husband for something, simply say, "I want you to consider it because I want it and you love me." When children ask for a new bike, they don't go into the 13 reasons. They say, "Mom, I sure would like a new bike" knowing that they have sway with you because you love them.

If your husband says a quick no, table it and know that you will properly, respectfully, re-appeal that decision later. You will not badger him (later, we will discuss when the time to re-appeal is right and when it is time just to accept his decision). We will need to deal with the manipulative nature of most women's hearts when we discuss this. Obviously, this technique of asking should *not* be used selfishly to ask for a larger diamond ring when resources are tight. I am talking only about needs and wants you have that are legitimate.

We have barely begun our study of the 8 A's so this may seem a little premature to say. But... I have found that after women consistently pour all the 8 A's into their husbands—and don't bulldoze them for *many* things—husbands usually comply as they now *want* to make their wives happy.

More to come...

DAY 5
A Few Random Tips

Here are three random tips that I have learned over the years.

Tip one: Husbands listen best when their hands are engaged so their minds are free. Examples are when men are painting, washing the car, planting flowers, or driving. Bring up topics when their hands are busy if you want to encourage better listening.

Tip two: Here is a sentence to say if your husband raises his voice to you. (You have given up raising *your* voice, right?) According to Gary Smalley, men are buffalos and women are butterflies. A rock hurled at a buffalo will barely faze the beast, but this same rock will seriously wound a butterfly's delicate wings. (The phrase *beauty and the beast* will always be true.) When your husband raises his voice, often he is not aware of how hurtful this is to you because he does not understand what a fragile emotional constitution you have. That's why men are exhorted to "live with their wives in an understanding way" (1 Pet. 3:7). Men talk roughly to each other all the time and are not offended (notice how coaches talk to players). Don't decompose and start a meltdown if your husband does this to you. Simply say in a sweet (not commander) voice, "Please talk to me as if you love me." Don't fall apart. He will calm down and you can resume the conversation. However, don't do this *until you have earned the right to use it*—that is, you have gotten rid of the emotional turmoil that you bring to the marriage, are accepting him, and are now filling him with the 8 A's.

Tip three: One great way to honor your husband is to brag on him to the kids. "Did you guys know that Daddy is a great basketball player?" "Hey, kids, let's be quiet. Daddy's been working hard all week, and he needs a little rest and quietness." "Isn't Daddy generous to take us out to dinner?" A man longs for the admiration of his children, and you, as the mom, have huge influence over the children. Don't ever be selfish and rob the children of their close relationship with their dad by talking behind his back to them. That is soooo selfish, and women with resentment toward their husbands do it all the time! *You are hurting your children by keeping them from admiring their dad.*

Years ago, a woman called me and told me that her husband was having an affair. She thought that the kids should know so that they would not marry a reprobate like their dad. "No, a thousand times, no," I said. "Don't bring kids into the marriage problems, even with adultery issues." The marriage has since reconciled, and the kids still don't know about the father's indiscretion. They adore their dad, and the family now enjoys great, fun times together. Don't punish your children by robbing them of a close relationship with their dad because you are angry at him. Deal with your marriage problems without involving your kids.

Prayer

Lord,

I'm a little slow getting onboard with laying down my life and becoming the woman You want. Please do the work in my heart to soften me to hear Your thoughts.

Although my home is an important responsibility, the mundaneness can be so exhausting. I feel I have a lot of gifts to share with the world! Yet I know that in Your time, you will allow me to use those gifts. For now, I am to be a *good manager of my home* and *look well to the ways of my household*. I don't like this assignment, Lord, but I hear You and will obey.

God, You know I want a happy heart. I want a heart that encourages others just by my presence. Please grow that in me. Right now, I am still a clanging cymbal, as we both know. I want to be that woman who is a delight to others. Teach me how to leave my burdens on the shelf in heaven, knowing that You have plans to prosper me. Calm my fears about the future and know that You will show up with grace when I need it. God, I want so much to be this woman in Proverbs 31!

Without You, I judge others harshly. Without You, I am a gossipy, slanderous, lazy woman. Without You, I am dishonest and self-seeking. God, I need You so desperately! Somehow, someway, make me an excellent wife, a woman of noble character. I know this task is equal to walking on water, but You've already proved You can do that.

I pray as a child who greatly needs much help, in the name of Jesus,

Amen.

WEEK 4

Assignments and Group Discussion Questions

1. Spend time thinking about if you look well to the ways of your household (Proverbs 31) and if you are a good manager of your household (Titus 2). What are the major things you could you do to improve? (Even tiny things, such as packing lunches or getting clothes out the night before, make a difference in how smoothly your home management runs.) Are your children well cared for? Is your home clean and organized? Are you having wonderful healthy meals? What is important to your husband in this area? What is God saying to you through these verses in Proverbs 31 and Titus 2?

2. How do you score with the verse, "She can laugh at the days to come?" Which of the seven applications spoke to you? Are you a woman who can laugh at the days to come?

3. Are you still struggling with fixing your husband? Are you still wanting to confront him and demand that he change now?

4. You just put your big toe into the pool of *asking your husband for what you want*. Do you see the tendency you have to manipulate your husband? Are you willing to be a woman of prayer and ask God to give you pure motives?

WEEK 5

Fourth A: The Attention Lesson

Contents

Day 1: Inattentiveness Sets in after the Wedding
Day 2: The Art of Being a Good Conversationalist with Your Husband
Day 3: An Effective Way to Show Your Husband Attention: Ask His Opinion!
Day 4: An Important Area in Which to Show Great Attention to Your Husband: His Food!
Day 5: If You Have a High-Maintenance Hubby

Please read chapter 5, "Fourth A: The Attention Lesson" in *Wife School* before you do this week's study guide lesson.

DAY 1
Inattentiveness Sets in after the Wedding

The opposite of giving attention is *inattentiveness*. An extremely common occurrence after a few months/years of marriage is that the husband's honey-do list no longer gets the priority it once did.

"Did you pick up the dry cleaning I asked you to pick up?" your husband asks.

"Uh-h-h," you say. "It was a busy day. Sorry, I forgot."

"I think I taste mayonnaise on this sandwich," your husband says. "I don't like mayo. Remember?"

"Well…uh…I forgot because I was trying to get the kids out the door," you say.

Inattentiveness is the *opposite* of filling your husband's tank with the 8 A's. It is *draining* the tank. Be on the alert to your husband's requests and preferences. I am not exaggerating when I tell you that if my husband asks me for something (as this is a weakness for me), I will sometimes tape a note to my bathroom mirror. You are probably not as dense as me, but do what works for you.

Examples of inattentiveness abound everywhere. One husband said how hurtful it was that he had written a book and that his wife wasn't even interested in reading it. If you are not interested in your husband's job, goals, or hobbies, it is highly likely that he is vastly disappointed in you *as a wife*. Men long for their wives to be extremely attentive to them in all areas.

Proverbs 31 says, "Her husband has full confidence in her" and "She does him good, not harm, all the days of his life." This does not describe a wife who forgets her husband's honey-do list or who is uninterested in his preferences and interests.

Thirty years ago when I was a new believer, I had a wedding luncheon for my friend Gayle. Her father and mother arrived at the event, and the first thing Gayle's mother said to me was, "Could you please get me a cup of punch for my husband?" Being a new believer and having no idea about marriage, my thought was, "Why can't he get his own punch?" I now understand how wise wives give their husbands this kind of attention. That woman was Joyce Rogers, wife of the late world-famous evangelist and pastor Dr. Adrian Rogers.

DAY 2
The Art of Being a Good Conversationalist with Your Husband

In chapter 5 of *Wife School* this week, you read the section where the Genie instructs Jessica to "hit the ping pong ball back" to Matthew. We will build on that discussion.

Imagine you are having a conversation with a friend about a topic that you truly care about. You go off about this and that because you are very excited about this subject. Then your friend makes a comment and takes the conversation in a completely different direction. Why, you didn't get to talk about all you wanted to! In contrast, imagine you are having lunch with a dear friend, and she sits and listens, letting you talk and think and turn over your subject and then think and talk some more. What a difference in the friendships. How we yearn for friends who will listen until we have been completely emptied and heard.

Your husband is the same way. The problem is, you are bored with many of his topics. You do not want to hear about the same business proposal again. You do not want to hear about his workout again and how many reps he did. It is normal for wives not to be interested in many of their husbands' details, but we Proverbs 14:1 women are not normal. We are Marriage Champions. So you must learn to hit the ping pong ball back to your husband until he is through talking about a subject. Being this kind of good listener—where you pay rapt attention, ask good questions, and don't give too much advice—is about as rare as finding loose hundred dollar bills. So many affairs start because someone else had time to listen, understand, and be interested.

When I got my master's degree in counseling, the very best thing I learned during the whole program was a skill called Active Listening. What you do (and this takes lots of effort and practice) is to listen incredibly attentively so you can figure out how the other person is *feeling*. Then, you reflect back the feeling. For example, pretend your husband mentions the fact that today at work, the boss overlooked his contribution to the project. Because you're listening for a *feeling* to reflect back, you could possibly say, "That must have been very discouraging after all that effort you put into the presentation." See? Your husband will feel *heard* because you listened so well that you understood his feeling underneath. (Be careful, though. Sometimes, your husband will say, "No, that's not how I felt." Be humble, and try again.)

Let's look at another example. Say your husband plays church-league basketball. You are not particularly interested in basketball (in fact, you think he should be home studying his Bible, painting the den, or playing with the kids), but your husband is having a blast playing. When he comes home, maybe you ask, "How was your game?" Your husband says something like, "We won, forty-six to twenty-eight." Then most likely, if you are like many wives, your response is, "Do you want one or two pieces of chicken for dinner?"

I promise, your husband would like you to ask some good questions to draw him out. This takes work, effort, and time. If you make a bland or common statement (e.g., "Tell me about it"), some men will talk, but most men will go blank. But if you can genuinely learn enough about basketball to ask intelligent questions, he will open up. So you might say, "Were you able to hit your three-point shots tonight?" Men love to talk about their interests *but only to interested parties*. Learn your husband's job and activities inside and out. You don't have to participate in all his activities, but you had better know about them and be interested in them. Wives have an inside track to know and care about a husband's life, and if she doesn't, he will feel a deep disappointment.

As you know, an expectation we all have from marriage is for someone to be wildly interested in our details. I will continue to be annoying and remind you that wise women *have two standards*: the one they give and the one they expect for themselves. In all of life, the *emotionally healthy people think about how to give and are not easily offended because no one is pouring into them.* In Young's Literal Translation of Matthew 20:28, "the Son of Man did not come to be ministered to, but to minister." Let that model set in. Learning to *think about filling others* is a habit to learn. When self-pity creeps in ("What about someone listening to me?"), pinch yourself, and remind yourself that you have to learn to think like an emotionally healthy person. (People with addictive personality traits all struggle with being easily offended and with never getting enough attention, respect, and high treatment.)

DAY 3
An Effective Way to Show Your Husband Attention: Ask His Opinion!

Humans long to *give their opinion*. You do. Your husband does. We want to give our opinion, have someone listen, and then have someone *admire* that opinion. Sometime after marriage, though, women quit listening to their husbands' opinions and instead begin to stuff their husband's minds with their own opinions. Of course, it is fine to give your husband your opinion. But remember, he likes to be asked about his.

Ask his opinion on subjects such as the sermon at church, the subdivision's covenant, the school's policies, and the food at his job. The list is virtually endless. Make your marriage a place where your husband is given the opportunity to give his opinion. He longs to give his opinion, to be truly listened to, and then to be applauded.

Just know that you can't blast him when he says something you disagree with. It is all too common for wives to say, "Really? You think that? My mother doesn't think that, and I don't either."

James 1:19 says, "Everyone should be quick to listen, slow to speak." Your marriage should be the place where you are the best listener in the world to your spouse's opinions.

DAY 4
An Important Area in Which to Show Great Attention to Your Husband: His Food!

The Proverbs 31 woman was described as "merchant ships, bringing her food from afar." I think this verse talks about the effort she expended to bring beautiful food to the family's table. I heard a sermon once where the preacher said, "The Proverbs 31 woman didn't just throw any ole thing on the table but took pains to make it wonderful." I agree with that. Food preparation is a major way to make your husband feel as if you are depositing the A of Attention.

My husband has always been easy to feed. But ever since he got sick four years ago, we are on a very strict Paleo diet. He can have no sugar and no refined starches, as those items feed inflammation (something that harms his autoimmune disease). Even though we have no children at home anymore, I have never cooked so much in my life. I now feed him a cooked breakfast, pack his lunch (often leftovers, thank goodness), and then prepare a nice dinner. In order for him to have a lovely dinner and stay in the confines of his diet, I plan and shop and prep and cook. He has to be careful at every meal. No cheating because his disease could be life threatening if it flares. I am naturally *not* a little cottage wife who likes to whistle and dust, the proverbial Snow White. But early in my marriage, I saw the calling to have beautiful food in my house to nourish my family's bodies and souls. Even now, when my family enjoys a meal I have prepared, it gives me pleasure. (I am not a fabulous cook as some of you are, but with effort over the years, I have improved immeasurably.)

With the current culture, we find ourselves busy beyond belief. Therefore, *throwing any ole thing on the table* is more common than ever. I want to look at food in a light that I hope will encourage you to think hard about the food you feed your husband and family. I admit, this is a soapbox for me, but I think it is necessary to confront *the quality of food* most women feed their families.

For centuries, the family dinner table has been a place of great meaning. In Psalm 128:3, the psalmist writes, "Your children will be like vigorous young olive trees as they sit around your table." *Eating together* has great meaning throughout the Scripture. This centuries-old tradition is worth discussing on many levels. But today, we will discuss only one.

Weston Price was a dentist known primarily for his theories on the relationship between nutrition, dental health, and physical health. He said that the aspects of a modern Western diet (particularly flour, sugar, and modern processed vegetable fats) cause nutritional deficiencies, and these deficiencies cause disease. Dr. Price studied and wrote about many *diverse native* cultures, including the Lötschental in Switzerland, Native Americans, Polynesians, Pygmies, and Aborigines.

Price argued that when these non-Western groups abandoned indigenous diets (their natural food from the land) and adopted Western patterns of living, they showed increases in typical Western diseases. He concluded that Western methods of preparing and storing foods stripped away vitamins and minerals necessary to prevent disease.

Studies such as Price's abound everywhere. An abundance of fast food, processed food, and junk food is just plain foolish. The human body is an amazing machine, and it can filter out some harmful substances, but it can't filter out a consistent overload of unhealthy food. God created natural food to perfectly nourish our extremely complex bodies. The complexity of natural food is actually staggering in the same way as the galaxies are staggering. Nutrition is a mind-boggling subject.

Because you are a wise wife, I encourage you to consider carefully what you are feeding your husband and your children. The Proverbs 31 woman went to a large effort to get beautiful food for her family, but *you just have to go to Kroger*. It's *what you buy* there that is important. Don't feed your family junk. Sugar is not love. Junk food is not love. Love your family, and feed them well with natural, healthy food.

If you sign up for a daily e-letter from Mercola.com, you will know more about nutrition in six months than many doctors. Dr. Josh Axe and Dr. Mark Hyman are two other experts that I follow because of their brilliance regarding *food*.

Yes, make beautiful food to delight your husband and kids. But be very mindful of the nutrition. If you study sugar and white flour and their damaging effects, you will realize that anything with those ingredients should be labeled with a skull and crossbones warning. How deceived we are as a culture that the amount of sugar we consume is ignored. An abundance of sugar causes all sorts of physical/mental/emotional problems. I think of Halloween, a day that overloads children everywhere with a kind of mild poison: sugar. Dear wise woman! Take the time to learn about nutrition.

DAY 5
If You Have a High-Maintenance Hubby

Giving attention to your difficult husband is tiresome because it is a daily job. Of course, your particular husband has certain things he cares about and things he doesn't care about. Some husbands care about an extremely neat house. Some husbands care if dinner is ready exactly when they get home. Some husbands want their shirts hung up a certain way. Some husbands…Well, you get it. Figure out your husband's preferences, and then make accommodations for him. The point is, all husbands care if you pay attention to their schedule, their preferences, and their comforts. All. Husbands.

If you have a needy, high-maintenance husband, then give him what he needs as far as attention. Filling up most husbands is akin to filling up a bathtub. Needy husbands are akin to filling up the swimming pool. No husband (unless he is mentally ill) is like the Mississippi River. You might have a tough job on your hands, but you, the Proverbs 14:1 woman, are up for it! Say no to some other things so your husband is happy with the attention you give him. If your child has learning disabilities, you go the extra mile to get him what he needs as far as education. If your husband needs exceptionally high emotional maintenance, go the extra mile. This is the husband you were given to love, so don't fuss. Instead, love him to the moon and back.

Reminder

Once again, I would like to say that this advice is *not* for women with husbands who are alcoholics, are abusive, or are committing adultery. Please contact your pastor or a Christian counselor for those issues. *Wife School* is for wives with *normal* husbands (annoying but not evil).

It is not good for man to be alone, and it is awesome to have a sweet marriage!

Prayer

Dear Father,

I feel so unworthy to come before You. In fact, as I sit in Your presence, I can feel the smut and dirt on my soul. I bring before You my tendency to manipulate things so they benefit me. I bring before You how easily offended I am when I feel overlooked or that I did not receive *high treatment* (as I know that is pride like Haman's). I bring before You my lack of concern for the poor, the hungry, and the needy. Instead, You know that I am primarily concerned about my comfort and success (and my children's, as again, they are an extension of me).

What do I do about this heap of dung? Where can I find relief for the guilt and shame I feel? Who can help me change?

For me to have great forgiveness and great freedom in my spirit and soul, there is no work I can do, but there is something *You did.* You chose to provide the Lamb! Not only do I pay nothing for this forgiveness, You give it freely and ask only that I now follow You and forgive others. Just like the unmerciful servant, I receive the huge ocean of Your forgiveness but then have trouble extending a bathtub portion to others, especially the man I was given to love. Show me my ocean of rebellion toward You and Your ways. Show me my utter reluctance to serve others (unless I somehow benefit). Show me how I want my name, not Yours, high and lifted up. Show me the Jezebel spirit that I have (although you know how hard I try to hide it from others). Clean me out.

May I be a branch on the Vine, receiving the Sap (John 15). May I be so full of You that when I get jostled, I spill the fruit of the spirit (Gal. 5). In my own strength, I am a worm. But with Your filling, I can have a gentle and quiet spirit (1 Pet. 3). In addition, You say I am of great worth in your sight. Imagine that—me, a Jezebel, trading my spirit for Yours and becoming a woman of great worth. That is more unbelievable than when You fed the five thousand! God, remind me over and over again of this great exchange. I bring my menstrual rags of good works (Isa. 64:6) to you. And somehow, someway, You will use nobody-me to do Your great will. Amazing. Incredible. Mind boggling.

I don't deserve this, but I do love it, God.

With great gratefulness and a new willingness to forgive even those who have hurt me,

And in the superior name of Jesus,

Amen.

Assignments and Group Discussion Questions

1. How would you rate your natural attentiveness to your husband? Is this an area of strength or of weakness?

2. How are you at hitting the ping pong ball back? Are you good at asking questions to draw your husband out and get him to talk more? Are you a naturally good listener? How might you improve in this area?

3. Do you frequently ask your husband's opinion, or are you usually interested only in filling his mind with yours? How could you improve in this area?

4. Do you make a big effort to have regular family meals? What do you know about health and nutrition? Are you aware of the disaster of sugar and the necessity of eating whole, natural food? Discuss your current views and also what you think you might need to do differently.

5. Have you made peace with the concept of how much work it is to be a fantastic wife? Do you realize that it is a sowing and reaping world? Do you understand that the only way to a husband's heart is to win it?

WEEK 6

Fifth A: The Activities Lesson and More...

Contents

Day 1: Thoughts about the A of Activities

Day 2: What If You Run Out of Energy to Pour into Your Husband?

Day 3: Why Is Respecting Your Husband So Important?

Day 4, Part A: Understanding Men's Tendency to Be Inconsiderate

Day 4, Part B: Beware of Not Feeling Appreciated

Day 5, Part A: Thoughts about the Clothes of Christian Women

Day 5, Part B: When Your Husband Wants You to Work Full Time outside the Home

Some of you are seeing huge changes in your marriage, but some of you are still just trying to keep your head above water. This is only week 6 of our 22 lessons. On top of that, three of the most important A's—Approval, Affection (sex), and Authority—have not yet been studied! Be patient. We are still planting the seedlings. Then it's growing season. Remember, "Love never fails" (1 Cor. 13:8).

Please read chapter 6, "Fifth A: The Activities Lesson" in *Wife School*.

DAY 1
Thoughts about the A of Activities

Some couples don't struggle with the A of Activities. For example, my sister-in-law and brother share many interests. They both like to antique shop (he likes to find items to fix up the garden/yard and she likes dishes). Also, my sister-in-law loves football (the Dallas Cowboys), and he's the doctor on the sidelines. The A of Activities has been easy for them for the entirety of their marriage because many of their natural downhill streams are in the same direction. This isn't so for everyone.

For example, my husband and I have to work on this A. David likes sports, and I like...well...books. After *extensive* work, we have figured out *some* activities we enjoy together. We both enjoy going to seminars to learn. Recently, we went to a Dave Ramsey event to learn how to grow and run his business better. We both enjoy Bible study, and we participated in a yearlong discipleship ministry called Downline. Naturally, we enjoy anything with our kids (basketball games, outings, dinner, etc.). We both like good movies, plays, or concerts (but I'm really picky about which ones). After that, we have to work at this A. I am somewhat of a homebody, so I have to push myself to go out and do the many activities that my sweet husband enjoys. Many couples have to work hard to find mutually enjoyable activities, so don't be discouraged if your marriage is like ours.

Having date night is very important when you have kids. Family activities are awesome, but it is important for you and your husband to focus on each other. We women are frequently reluctant to do that, and I understand. You can't ignore this A because *fun and play* are often very important to your husband. You have to make this work for *your* marriage. There is not a formula. But a marriage can get boring if you do not continue to have fun and play in the partnership.

Just a hint to know when you are on a date with your husband: he wants to know if you are having a nice time. Tell your husband if you are enjoying yourself. Give him a little kiss, smile, or squeeze. He will take it personally and feel good that you are happy. Just lean over and whisper to your husband, "I'm having a good time." In other words, *be a good date*. Smile. Thank him for dinner. Tell him how delicious the crab cakes are, as in the old days when he was paying and you were on a date. We women can settle into talking about what's wrong and "how cold and tired" we are. Really? Is that being a good date? It is said that women start trying to change men the second they are married but conversely, men never want their wives to change *from when they were dating*. (We fixed ourselves up and were in a good mood, remember?) We wives need to listen up!

DAY 2
What If You Run Out of Energy to Pour into Your Husband?

One woman in my *Skinny School* class has not been able to do the work to plan, prepare, or track her food, which are tenets in the program. When we dissected her situation, we found that she is so ultra-busy with her school-age children, housework, job, and volunteer work that there was simply no energy left to put into figuring out a new eating program. I explained to her that humans only have a certain amount of willpower/energy points a day, and when we run out, we run out. Her busy and hectic life left her without any reserves to invest in a new endeavor.

I once read—and I'm not sure if this is true—that President Obama couldn't quit smoking cigarettes while he was in office because after trying to solve the world's problems each day, there was no energy left to apply to quitting smoking. Whether that story is true or not, the principle is. We are just humans, not gods. We are finite creatures.

Now I say the same to you about your marriage. If you are running the PTA, running the women's ministry at your church, handling three energetic preschoolers, working forty hours a week, managing your house and your aging mom and still want to love your husband to the moon and back, well, forget it. You will be out of willpower/energy points. Vince Lombardi said, "Fatigue makes cowards of us all." You can accomplish only so much in every twenty-four hours, so be incredibly intentional about what you give your time and energy to.

Again, camp in Titus 2. Go down the list of the younger woman's responsibilities. If you can't outrageously love your husband and children, have a happy heart, take care of your household, then you have to stop there and get those priorities right. You can't take care of a family on an empty tank, and that is your priority in this season. Again, learn to say *no* graciously to others. Give up time wasters (too much social media, TV, etc.). Margins are necessary because cars break down, dishwashers overflow, parents get sick, and children have issues that need addressing. Quit trying to be Superwoman. Instead, just attempt to be Titus2Woman.

DAY 3
Why Is Respecting Your Husband So Important?

The movie *The Godfather II* was on TV a month ago. One of the brothers, Fredo, who has no influence in the family, says to Michael Corleone, the brother with the power (played by Al Pacino), "I just want some respect." The brother saying this is pitiful and sad, but yet I was reminded how all men want respect. It is wired into them.

As you read the next section, you are going to want to throw it down and start stomping on it. Just remember that God inspired Paul to write this.

In Ephesians 5:33, Paul wrote, "and the wife must respect her husband."

If that's not bad enough, Young's Literal Translation says that "she (the wife) may *reverence* the husband."

Again, I recommend Scripture4all.org to you. Click on "Greek-English Interlinear," and then you can follow along with the following. Warning: rough water ahead.

The Greek word for *reverence* in that verse is *phobetai*. Scripture4all.org translates it as she "may be fearing." If you research this Greek word (Strong's G5399), the word has several meanings. This word is often used in the New Testament for *fear* and *afraid*. (You can go to blueletterbible.org and find twenty examples of this.) Another meaning of this Greek word is "to reverence, venerate, to treat with deference or reverential obedience." This is the meaning we will discuss. Remember, I warned you about the rough water.

In my opinion, no husband is worthy of being *reverenced* as he is a human and all humans are broken. *If* husbands are worthy or not is *not* the point. The point is that *God* wants wives to treat their husbands with reverence and deference. It is the *position* of husband that we honor. When the judge comes into the courtroom, we all rise. We don't rise for the man; we rise for the *position* of judge. You don't rise when you see that judge in a restaurant. You are to treat your husband with reverence, not because he deserves it but because *how you treat your husband* is a picture of how the Church (a believer) is to treat her husband, the Lord. Once we see the spiritual analogy, *we can soften to the command.*

I actually think this verse gives a lot of freedom to wives. Instead of respecting or reverencing our husbands because they deserve it, we respect and reverence them because *God has asked us to do this for Him.* I can buy into that. I can obey that. It may not be easy, but I can get my mind around this analogy that God gave us. This takes faith. This takes understanding.

I have a very nice husband who has integrity that is off the chart. But I still have trouble reverencing him, a mere human, even though he is a very good man. Again, whether he deserves it or not is not the point. *The point is this is God's will for wives.*

Exhale. That was pretty rough, I know. Go get a cup of hot tea, and read the rest of this later. Whew. Glad that's over. 😊 (Lesson nine, the A of Authority, is coming down the tracks in four weeks. It is *not* going to be pretty, friends, not pretty at all. This was a warm-up for that lesson.)

DAY 4, PART A
Understanding Men's Tendency to be Inconsiderate

You have been in *Wife School* now for six weeks. You know the baseline principle in *Wife School* is to focus on how you love and give, not on how you are loved or given to. Actually, this section was strategically placed after the reverencing-your-husband section so I wouldn't be misunderstood. With the prior biblical concepts in mind, I offer the next section with trepidation that I will be misunderstood. For example, if this next section were quoted out of context, it would be easy to call *Wife School* a manipulative program. But I am counting on you to have greater understanding than that. So let's proceed.

Many of you are dealing with issues in which your husband is very inconsiderate of you. The next two examples may seem small, but the principles apply in the same way.

An older wife told me that she and her husband were invited to a Halloween party and were going out on Halloween night. She did not want to receive trick-or-treaters because she and her husband were leaving for the night. She asked him to please keep the lights off in the house until they left so the trick-or-treaters wouldn't stop by. Her husband flipped on the laundry room light. She asked him again to please keep the lights off because she had no candy for the kids. He went upstairs and flipped on another bedroom light. Again, she sweetly said, "That light can be seen from the street. It is almost time to go, and I don't have any candy." A third time, he flipped on a light, completely ignoring her request again. He finally said, "If they knock on the door, just don't answer it." But she didn't want neighborhood kids knocking on the door and her not having any candy to give them. The situation was small, but the insensitivity to the wife's requests was not small in her opinion.

Another example is that a wife (wife A) bought a friend (wife B) a small Christmas ornament that she knew would delight her friend. Wife A knew that her husband would see wife B's husband in the next few days (they were involved in some church activities together). Wife A asked her husband to take the ornament to wife B's husband so he (husband B) would give it to his wife. Husband A forgot. Then, wife A asked him again. He forgot again. This went on three or four times. Wife A was frustrated that her husband couldn't seem to remember her request.

Not that this is right, but men tend to evaluate whether they think your issues are important and then make a decision through their *male mind* whether they should do it or not. A lot of our female stuff is not important to them, as you will discover (turning off lights during Halloween, giving ornaments to friends, etc.).

I gave you unimportant examples on purpose because that's not the point. The point is that men will often feel your issues are not important and won't comply with your request. You have to fill their tanks and then, in a sweet way, say, "I know this isn't important to you, but it's important to me as a woman. So could you please do it?" That somehow frees them when they realize that although your request is *not* important to them, they can still do it because it is important to you, for the standard is different for what is important to women.

Remember, when your husband does something for you that he doesn't really want to do, you do the one-two punch of thanking him. The first time, say, "That was so nice of you. And I especially love it because you didn't think it was necessary, but you did it just to make me happy. Thank you!" And then the killer/knockout punch comes when you thank him hours/days later. "I was thinking about how you don't have any need for *x* or *y*, but just because I asked you, you did it for me. How understanding and unselfish that was of you. That really meant a lot to me. Thank you." A sweet kiss on the cheek or a nice smile is good here.

The scripture says to husbands, "Live with your wives in an understanding way." Why? Because we are so ridiculously different from them, and they can't treat us like *the boys*. But men don't usually get this the first five years of marriage (or more, unless you teach them).

When your husband doesn't live with you in an understanding way and is inconsiderate, don't begin a meltdown with accusations. If you are living the 8 A's and he disappoints you in a *big* way (overlook the little things), say, "I guess you didn't understand how important this was to me or else I know you would have considered it." No emotional hissy fits. Try to overlook everything that *you possibly can*. No tears unless the transgression is gigantic. (Just so you know, the more you cry, the less effective it is, so try to keep back the waterworks. Women are notorious for trying to manipulate husbands with tears.)

Husbands have been civilized by wives for centuries. Otherwise, husbands wouldn't bathe, they would tee-tee in the backyard, and many men would be semi-slobs. (Have you ever visited a fraternity house?) But they are to be *called up* by the sweetness and softness of their wife, not by some army general barking orders.

Sorry, but it takes many men around five to ten years to get this. My husband is only a shadow of who he was thirty years ago (as far as how he treats me). David still opens the car door for me. Early in the marriage when he did it, I said over and over again, "I can't believe how I'm treated like a queen and you open my car door for me. It makes me feel like a million dollars." Every six months or so, I still comment on him opening the car door. Husbands want to please us. Just be adorable and grateful and give it five years. *Catch them doing things right* and *praise them*.

Another example might be, "You just listened to that whole long story of mine, and I know you aren't really interested in the drama going on with my friends. But how wonderful to have a husband who listens well until I'm through! That makes me so happy." Then add a sweet smile or little kiss.

Another wise woman said to her husband, "I can't believe I have a husband who lets me take a nap and watches the children. How sweet is that? I certainly married well." The *normal* wife expects her husband to watch the children; the *wise* wife expects nothing and thanks him all the time.

Women! This is not rocket science. This is female wisdom of the ages. Be sweet, grateful, kind, and soft. Your husband wants to please you. That's why Adam ate that apple in the garden. Eve wanted him to, and he wanted to please her. (Hopefully, God is leading your husband, and your husband will be man enough to stand up and say *no* to you when you are out of God's will. More on this unpleasant situation in week 9.)

Just to recap: many men come into marriage and are very inconsiderate because they do not understand your womanly mind. Give it some time. Things mightily change when women are wise.

DAY 4, PART B
Beware of Not Feeling Appreciated

A few years ago, a woman of influence whom I respected called and asked if I would meet with her niece, Suzie, who was having serious marriage issues. It wasn't a very good season for me to add a new commitment, but she sounded rather desperate, so I acquiesced. I met with the girl many times, and that doesn't count the phone calls and emails. We made a lot of progress.

Later, I saw this woman of influence out, and she didn't mention all the hours I had spent (at her request) to help her niece. Before we parted, I casually asked, "How's Suzie doing?" Now here was her chance to gush me, to tell me how wonderful I was that I spent so much of my free time helping her niece. Nope. It didn't happen. She just told me that Suzie was now pregnant.

When we actually parted, I was like a dog with my tail between my legs. Forlorn. Discouraged. I even said things to myself such as, "Well, I might have to think a little harder before I take on a new counselee next time if I'm going to get appreciated like that." (You can stop gagging, haha. I know this is a pitiful way to think but this was my honest initial reaction.)

The point I'm trying to make with this pathetic story is, *I didn't feel appreciated*. If our goal in doing service is to get appreciation, *we will be disappointed*.

This is really true with your husband (and someday, adult children). Giving up expectations that your acts of kindness will be appreciated is very wise. Now that you are pouring the 8 A's into your husband, you might be like most wives and think, "Mmm, I bet he's going to like this and thank me." Warning: you are setting yourself up for disappointment. Give and love and then get your appreciation *from the Lord* (Col. 3:23). Serve others because that's *who you are*, and that's *what you do*. Release those you serve from appreciating you. Here we are again with our double standards: we appreciate everything the husband does, but we don't expect appreciation from him. You know what happens when he *does* appreciate you, right? You are grateful to Jupiter and back, and you write it on your Turquoise Journal lists!

DAY 5, PART A
Thoughts about the Clothes of Christian Women

In this section, I would first like to give you a few thoughts about how men feel about women's clothes, and then we will look at a couple of thoughts about what the Bible says about women and clothes.

Men usually like feminine clothes on women that are soft and *decidedly female*. Men like cashmere (soft), bright colors, soft textures, and dresses. Wear something soft and colorful, and hear what your husband says. Dress for your husband. My husband likes a tailored look, whereas I'd rather dress with jeans, leather boots, and leather jackets. The tailored stuff is boring to me, but that's what he likes. We are to reflect our husbands. The way we dress reflects to the world *how they take care of us*. Again, there are no rules, only principles and suggestions.

This is not very difficult. Simply ask your husband his opinion.

Let's briefly look at what the Scripture says about clothing. In Proverbs 7:10, the Scripture says, "Out came a woman to meet him, dressed like a prostitute." So there is definitely a way to dress that conveys we are immoral women. In contrast, the Proverbs 31 woman was "clothed in fine linen and purple." That sounds more like a *regal* look, doesn't it? We have to admit that how we dress says something about us. I am not giving absolutes, but the principles are pretty clear: *not raunchy but tasteful.* (There is a lot of gray area here, aren't you glad?)

There are some specific instructions in 1 Timothy 2 about how women who are going to worship should dress. The Scripture says women are to dress with "modesty and decency." In church a few months ago, a girl who was wearing shorts was sitting a couple of rows ahead of us and was shaking her booty to the worship music. My boys were all observing *the bounce.* I wanted to tap her on the shoulder and say, "Quit shaking your booty in church!" Men go crazy at a booty that is shaking. Shake yours at home in the bedroom, but please don't shake it at church.

A few years ago, I heard a respected preacher in Tennessee talk about his congregation as "fried chicken: breasts, thighs, and legs." I know we women like to show what we've got—to flaunt our stuff. But scripture is specific that when you go to church, be especially mindful to be modest. Men are distracted by bare skin and super tight clothes. Don't be *that* woman.

I was at a basketball game a few months ago, and a mom showed up in a very short tennis dress. Every single person in that gym was looking at her thighs. Then, a few months after that, a mom at a Meet-the-Teacher event was there in *short* shorts. Both of these women claim to be Christians. I'm just giving you my opinion here (and yes, maybe I was a little jealous of their great legs, but that's not the point). The point is, I really feel it was inappropriate in those *settings* to dress like that. I said I wasn't giving rules, and please know that each of these situations calls for unique discernment. It's one thing to be in shorts and exercising. It's another to be at an event where everybody else is dressed in regular street clothes. You will have to figure this out. You can look nice and wear fitted clothes; just don't dress raunchy or tacky. It's beneath your station in life as a godly wife.

We get so mixed up. We wear low-cut blouses out in public and then wear flannel cover-up nightgowns to bed with our sex-starved husbands. I'm not saying to dress like a nun. I'm saying that we are all to be mindful of how we dress, especially when we go to public worship.

DAY 5, PART B
When Your Husband Wants You to Work Full Time outside the Home

This section is written for those of you whose husband wants you to work full time outside the home, and your heart is to be home. (Skip this section if it doesn't pertain to you.) I have a lot of compassion for you. The following are suggestions, not rules. Take what is helpful to you, and throw the rest to the wind. This is a difficult situation. But I see miracles happen in marriages when women understand a few concepts.

First, live the 8 A's. Get rid of your resentment, and persuade your husband that you know you were created for him (1 Cor. 11:9), that you want him to be happy and successful, and prove it. This will open him to your influence.

The next thing is to pray like a madwoman (see the parable of the unjust judge, Luke 18:1–18). Beg, plead, ask, seek, and knock in prayer. Believe that God *has plans to prosper you* (Jer. 29:11). Tell your husband that you are asking God—in maybe a year or so—to make provisions so that you won't have to work full time outside the home. Giving him this yearlong timetable takes any immediate stress off him. Tell him your heart is to work part-time or to work from home. If he says that is ridiculous, then respond calmly with, "This is a desire of mine, and I am asking God for a miracle." He cannot argue with that. If he is again rude—for example, "Good luck on that"—let it go.

Then, carefully consider your lifestyle. It is definitely difficult to *downsize* lifestyles. But it is crazy to take fancy vacations, drive new cars, live in a big house, and go out to eat often and then for you to work full time outside the home! Camp for vacations, drive older cars, move to a smaller house, and eat at home. Then, start *not* spending money wherever you can. If your husband wants to go on an expensive vacation, say, "Honey, could we camp? I am trying to find ways not to spend money. I want so badly to be home so I can focus more on you, our children, and our home."

Don't get on him too much, but *you* start cutting back. Cut back on Christmas (do something free for a present exchange with extended relatives so you can save money for the kiddos). You don't have to have new stuff; you really don't. I know you want it. I know! But we have to get straight on the fact that we don't get everything in life. Giving up one thing means we get another. I repeatedly like to use the example of giving up sugar (something we like) for health and thinness (something we like better).

Start researching *working from home*. Ask your husband his goals and his opinion. How much money do we need to save? If you can (please do this), go to a Dave Ramsey course and get your finances straightened out. Finances are a huge area of conflict for couples. Getting on the same page as your husband with finances is one of the smartest things you can do for your marriage. The Proverbs 31 woman helped with the income; so can you. But the burden to provide lies mostly on a man's shoulders. Many men want their wives to work to help with the financial stress, and this is understandable. But when your husband feels as if it would profit him and your family for you to be home more, he will begin to help find ways for you to do this. Husbands want to please adorable wives. They do.

There is not an overnight fix for this. Don't put a time limit on this huge goal, but at least in your heart know it will take months and maybe a year. When a wife really does have a quantum switch in how she treats her husband, she will notice a quantum switch in how her husband responds to her. If your husband just agrees to *think* about it, thank him. Then later, *thank* him again for just agreeing to *think* about it. Wise wives praise and appreciate the little things.

I am not trying to take an overwhelming issue and make it simple. These are some thoughts for you to put into your pot to stir. Wise women are kind and patient but persistent.

We all have sorrows and battles. This one is yours. It is amazing how husbands change their minds in response to wise, prayerful, loving, noncritical wives.

A Verse to Encourage You

"Let us not become weary in doing good, for at the proper time we will reap a harvest if we do not give up" (Gal. 6:9). Persevere, my *Wife School* friend, as in time you will reap a harvest if you do not give up.

Prayer

Dear Father in heaven,

For now, You have allowed sorrow and grief to remain on Earth. To be honest, I am feeling both of those enemies right now. My heart is burdened. You say to come to you, *all that are weary and heavy-laden* (Matt. 11:27) and that You will give me rest. You are not far off. You hear when I call. Please bring your kindness to me and to those I love. Please answer me in my hurt and disappointment. Please show me how to handle the problems that are sitting on the table right before me. Please pour Your wisdom and grace into my situation.

I trust You right now to untangle these knots, though I don't see how You are going to do that. But You just say the word, and it happens (Matt. 8:9). You are not a human, bound as I am, by time and strength. You can work through my weaknesses and mistakes. Thank you, God, for listening. Matthew 7:11 says, "If you then, being evil, know how to give good gifts to your children, how much more will your Father who is in heaven give what is good to those who ask Him!" God, I'm asking. I'm asking really hard.

I lay these requests before You. My soul waits for You, Lord, more than the watchman waits for the morning (Ps. 130:6).

In Jesus's name,

Amen.

Assignments and Group Discussion Questions

1. What activities do you and your husband enjoy together? Is the A of Activities a strength for your marriage or do you need to work on this?

2. Between zero and ten, where is the resentment dial pointed in your marriage (with ten being high)? What is God telling you to do in this area?

3. Do you have energy to pour into your husband? What needs to be pared down in your schedule so you have more energy for making deposits into your husband's tank? Did the word *reverence* throw you? How do you feel about this command from God to treat your husband with reverence?

4. Now that you are pouring into your husband, are you struggling with not being appreciated for that?

5. How did you feel about the section on men's tendency to sometimes be inconsiderate with their wives? What are your thoughts about this section?

6. What are your thoughts about women, modesty, and clothes in church?

7. If your husband doesn't want you to quit your full-time job, what thoughts do you now have about asking him to consider a different future situation?

WEEK 7

Sixth A: The Approval Lesson

Contents

Day 1: Thoughts about the A of Approval
Day 2: When Your Husband Is Selfish with His Time
Day 3: Something Only a Man Can Give to Your Kids
Day 4, Part A: Understanding Your Need to Release Emotional Tension
Day 4, Part B: Tips for Traveling with Your Husband
Day 5: Dealing with Difficult Parents/In-Laws

I have a journal where I write down ideas and thoughts I want to keep. When I go back to review it, I wouldn't even believe that I wrote it, except that it is in my own handwriting. Friends, collect good sentences and thoughts, and then bathe your mind with them. That will change you. There are many extra blank pages in the back of your Turquoise Journal just for this purpose.

Please read chapter 7, "Sixth A: The Approval Lesson" in *Wife School.*

DAY 1
Thoughts about the A of Approval

In chapter 7 in *Wife School*, the Genie tells Jessica that "spouses can read between the lines to hear if the other spouse communicates approval." The overall approval rating that one feels from his or her spouse is often indicative of that person's satisfaction in the marriage.

The power we have over our spouse's self-concept is gigantic. I was at a career-planning seminar this fall with one of my sons and the speaker said, "If our spouse is for us, it doesn't matter who is against us." Giving—or denying—approval in marriage is either healing or destroying. "Gracious words are a honeycomb, sweet to the soul and healing to the bones" (Prov. 16:24).

As we learn in chapter 7, a surprising concept to many wives is the fact that when they share many burdens with their husbands, husbands take it personally, as though they are not good providers/protectors. Here are a few examples: "I hate driving this old piece of junk." "Look at all those people flying in first class with the extra leg room and special drinks. That must be the life." "No wonder she always looks so good; she has a maid and a personal trainer." "I wish we had more money so we could send the kids to private school." "Their kids are super talented. The father spends all Saturday afternoon playing ball with his boys." Those statements often communicate *disapproval*.

We are simply sharing our thoughts, but our husbands are thinking, "She would be happy if I provided/protected better. I am inadequate." Then they do the thing we hate: withdraw.

Of course you can share your burdens with your husband, but be mindful of his "inadequacy radar" and make accommodations to communicate approval. Let's take the examples in the paragraph above and see if we can come up with better sentences.

"I hate driving this old piece of junk" could be better reworded like this: "This car has two hundred thousand miles on it. Maybe we should consider getting another car in the near future."

"Look at all those people flying in first class" should just not be said. Be glad you can afford to fly at all.

"No wonder she always looks so good; she has a maid and a personal trainer" makes a husband feel as if you are unhappy under his watch. If you want/need household help, then consider putting that request on your list of things you want/need. We will soon discuss how to ask for the top things on your want/need list. But throwing out random statements that communicate your discontent is not wise or loving.

"I wish we had more money so we could send the kids to private school" might be reworded as, "Educating our children in the right environment is very important to me. I'd like to discuss this and get your thoughts on this issue." There are no issues you cannot discuss with your husband. But again, be mindful of not communicating discontent with his provision.

There is a better way to communicate to your husband that you'd like him to spend more time with the kids. One idea is to *catch your husband playing with your kids* and give him a one-two punch. A one-two punch thanks him the first time and then tells him again how happy you are to see their faces light up when he gives them attention. Men are drawn to praise and tend to repeat what gets appreciated and admired.

Death and life are in the power of the tongue (Prov. 18:21). Never forget that. It is one of the most powerful sentences to help your marriage. Death and life. Tattoo that verse on your brain.

We get to be honest with our husbands. But remember, we are to speak the truth *in love*. Letting whatever feelings we have tumble out is not speaking *in love*; it is speaking only *in truth*. The command is to do *both*. Be mindful that your husband has a tendency to hear your complaints as *an indictment against his provision*. Men with grumbling wives do not feel approval from them.

I was talking to a group of young women, explaining how men are roosters and want to be the biggest rooster in the chicken yard *especially to their wives*. A young woman mocked her husband by saying he was a ridiculous rooster and wanted to be at the very top of the pecking order as if this were awful and terrible. Women, realize that *most men are like this*! They want to be heroes to their wives. Often I hear a repulsion from wives toward their husbands' fragile, easily cracked, egg-like egos. I think it would be helpful if men would carry a warning label on their chest: "I am a man with a big and fragile ego. Therefore, if you are my wife, please handle with care!"

The fact that most men are wired this way should calm you down about having to pour into—and handle with care—his ego. I've quoted Ruth Bell Graham before but again I quote her brilliant statement: "God called you not to make your husband good, but to make him happy." Friend, let God humble your husband, not you. God is working on him to humble him. But that is *not* your job.

Your husband wants you, the wife, to think he is Superman. If *most men* are like this, then we wives had better wise up and adjust our communication so we don't set off their inadequacy alarms. Your husband isn't some huge psychologically needy individual. He's most likely a normal husband. Some of the very best husbands, the very best Christian men, have fragile egos.

A Christian man should be working on his humility because of his call in Christ, but his baseline desire is for a wife who is mindful of his need for *much encouragement and affirmation*. Your role is not to set him straight about all his weaknesses—of which he has many. You are not the coach, the teacher, or the mother. You are the wife who does him good all the days of his life.

The best environment for another to change and grow is one of *approval and acceptance*. We don't believe that. We think barking at husbands and criticizing them is the best way to help them grow and change. We women can be such dummies.

Finding contentment is one of the most difficult assignments that God gives women. It is *absolutely opposite* to our natural inclinations. This will be a lifelong battle for most women (there are a few Snow Whites out there who are happy to whistle and dust, but just a few). Finding contentment in the Lord is one of the best gifts you can give to your husband, as you will be able to sincerely communicate approval when your expectations are reduced.

Because our expectations as wives are so enormous, men continually feel a stream of disapproval from us. This is not an optional subject for a wife. Get your heart happy in the Lord, and learn how to communicate approval to this man whom you were given to love.

I cannot tell you how many times God has pricked me with thoughts such as, "Your husband, not you, was right about how to handle that." When I say to David, "You were right about that, and I love the wisdom/knowledge you possess and how it protects me," I communicate my approval to him. Be humble, and tell your husband how he was right and you were wrong about an issue. Write down in your Turquoise Journal the things your husband does better than you. Then, *tell* him. He needs to feel your approval for how he does life.

DAY 2
When Your Husband Is Selfish with His Time

Men need hobbies and time to relax. Helping your husband find some time to do this is a gift you give him. Many husbands greatly appreciate your giving him the green light to some time for himself (and not feeling guilty about it).

However, with that said, some husbands neglect family responsibilities (in the wife's opinion) because of extremely intense and demanding hobbies. Some husbands are on golf teams and travel many weekends with their buddies, leaving their wives home with the kids. Some husbands are training for triathlons, bodybuilding competitions, bike races, or they work out for many hours, again leaving their wife with the responsibilities at home. I know of many wives whose husbands hunt every weekend once the season opens. And don't forget good old TV. Many men love ESPN, the NFL, and the NBA.

Realize that you are not angry about the individual activity or sport. In fact, if your husband had unlimited time and resources—and you and the kids had the help and attention you needed—then you would be fine with his bowling, mountain climbing, or volunteer work. You are not angry at *golf*. It's the *limited situation of time* that is the problem, as well as the unmet needs. After the children are much older and the demands are fewer, many women are no longer upset if their husbands intensely pursue hobbies. But in this season, the hours are few, and a husband being overly active in activities outside the home (in the wife's opinion) can be a great source of conflict.

As you will see throughout *Wife School*, many problems have the same answers. Always remember that husbands are better *coaxed than commanded*. We remember that husbands change only when *they want to* and that we increase their desire to please us when we live the 8 A's and get hold of our emotional turmoil.

An obvious principle is to encourage your husband's enjoyment of family time by bragging on him in front of the kids and doing activities as a family that *he* enjoys. Thank him for every investment of time he pours into the family, large and small. Learn to look for opportunities to say, "I can't tell you how soothing and fulfilling it is to me to watch you play with the kids and see their happiness. What a gift to our children to have a father like you." When you ask him for more family time, you don't want to bash his hobby, such as, "Why do you waste all that time on that stupid hobby?" (You know better than this by now, don't you?) You want him to enjoy his interests and tell him that. You like him to be happy, and you know how much he enjoys activity *x*. So you don't want him to quit; you simply need to figure out together how to (insert the need here).

If he barks, try to soothe him. "A gentle answer turns away wrath" (Prov. 15:1). When he sees that you are not trying to force him to give up his activity, only to get some needs met, then he is more willing to consider your requests. If the conversation goes south, just say, "Well, we can think about it. I really care if you are happy, and I know you relax/enjoy when *x* is happening. I am just trying to figure out how to get need *y* met."

Men like this rational approach. No bashing. No hysterical demands. Just state what your needs are, and let them stew around in his pot. He may act rude and insensitive, but if you are living the 8 A's, the ground of his heart is being plowed, and he will want to consider your requests.

Again, this takes months and even years. Don't expect him to change by Labor Day. Most men are extremely reasonable when a sane, loving, adorable wife asks for something. It's the angry, demanding, critical wife whom a man tries to escape. Proverbs 21:9 says, "It is better to live on a corner of the roof than to share the house with a nagging wife." Men hate few things worse than a nagging, upset wife. (But you have taken steps to get rid of *that* woman, right?)

For centuries, wise women have had husbands who are selfish with their time. But with strength, tenacity, and perseverance, these wives have made princes out of toads. I have seen the most immature, egotistic husbands want to move into responsible manhood with the right wife. Again, we can stomp our feet against heaven, but the fact that the "wise woman builds her house" while "the foolish woman tears hers down" is true. The call for the wise wife is to have an ability to suffer, be humble, and yet persevere with kindness. Your husband has to *want* to change. I've never seen a man change because a woman *let him have it* or because she called him a dope.

For your birthday or Christmas, ask to go to a marriage conference (marriage conferences are not nearly as threatening as counseling). Or ask him to read *Husband School, Where Men Learn the Secrets of Making Wives Happy.*

Become the godly woman of the century, learn to pray like a madwoman, get your needs met in the Lord, rock the *Wife School* principles, and get ready to see the Red Sea part. Humans *respond* to other humans. Your husband has no choice but to respond to the new *you*.

Again, try not to demand that this happen soon. Give it a year or two. How old are you? Don't you have this kind of energy and time for the most important relationship in your life? Men change all the time *when they want to*, and they *want* to change when you meet their 8 A's.

DAY 3
Something Only a Man Can Give to Your Kids

Many years ago, Gary Smalley wrote a book called *The Blessing*. In this classic, Smalley discusses Old Testament examples of when fathers gave their children a blessing. Being older now, I have experienced watching various families in which the children either did or did not receive the blessing from their father. We women have to wrestle with the fact that God made families a patriarch institution. Although women are incredibly important in the family, there is something about a wise, godly, faithful father who blesses and loves his children that you, as a woman, cannot give your children.

Women love their children beyond belief. You know this. You know that you would cross a narrow board between two skyscrapers to save your children. Somehow, God zaps women with this love after childbirth that even surprises us.

Many men do not naturally have this same zapping. (If your husband is one of the few who got this unquenchable love for your children, then thank God for him.) John the Baptist came in the spirit and power of Elijah, and one goal he had was to "turn the hearts of the fathers to the children" (Luke 1:17). This infers, of course, that the fathers' hearts were *not naturally* turned to their children. Don't get angry at your husband because he does not have womanly hormones. One of your jobs in being a wise wife and building your house is to "turn the heart of your husband to your children" and "turn the heart of your children to their father." Praising Dad to the children is one of the wisest and kindest things you can do for your children. Their closeness with Dad gives them inner stability and security that you cannot give them. Never be jealous of their relationship.

When I lived in Virginia, a woman told me that she told her husband she was jealous of how he picked up their little girls and loved them. Therefore, the husband quit doing this to his little girls. Isn't that the saddest story? Can you believe how ignorant and foolish that woman was? Oh my goodness! Praise your husband to the moon and back when he loves and adores your children. He is pouring iron into their veins.

You will lose a lot of control over your teenage boys when they get around eleven, twelve, and beyond. They will love you, but they don't want to be a girl. They want to identify with manly Dad. So if your husband is close to your boys, he will be able to influence them. You will always influence your boys, too, but not in the same way as Dad. Your daughter will more likely develop the ability to say no to bad boys when she gets love, attention, and affection from her daddy. Women, you don't love anything more than your children, so get this right. Stir up the affections of your husband toward the children. Tell him all the cute things they say about him. Tell him how they admire him. *Build your house. Build it!* God gave your husband the leadership but gave you the greater power of influence!

OK, I'm calming down. But I see women stealing the hearts of their children away from the husband all the time because the woman is resentful toward the husband and wants to punish him. You are punishing your children if you do this.

Yesterday, one of our six children had an unpleasant situation. We were on a conference call with him and a fourth person. My sweet husband talked and spoke with such love and protection for our child. I wanted to cry, watching how my husband rose and defended the child. The child's heart was more open to David than I've ever seen. It was beautiful, simply beautiful. The security it gave our son to see his father's affection and respect for him was very emotional to me. Women, you build your house by helping your children love and respect their father, and vice versa.

My think tank friend, Kendall, has helped me see this even clearer in the past few years. If your mom didn't live this, then you need to witness it in another woman. This is too important to mess up.

DAY 4, PART A
Understanding Your Need to Release Emotional Tension

Soon we will discuss the A of Affection, which is the chapter on sex. Your husband, if he is in the 80 percent of men, regularly builds up sexual tension that needs to be released. But if you are in the 80 percent of women, you regularly build up *emotional* tension that needs to be released. Today we are going to discuss what you can do about *your need to release emotional tension.*

Just as there is a continuum of men with a high sex drive and some with a low sex drive (and all of that is normal and fine), there is also a continuum of women with high emotional natures and some with low emotional natures (and likewise, all of that is normal and fine). *However,* just because you are a woman with a high emotional nature, it does not give you license to spew out your emotions. That's crazy. A man has to keep his sexual desires in check, and you are called to keep your emotional crazies in check. (We have discussed the problem of emotional turmoil numerous times.)

A man needs to have sex with his wife to release sexual tension. And you need to *talk* to release your emotional tension. Your husband can have sex with only you, but you can release emotional tension with several people. Sisters, best friends, and mothers (the ones who listen and don't give too much advice) can all help you with releasing emotional tension. Talking and being heard is incredibly therapeutic to a woman.

Many women want their husbands to be the primary person who gives them emotional release (like me, for example). That is fine, but try not to wear him out too much. God gave us other women to talk to because men usually don't want to talk as much as we do. Have several trustworthy women you share with so you don't wear out any one person too much.

Many women have found that exercise is an incredible means of reducing emotional tension. A great workout or a fast walk can be amazingly helpful to dial down emotional crazies. Praying out loud and walking seem to calm me down a lot. Journaling is another tool wise women use to help them sort out their frustrations. We have many twisted knots, and talking helps us untie those knots.

I understand that you want your husband to be your primary source of emotional release. Once you are eager to meet his need to release sexual tension, he will be much more willing to give you the time and energy to listen, which releases your emotional tension. Just remember, he has no idea that your emotional tension equates with his sexual tension. Most of the time, men think we women are a little emotionally unbalanced. (Actually, haha, we can be.) But when we release emotional tension by talking, we become more balanced.

Girls, we have a real need to talk! Women have gathered for centuries in knitting circles, have washed clothes in the river together, or have gone to the market together. When you recognize you are in an emotional hissy, realize it's time for a good chat. But remember, husbands don't have this need, and most husbands don't understand it. (Guess who the lucky duck is who gets to teach him?)

The lesson next week is the sex lesson. Oh dear. Oh my. It's coming. And your husband is going to love it.

DAY 4, PART B
Tips for Traveling with Your Husband

As you know, we women are very opinionated, and trips seem to present many situations in which those opinions tumble out. Which rental car should we pick? Which restaurant should we choose? Which side of the bed do you want? What type of clothes are we going to wear on the plane (dress-up or jeans)? How much should we tip? If you are like most women, you have all sorts of opinions on *everything*.

One thing to try to do on trips is *try not to criticize glitches*. Opportunities for glitches abound on trips: the airplane's tardiness, the hotel room's poor view, the service in the restaurant, etc. Instead, try to comment on everything nice you can.

This past weekend, David and I took a trip. When we arrived at the hotel, one of the lamps didn't work, one of the electrical sockets didn't work, we couldn't figure out the TV system, and the refrigerator wasn't cooling. But instead of complaining and criticizing the hotel (because my husband planned the trip and arranged for the hotel), I just called the front desk three times. They sent up very friendly, helpful people and fixed everything in ten minutes. After everything was fixed, I could honestly say, "This is a very nice room. I'm going to like being here for three days." This may seem small, but instead of criticizing inconveniences (because they will happen for the *rest* of your life), just roll with them and thank your husband for the nice things. Do you see how much more pleasant of a companion you are?

Trips always have the unexpected glitch. Get the glitches fixed, don't complain, and focus on what is nice. Say true things such as, "I've enjoyed just traveling with you today" (with a smile). A husband *loves* a grateful, contented wife. He feels as if he's providing the trip and you're happy about it. It's the difference between night and day for a man to have a happy, contented, noncomplaining wife! We women can be such dopes!

DAY 5
Dealing with Difficult Parents/In-Laws

Many of you adore your parents and in-laws, and that is fantastic. *Rejoice greatly*! This section is not written for you. It is written for women who struggle with difficult parents or difficult in-laws (or both).

In chapter 19 of *Wife School*, the Genie discusses these principles extensively. But for now, I want to remind you of a couple of principles.

To begin this discussion, please remember that the fifth commandment in the Bible is to honor your parents. In a previous lesson, we discussed how we are not necessarily called to have affection for those who have mistreated us, but we are to forgive them and to treat them with agape love—that is, doing good to them. In the case of parents/in-laws, an additional command to honor them is given.

Let's discuss honor. We previously discussed how we honor the judge by standing when he comes in the courtroom, but we don't stand for him in a restaurant. We honor the *position* of judge. Honoring our parents/in-laws is a biblical call because of their *position* as parents/in-laws. We don't decide we will honor them if they deserve it. We don't have to be best friends with them, but there is a call from God to treat them with honor. When you marry, you become one with your spouse. Therefore, his parents are now a type of parents to you, and the call to honor them is now binding to you, also.

Think about if you are in a courtroom, and the judge says something you don't like. You don't go haywire. You react with, "Your Honor, if I may, I'd like to address the court with another perspective, please." That's honor. Treat others with great respect, even though they don't deserve it.

A young woman once told me that her mother was extremely critical of her. The young woman's mother came to help her when she (the young mother) had a baby, and she *did* help in many ways. But the young mother couldn't wait for her mother to leave because she continually criticized the young mother. "Don't you have more food in the freezer? That's such bad planning." "Look how big your stomach is. My stomach wasn't big like that after I had a baby." "How do you live in this mess? Your kitchen drawers are a wreck." "Your other children certainly look raunchy. Can't you dress them better?" And on and on. Can you imagine the emotional turmoil that this new mother felt, having her hormones all jacked up and then her mother criticizing her at every turn? So let's pull apart and analyze this young mother's situation.

After you are married, your husband is your new authority. You are now a new unit. The husband leaves and cleaves from his family-of-origin and you two are now the new family. You and your husband decide how much you see the in-laws and your parents. When relationships are strained with parents/in-laws, a wise practice is for you and your husband to decide how often you are going to get together with them and also how often you feel you should communicate by phone/text, etc.

For example, this same young girl from above, along with her husband, decided that her mother could come visit four times a year and stay four days/three nights each visit. When her mother planned her trip, the young mother said, "We are thinking you could come Thursday through Sunday." Her mother started a meltdown.

"Three days? That's so selfish of you. I don't understand why you are telling me how long I can stay."

The young mother was physically shaking. She had never stood up to her mother before. The young mother said respectfully, "We are glad you are coming for a visit, and Joe and I have decided that with how busy our lives are, four days/three nights is a good length of time for a visit."

Her mother again lashed out. "That's stupid that you are telling me how long I can stay. Selfish and stupid."

The young mother again, with great self-control (although she was still physically shaking), said, "I want you to enjoy your visit, and we have some fun outings planned. But Joe and I decided that three nights/four days is the right length of a visit."

The young mother insisted on honoring her mother, but she was no longer going to be *bulldozed* by her. After you are married, *you and your husband decide what the boundaries are.* It is even good to write them down so you can be sure you are both on the same page.

This young mother told me, "I dread the week before my mother comes, and then I mull over her visit for days after she leaves."

I said, "Don't do that. You get to decide what you think about, and don't waste the week before she comes by dreading it. Simply say to yourself that you will gear up for four days/three nights and try to overlook things. You will honor your mother and treat her with great respect. When her trip is over, it is over, and you won't mull over it. You choose to set your mind on something else. After you once (or twice) process what you learned from her visit, it is not helpful to keep mulling the situation over in your mind, so don't your waste time thinking about it. Get distracted by thinking about something else."

Remember, *you* get to set the boundaries with your parents/in-laws when you are married. You and your husband are now in charge of how much and when you see the parents/in-laws. Remember the principle: honor them. But that does *not* mean *they* get to set the boundaries. *You* set them. If they react, honor them. If they decompose, honor them. But hold to the boundaries you set. *You now have all the power.* They don't want you to know this. They try to act as if they still have the power. They don't.

To summarize, you are called to honor your parents. If they are in need, you are called to help (see Matt. 15:3–6 and 1 Tim. 5:4). But you do not have to have phileo love for them (love with affection), only agape love (doing them good). This releases many of you from the guilt you have toward parents/in-laws who have mistreated you (see previous lesson on resentment; you *must* forgive them and do them good). However, honoring your parents does not mean they get to tell you what to do or they get to be in charge or even that they get to ramrod you with whatever they want. No, you and your husband are *now in charge of your new family unit* and you set the boundaries. You focus on forgiving, agape-loving them, and honoring them.

The young girl in the above example is now years down the road and her mother has given up some of the earlier hysteria. But the young girl has continued to endure some criticism from her mother over the years. She still chooses to forgive and honor, forgive and honor, but to *set firm boundaries with her mother.* The relationship has now healed to an extent, but her mother still comes in with some sharp needle jabs. The young mother says to herself, "Honor, forgive, and set appropriate boundaries."

Life is not easy; it is messy. We understand that, and we choose God's principles when we have a mess. Don't focus on your problems. Understand the principles, try to solve your problems the best you can, pray like a madwoman, and then move on and focus on all the good stuff in life (of which there is so much). Give up the fantasy of an uncluttered life.

Just FYI, I have written the book *Happy School, Where Women Learn the Secrets to Overcome Discouragement and Worry* (as well as the *Happy School Study Guide*) to help you learn how to think correctly about your WMDs (What is Missing and Disappointing), such as difficult parents and in-laws. I hope you and a few friends will go through that study when you are finished with this one.

Prayer

Father,

When I think about You and Your goodness, knowledge, and power, it is as if I'm thinking about the vastness of the heavens. And when I think about my inner qualities, it is more as if I'm thinking about a little mud puddle. Sometimes I feel so small and self-centered. Please pour Your character into my heart, which desperately needs reworking.

I think about all the multitude of blessings You have left on my front doorstep, and like a spoiled child, I stomp my foot because there are not more. Please forgive me for letting small things upset me. Please give me a heart of perennial gratefulness. Help me be glad for our health, indoor plumbing, safe neighborhoods, good schools, Kroger, friends, freedom to worship, our eyesight, my children's laughter, and my husband's job. Help me focus hourly on all I have instead of the things I don't have.

My husband does much that I do approve of. Alert me to when he does something that I approve of so I can tell him. Help me be a wife who focuses on all that he gets right in life, instead of the portion where I think he misses it. Help me see where I miss it, and help me turn from those mistakes.

Thank You, God, for the unequalled earthly joy of intimacy and closeness in marriage. Give me the perseverance to deposit the 8 A's daily into my husband's empty tank.

In Jesus's name,

Amen.

Assignments and Group Discussion Questions

1. Knowing that "giving—or denying—approval in marriage is either healing or destroying," how would you rate your approval and its effects in your marriage?

2. Are you still trying to make your husband *holy* instead of *happy*, or have you given that job back to God?

3. Knowing that the best environment for another to change and grow is one of approval and acceptance, how would you rate the environment you have in your marriage?

4. After reading the section on "When Your Husband Is Selfish with His Time" (assuming your husband is guilty here), how have you changed your strategy in dealing with him?

5. Do you understand that there is something only a man can give your kids? What are your thoughts on this section?

6. Did you realize you have a need to release emotional tension that is mainly met by talking? Discuss your thoughts about your emotional tension.

7. What are your thoughts about the next time you take a trip with your husband?

8. If your parents/in-laws are great, skip this. But if you have difficult parents or in-laws, what principles do you need to think about adopting for the future?

WEEK 8

Seventh A: The Affection Lesson

Contents

Day 1: More Thoughts about the A of Affection
Day 2: Bump. It. Up.
Day 3: When You and Your Husband Disagree about How to Handle Something
Day 4: The Financial Pressure that Most Men Carry
Day 5: Give Your Husband Time to Change the Way He Perceives the New You

To start this lesson off, I want to be clear that I am not setting myself up as an expert on the A of Affection (sex) in any way. What this section is attempting to do is discuss how your husband feels and what your husband wants. This material is from the books I have read, as well as the truths I have learned from the women I have counseled and mentored over the past twenty-five years. What I've mainly learned is that the A of Affection makes husbands ridiculously happy! There is much more you can learn about the subject of sex with seminars, Christian sex counselors, courses, and books, and I wholeheartedly encourage you to explore that material further.

DAY 1
More Thoughts about the A of Affection

If I could give only three pieces of advice to a woman about making her husband happy, the three pieces would be (1) stop the emotional turmoil in your relationship (quit criticizing, giving so much advice, and being argumentative), (2) find a way to praise and encourage your husband in a genuine and meaningful way that delights him every day, and (3) *drum roll*...figure out how to make your husband happy in your sex life. Those pillars seem to make more of a difference than any other three pieces of advice. (Of course, walking in the Spirit with a gentle and quiet spirit supersedes all this advice, but I am assuming you know that.)

In the past few years since *Wife School* has been out, the chapter on sex has initiated more feedback than any other. Women are simply not aware of how men feel about sex. When we understand that husbands care *colossally about our sex life*, we can *adapt* our behavior, and then husbands get happy.

I'm not sure what you need to do in your marriage to *up* your sex life. Maybe it's just have sex more often. Maybe it's to be a more engaged partner. Maybe you need to be creative and do something, such as buy some outfits (men are stimulated by sight; see the next section). Tweak this area of your marriage until your husband is happy. No man can adore a woman who doesn't meet this important need of his (well, 80 percent of men are like this).

Many men have godly wives who are rock stars at homemaking, rearing children, and serving others. But mark it down: if you are not an interested, engaged partner in the bedroom, then you are not a queen in his mind. Therefore, decide that you will be amazing in this area.

The section on *willingness* being the first step in sex is probably the most helpful piece of advice in chapter 8 in *Wife School*. If you knew how many women secretly told me that they are not very interested in sex (or are not easily aroused), you would be shocked (or then, maybe you would just be relieved). So many women feel like this. When women realize they are normal, and there is nothing wrong with their husbands or them, women feel a great sense of relief.

You intellectually know that spouses have different appetites for different needs. But we still beat ourselves up and tell ourselves that we are not compatible. Hogwash. Your husband is a man and has a huge hunger for sex, just like 80 percent of all men. You are a woman and have a huge need for emotional intimacy that he doesn't have. I know you'd like *him to go first* and meet your need for emotional intimacy, and then you'd be more willing to more actively and frequently engage in sex, but wise women don't live their lives waiting on husbands to meet their needs. They meet the husbands' needs first and then ask for what they want.

A wise woman builds her house by *constantly* thinking about how she *loves and gives*, not about her own self-pity because others don't love and give enough to her. The day you say you will become a woman who takes responsibility for your own needs and let your husband off the hook of your high, unrealistic expectations will be the day your marriage begins to turn around and soar.

If you feel your sexual problems in the marriage are very substantial, go to a Christian sex counselor. There is a lot of help available, but you have to seek it out.

See sex as an opportunity to grow your marriage, to pull your husband's heart to you, and to love your husband in a language he can hear. And that brings us to...

DAY 2
Bump. It. Up.

(I almost didn't include the following section for the obvious reason that it is rather explicit. But I feel obligated to include it. So, here goes.)

We can learn from negative examples in Scripture. For example, remember how we learned to drip some honey from the prostitutes? Now we're going to learn something new from another negative example.

In John 14, the daughter of Herodias danced for Herod and pleased him so much that he promised to give her whatever she asked, up to half his kingdom. I feel relatively certain that alcohol was involved in this scene, but the truth remains that men are *stimulated by sight* and like to watch women dance. I mean, look at strip clubs. Please don't misquote me or get me wrong. Please! I am only pointing out the obvious: *men enjoy women dancing while they are scantily clad.* Have you ever noticed how men are mesmerized when they watch the Dallas Cowboys cheerleaders? Please hear me, I am *not* giving you specifics and *not* telling you what to do, but I am telling you that husbands—*Christian* husbands—enjoy watching their wives *move*, and they doubly enjoy it when their wives are barely dressed. Again, you know how against strip clubs I am, if you know me at all. And I detest the sin of porn and its horrible effect on men. (I am certainly not giving men a pass on any inappropriate sexual sin!) But I am telling you that men *love* to be stimulated by sight, and this is legitimate in marriage. Because we women (80 percent of us) don't have this sexual craving, we tend to ignore it in our husbands. (It's the same as men not having a need for emotional intimacy, so they tend to ignore it in wives.)

Here's my advice to you: bump it up a notch, women. Bump. It. Up. You may think you're chubby and not a supermodel, but according to everything I've heard and read, *most* men don't care. They like the effort you are making to stimulate them. So…Bump. It. Up. Many of you are embarrassed at this advice, and believe me, I'm embarrassed writing it. But we all need to be reminded. The enemy wants *feisty sex on TV* and *boring sex in the Christian marriage.*

Remember, you are all the sex your husband legitimately gets. Again, I am not excusing him for any inappropriate behavior, but I am telling you that 80 percent of husbands care about this area in a huge, gigantic way—and most wives are not knowledgeable in this area.

If the kids are at your mom's and you have a date night, tell your husband you have a surprise for him before you go out to eat. Meet him at the door in an *outfit*. And then, have some music or candles lit. Bump. It. Up. Men love this attention, and many have difficulty asking for it. You are creative, right? Use some of it in this area. An adorable newlywed I know bought some cute Santa outfits for her first Christmas with her husband. I promise he will remember that, and he will never remember the gray sweater she bought him.

I can hear your thoughts: "Ugh. I don't care about that. That doesn't excite me at all. In fact, that sounds like another thing to put on my to-do list." Remember, we are to love husbands in a language they can hear. And most husbands hear the language of sex in all caps and in italic.

If you feel uncomfortable with your body, then get a sarong to feel a little more covered. Don't just ignore this. Men love nakedness. Again, I am not suggesting that you dance (but then again, I'm certainly not suggesting that you don't). *I am only telling you the obvious,* which is that men love it when women dance or *move around* and *are scantily clad.*

Put away the flannel nightgown and bring it on. Christian marriage is where it should be happenin'.

And be sure to bump it up on vacation. (Husbands think vacations should have extra sex, just FYI.)

You will have to experiment to see what delights your husband. Even the most stone-faced husbands will usually communicate their approval when wives *bump it up*. If you try something and it doesn't hit his button, then try something else, and don't get offended. (If you are in the 20 percent who wants sex more than your husband, read chapter 32 in *Wife School*.)

Women are usually real idiots about men and their desire for good sex. Don't harm your marriage by ignoring this important area. You want him to be happy, and this area is at the tip-top of men's lists. They hate to beg for it, so here is your opportunity to surprise and delight him.

No, this isn't about you. And yes, it's a lot of work. But it is the right way to love a husband. And on top of that, as you now know, *it opens his heart toward you.*

DAY 3
When You and Your Husband Disagree about How to Handle Something

One of our six adult children made a choice in which my husband and I both didn't approve (imagine that, a child making a choice with which we didn't agree). One morning before church, we were discussing how to handle it. I was going on and on about what needs to be said, what I thought, yada yada, etc. My husband felt differently. He thought x, and I thought y. I could feel the tension between us as we disagreed on something that was very emotionally charged.

You and your husband could disagree about how to handle finances, in-laws, church-related situations, or any of a thousand subjects. There will be many topics in which you vehemently disagree. You must have a strategy for these times.

How couples handle conflict is a major component of their relationship. We will discuss two subjects in this section: (1) your behavior when you and your husband disagree and (2) your reaction if your husband is rude, inappropriate, blaming, or critical. First, we will address your behavior.

As I say over and over again in *Wife School,* emotional turmoil is something husbands *hate.* To illustrate this principle again, let me tell you about an unsaved young woman I met with this week who is actually pretty smart about men. (She certainly gets the sex thing and that men care so much about it. She shows up at the airport to meet her partner in boots, a long trench coat, and nothing underneath. I know, I know, I don't have the nerve for this either, but I am impressed by it.)

Anyhow, she thought that she should be able to be honest and genuine and therefore let her emotional despair spill out. She felt she was *entitled* to this in a close relationship. I asked her if she treated her business clients like that.

"Of course not," she said.

"Why do you treat the most important person in your life like that?" I asked. "Why do you not tiptoe and say hard things in a sweet way to him as you do to your clients?"

This savvy woman said her mother treated her father disrespectfully (they are now divorced), and that's all she has ever known. It was an aha moment—that is, we should treat our husbands the nicest of anyone.

"That is so much work though!" she said.

"Isn't your business a lot of work?" I asked. "Isn't your fitness and eating a lot of work?" (She is super fit and in incredible shape.) "Then, why do you think that your number-one relationship in the whole world wouldn't be a lot of work?"

We women think we have a right to let our ugliness roll out of our mouths with our spouses. Women, it's idiotic. Even if your husband is immature with his tongue (we will discuss that in a minute), *you* must have self-control. I love that self-control is in the Titus 2 short list for young women.

When you and your husband begin a disagreement, flip the switch, and hear the warning sirens go off. Say to yourself, "I am entering dangerous and deep waters. I need to watch my tongue."

Then, use mature dialog. Ask questions such as "What is your opinion?" and "How do you see it?" If he says ridiculous things, instead of jumping down his throat, say, "I'll need to process that. That's different from what I was thinking, so I need to think about it." How much better it is to buy some time with sentences like this instead of barking, "That's why you have trouble at your office because that's how stupidly you think!"

John Gottman, one of the premiere marriage experts in the country, says you can tell a lot about a marriage by how conflict is handled. It's true. Do you stoop to disrespectfulness? To sarcasm? To giving the silent treatment? How immature! Just stop it. Stop it. We all have to grow up and slap ourselves and say, "Wow, I need to treat my husband respectfully, even when he's driving me crazy."

Back to the conversation between my husband and me: I was a little unhappy about how the conversation was going, to be honest. But I made a choice to tell my husband what I liked about what he said, that I would think about it some more, and that he had a good idea about *z* (although I didn't tell him I didn't like *x* and *y*). I tried to compliment him on any aspect of what he said. One thing I said was, "You are a great logical thinker, so let me think about all of this for a while."

Later, I was able to think of something else he said that was true and good, and I said to him, "I liked your point about *xx*, and I feel that helped me." We actually did resolve the issue finally, but I never decomposed into emotional hysteria, *although I felt like it*. (See chapter 9 in *Wife School* on the A of Authority if you can't resolve the issue together.) Death and life are in the power of the tongue, and you will never have the marriage of your dreams until you can get control of that contentious, argumentative, critical tongue. If you learn nothing else in *Wife School*, learn that you must muzzle that viper. It can destroy your marriage (or take it to new heights).

We are sinful, self-absorbed human beings, and you will never be a completely pure and holy woman while you are on earth (although you can certainly grow in this area). But you can learn to speak respectfully, no matter how upset you are. If you refuse to be respectful, you suck the affection right out of your husband's tank.

Let's discuss if your husband is rude to you during a conflict. If he begins name-calling or rude comments, give him a couple of nice warnings (again, no commands but sweet requests). I like the sentence (said in a very soft voice) "Please talk to me as if you love me." If he continues to bombard you with disrespectful comments, say (without any negative emotion), "I'm sorry, but I am going to have to go for a walk (or go to the grocery store) because I don't feel respected when you call me names. I'll be back in an hour, and maybe we can resume this conversation when we both calm down." Then leave. He can't mistreat you. Men don't respect women they can mistreat. But don't bash him. Model humility coupled with self-respect. You don't dish it out, but you also don't take it.

Later, you might study chapter 13 in *Wife School* and give him a word picture about how you feel when he talks disrespectfully to you. I often counsel women to use examples from the husbands' work. For example, you could possibly use an example of when his boss talked disrespectfully to him. Word pictures are powerful but must be used sparingly.

I can hear your thoughts from across the ocean: "This is *so* not fair." Who said life was fair? We're not going after fairness; we're going after a great marriage, and this is how the wise woman builds her house. She throws pillows around her husband all the time, worrying about his ego, building him up when no one is building her up, and appreciating him when no one is appreciating her. This is how wise women earn the love and respect of their husbands, by doing what is *uncommon*.

Don't go for average; go for amazing. I can honestly say to women that nothing on this side of heaven is as fulfilling as a fabulous marriage. It is worth your all-out effort. And yes, it takes months and years.

In the past two weeks, a woman told me that after having practiced *Wife School* for several months, her husband said to her, "On my drive home tonight, I was thinking about what was really important to me in life, and guess what it is?"

"What?" she asked, thinking he was going to say something about helping people in his business.

"You," he said. She broke down and cried, as this man is not the gushing type. She hugged him, and he also had big tears coming down his cheek. This woman has now earned that type of love from her husband *after years of doing it wrong*. You can earn it, too. Stay the course. Do and say the right thing, even when you don't feel like it. In return, you will eventually win your husband's heart, because *love never fails*.

DAY 4
The Financial Pressure that Most Men Carry

Years ago in a nail salon, the cover of a secular magazine announced an article entitled, "What Men Think About." This article said men think about work 30%, money 30%, sex 30%, and everything else only 10%. I remember how surprised I was at those numbers. *Why, that's not what women think about at all.* Women usually think about their children, their homes, their looks (weight), their relationships, etc. Men and women indeed think about different topics. Even if you work and you think about your work a lot, my hunch is that you don't think about money and sex as your husband does.

Men feel an extraordinary pressure to provide for their families. When my husband taught young men in Sunday School and polled them about their struggles, money was very near the top of every young man's list. This isn't surprising. Men feel a burden to provide that we women don't usually carry.

In contrast, women like to build their nests, so we are continually thinking about making the nest nicer, and this usually costs money. Women have to be wise about understanding the pressure men feel about paying for all our *nest-building ideas.*

Early in our marriage, I would list to David ways I wanted to improve my nest. I understood that we couldn't afford many of my nest-building ideas right away, but I wanted him to know what was in my heart (women long to be known deeply). What my constant nest-building dreams did to him, though, was put pressure on him. He felt that I wanted *so many things*. Many of the things I wanted were good, but I had no idea what a pressure he carried about money. This whole area of *how much stress men feel about money* is foreign to most women—just as men's sex drives are foreign to most women. But you are a wise woman, and you are learning the deep things about men so you can understand your husband in a way that he feels supported and loved.

Later in our marriage, David and I learned to make a list of things we wanted to purchase and prioritized them. I quit fussing about all that we didn't have (well, I got better). It frees husbands if you are only asking for a couple of things on the top of your list and not always barking about other things you want. A woman's want list can often be very long. If we are not careful, we can put unneeded pressure on our husbands.

Living on a budget is usually nonnegotiable for young couples. Having a budget (and sticking to it) takes truckloads of stress out of the financial conflict in the marriage.

One of my favorite financial marriage-conflict stories was when we were newlyweds and we made our first budget. I looked at the clothes budget, and it was one hundred dollars.

I was shocked. "A hundred dollars a month? I could never live on that!"

"A month?" David asked. "That's a year!"

We still hoot and laugh over that conversation thirty years ago. Learning to figure out finances is enormous to young couples. Having a budget and agreeing *not* to spend money outside the preplanned budget prevents much angst in the financial aspect of the marriage. There are many good Christian organizations that help couples with money: Dave Ramsey, Crown Ministries, etc. Don't let finances zap the affection out of your marriage. Get on a budget! Get a plan. If you want to have a "Maybe Someday Dream List," call it that, and then you get to tell him your dreams without putting pressure on him. Wise women learn how to communicate their hearts to their husbands without upsetting them.

Realize that finances are like sex to men in that men usually care much more about these areas than you do. We bless our husbands when we can understand their hearts and minds and live in consideration of their concerns. If your husband talks and whines about money over and over again, be sweet and attentive, and let him do this. He is a normal man, and you can soothe him if you will listen and be supportive. Men adore women who understand them and encourage them.

And that's you, right?

DAY 5
Give Your Husband Time to Change the Way He Perceives the New You

I am reading a book on how the brain is *plastic*—that is, it can change. But it changes slowly. When you begin to treat your husband differently, he is slowly replacing neural patterns that *this* is the new you. It might take months, if not a couple of years, to replace the deep grooves in his brain. The longer you've been married, the longer it will take. You can't expect his brain to realize quickly that you are a new wife and have new patterns of relating. Persevere. Husbands who have been very discouraged in the marriage can be completely brought back to life with wives who will persevere in giving them the 8 A's.

Mark it down, your husband's brain is being changed as far as how he perceives you if you are living the 8 A's. Give the guy some time for his brain to make new neural patterns. Honestly, he is afraid it is not going to last.

One More Thought

Scientists and psychologists disagree about how many positive interactions are needed to make up for a negative interaction. I have read that the number is three; I have also read that the number is seven. The brain seems to have a *negative bias* and gives more weight to negative interactions. A *hysterical outbreak* of yours will take many deposits to get back to zero. You don't want to undo all the benefits of your 8 A deposits with some accidental emotional escalation or with your sarcastic retorts. You are truly losing ground with those mistakes, so be careful with the fruit of your lips.

Next week is the hardest lesson of all, the A of Authority. Gulp.

Prayer

Dear Lord,

Here we are again. To be honest, I was hoping that I'd be farther along than I am. I was hoping that by this time in my life, I would be over some weaknesses and hurts, but honestly, I'm not. I'm still wallowing around in many of the same ditches.

But maybe this time will be the time I learn *to rest*. Maybe I'll give up my ridiculous expectations for others to love and give to me. Maybe I'll give up my insecurity. Maybe I'll grow in getting rid of wanting to impress others and instead, serve them.

Maybe this time will be the time I grow my faith, walk with You, talk with You, obey You, and relax *in* You. Trying to carry the weight of the world all the time sure hasn't worked in the past.

Maybe this time will be the time where prayer overcomes my anxieties and the year where I turn from my self-pity and exchange it for gratefulness. God, maybe this will be the year where my marriage takes a quantum growth step and I become a woman with a gentle and quiet spirit, which You said was of great worth in your sight.

And just so You know, Lord, I realize that You will have to show up to do all that. I've tried before to do it myself—and that hasn't worked.

So thank You for continuing to put up with me. Thank you for giving me another chance to live for You and do the work that You've assigned. May the thoughts of my heart be pleasing to You.

I love You, Lord. I really do. Thank You for choosing me.

In Jesus's name,

Amen.

Assignments and Questions for Group Discussion

Most of these questions are rather personal. Please pretend your husband is there listening when you share anything. Remember also that many of the other women present will go home and tell their husbands (and best friends, sisters, etc.) what you said so be very wise and discerning in what you share. Less is more.

1. Overall, how would you describe how you are doing with the A of Affection? What are some thoughts that you have on this subject?

2. In which ways could you Bump. It. Up. with your husband?

3. What is it like in your marriage when the two of you disagree? How could you take steps to improve that?

4. What kind of financial pressure is your husband under? What could you do to help him with this?

WEEK 9

Eighth A: The Authority Lesson

Contents

Day 1: More Thoughts about the A of Authority
Day 2: Learning to Make Proper Appeals
Day 3: The Beauty and Power of Empathy in Marriage
Day 4: When Your Husband Doesn't Obey Scripture
Day 5, Part A: If You Are Having Trouble Accepting Your Biblical Role
Day 5, Part B: A Story to Encourage You to Persevere

Actually, I am delighted to write about the A of Authority in *Wife School*. Understanding God's design for women in marriage is one of the most beautiful truths you will ever learn. A Christian woman's submission is actually a path to protection and blessing. Women have to renew their minds, though, and think like Christians—and not like the world. That is what we will endeavor to do in this lesson.

Be sure to read chapter 9 in *Wife School* before you read the following lesson.

May God richly bless you as you uncover the beauty of the A of Authority.

DAY 1
More Thoughts about the A of Authority

I admit that this A has been the most difficult of the 8 A's for me in our marriage. I grew up in a matriarch family (in which the father is only a figurehead and the mother runs the family). Many wrong, deeply ingrained modes of thinking had to be replaced in my mind. Therefore, I do understand your angst accepting the concept of your husband leading the marriage. Even though my husband is godly, smart, and caring, I have still wanted to kick the wall on this principle multiple times. What I have learned over the years is that submission to a husband is not so difficult when we realize that actually it is only an extension of *our submission to the Lord*.

When you and I can get our hearts around the concept that Authority *is God's order, God's best*, we can bow our hearts to it. Women *choose* to let their husbands lead them because this is *God's idea*. We know that we salute the uniform of *husband* in response to a God who created everything and therefore has a right to rule over us. Submitting to your husband is really about *submitting to the Lord*.

Please let me ask you the hard question that the Lord has so often asked me. Why haven't you completely bowed your heart to the Lord? It is in *not bowing our hearts to God* that makes us not want to bow our hearts to our husbands. The hardest question in your life is, Who will rule your life? You or God? Because when you and I allow God to be over us, then it is not so difficult to allow our husbands to be the leader in the relationship.

The battle is not about your imperfect husband. The battle is about your imperfect heart. The battle is that you want to choose how you live your life, instead of letting God choose. God has chosen that your imperfect husband lead the family. You must bow to that truth as you bow to God.

"No," you say. "I will not submit to this teaching. My husband is not worth following. He is not able to make good decisions."

Look at Abraham and Sarah in Genesis 12. Abraham was so selfish that he told the Egyptians that Sarah was his sister and let them take her into captivity so he could save himself. Why, one of the most important expectations we have from our husbands is to protect us! This disappointing husband let foreign guys have his wife to protect himself! How do you respect a man like that? What a downer it must have been for Sarah to respond sexually to Abraham again after he acted as he did toward her. I think God gave us this extreme example of failure in a husband so that we could see that our husbands have feet of clay, too. Yes, we want saviors for husbands; instead, they are Abrahams.

Sarah didn't submit to Abraham because he was a good leader. She obeyed Abraham because God asked her to *in her role as a wife* (see 1 Pet. 3 and Eph. 4:21–32). We women are called to submit to our imperfect husbands. No woman I have ever met has said this was easy.

Here is an example of one of my many failures in this area of Authority:

Many years ago, David and I were having some trouble with one of our five boys. This son would not *get with the program*. He kept pulling in another direction. David and I heard about a counselor in the West that was great with teenagers. We secured a telephone consultation. I can still picture the moment David and I were in his car in a parking lot, and we were having a telephone consultation on his speakerphone. We began to explain our problem to the counselor. We had just finished telling him the situation when the counselor says to me, "Julie, do you resist the leadership of your husband?"

What? *What?* Why was this counselor talking about *me?* We had just explained the problem was *this kid*, not me. I felt like a wild animal and that I had walked into a cage, and it had shut. "Well, yes, I do resist his leadership sometimes," I said. And then the conversation went from *bad to worse*. The counselor began to pin the independent spirit of our son on *my independent spirit*.

Intellectually, I knew that children learned to obey God and to submit to God by watching the pattern in the home, but I was still kicking against it. (The mom is the picture of the believer, and she submits to Dad, the picture of Christ. So if Mom doesn't submit to Dad, then the kids don't learn to submit well to Christ.)

Friend, I tell you this with as much compassion as I can, that not only will you lose your husband's affection if you try to lead the family, but you will lose God's protection of your family. (Thank goodness God gives us the concept of "beauty for ashes" when we fail.)

Wherever you are in your marriage, stop right now, and get under your husband's authority. It is the only path to blessing. You can be brilliant, godly, and a dynamo in getting things done, but until you are under your husband's authority, your independent spirit will wreck your home. I have watched marriages for thirty years, and there is no other path to blessing in a Christian marriage except this one. Your husband will make mistakes in leading. (We will discuss how to appeal in the next section.) But in the end, we women must submit to God, and God asks us to submit to the Abraham in our home. *Again, this isn't about his ability to lead*; it's about his God-ordained *position* to lead. Hand him the scepter. Go on, hand it to him.

David and I were out to dinner with a godly couple in October, and they told us about a disagreement they had had that was serious. It concerned how to handle an adult child. (Parenting seems to stir up much conflict in a marriage, have you noticed?) This couple discussed the issue and re-discussed it. She appealed and explained her thoughts. Neither would budge. They said, "We couldn't get past it." So they went to see a Christian counselor about the issue. The wife told us that almost as soon as they were in the session, she was smitten with conviction. The wise counselor had said, "When couples try and try, and seek counsel and do everything under the sun to come to an agreement—and can't—the wife must submit." My friend hated that. Hated it. And I understood exactly. Submission *does not* get easier as the years go on. You will wrestle with this biblical premise until the day you die. But because my friend truly loved the Lord, she responded well. This was about my friend and her spiritual walk with the Lord. It wasn't about her realizing her husband was right. It was about her seeing her husband's right to make the final decision, even if she disagreed.

Authority will be lived out in your marriage only when you can take the reins off your life and give them to the Lord. You will not be able to let your husband lead until you let the Lord lead you.

I'd like to remind you that Jesus was with his disciples for three years, and he repeatedly talked to them about humility. Even at the Last Supper, though, they were arguing about who would be greatest. It wasn't until after the resurrection that the Holy Spirit came and infiltrated these guys. It has to be the Holy Spirit who lives through you to give you submission. You can't do this in your strength. Pray until you give yourself to the Lord so completely that you are filled with the Holy Spirit. *Then* you can really start to turn your marriage around. Only a woman who is surrendered to the Lord can submit to a husband.

Often wives tell me a huge issue they have with submission is the smoldering resentment they carry toward their husbands because the husbands *do not love them well*. Women, we will never be loved in the fantasy way we want. We will never have the divine leadership we want in a mortal husband. His feet are clay, and our expectations repeatedly make us resent this person over us. But God is perfect, so we can allow God to rule over us. And his decree is that we allow our husbands to have final authority in the home.

Even as God surprisingly asks us to do good to our enemies, he again asks something counterintuitive: *let an imperfect man have the main authority in your family.* The feminists are up in arms over such a stance. Who would submit to an imperfect man without knowing that God is in heaven and has asked us as women to submit to our husbands? Your imperfect husband needs your forgiveness, probably daily. Don't demand he be God in order to lead you. God's plan is that a human, an imperfect human, lead you. Pray. And pray again. Get your heart soft and full of the Holy Spirit so you can forgive, submit, and bless.

This is something only a Christian woman understands. We don't expect the world to get this. We honor our husbands because God has asked us to this. This is the way God chose to create marriage. Submission is more about your relationship with God than it is about how wonderful a leader your husband is.

Over and over again, I see the godly influence of a grateful, servant-hearted, and meek woman on her husband. That is God's plan, for you to influence your husband through your godliness, your submissive heart, your humility, and your joy. Your energy must come from an underground stream, which you will find in prayer and surrender.

Friend, there is no other path to a godly family except this one. You are the woman, the heart of the home. And if you want godly generations to come from you, you really have no other choice.

DAY 2
Learning to Make Proper Appeals

When your husband gives you *a way to do things* and you feel it is not wise or in the best interest of the family, you may appeal to him. But we have to be careful about appeals; otherwise, they are just another manipulative ploy to be sure we get our way.

A while back over lunch, one of my best friends challenged me on the issue of appeals. She said to me, "You keep appealing until you get what you want." I have wrestled with what she said. I believe her comment helped me see a blind spot in myself. My goal in this section is to properly explain appeals so that we don't "keep appealing until we get what we want."

Several months ago, David and I sharply disagreed about an issue with the advertising in his business. Now on the onset, it would be easy to think that it is *his* business, so I should just shut up. But you need a little background to understand this example properly. I have an undergraduate degree in advertising. After college, I sold advertising for billboards; later, I sold radio advertising. After David started his business, I read ogles of books on advertising and marketing. And then, I became David's official marketing/advertising director for his business. I came up with the theme of his ads and his branding and wrote the scripts. Recently, I have been in the studio producing the ads. I give you that background so you can see why I felt my opinion should be weighed heavily. In fact, I thought it should be weighed *more heavily* than David's. I felt sure we should do things the way I saw them. We discussed the advertising issues several times and still couldn't agree to see it in the same way.

Responding to my wise friend's earlier rebuke, I handled this conflict differently. In an e-mail to my husband, I went over the data and again explained why I thought we should do what I suggested. But I was a little wiser this time. After I wrote what I thought the data suggested and what I therefore recommended, I wrote these sentences:

"I have given you every ounce of my opinion several times. There is nothing else to tell you. Now, I must take my hands off this decision and let you make it. If I disagree with your final decision, then I will cheerfully try to submit to your leadership. Thank you for listening to me and considering my opinion. You are a great husband, and I trust you always to make the decision that you feel is right and best for our family."

Friends, that was difficult to write because *I still felt certain I was right.*

I have now learned to say a version of The Paragraph before we enter into a conflict. Here is another example of what I often say to David when we venture into a heated area of discussion:

"I appreciate how you listen to me and that often you let me influence you. I also appreciate that you have a respectful discussion with me, let me give you my input, and that you are patient while we both go back and forth and discuss our views. But I want you to know that after I have exhausted everything I have to tell you, and we can't agree, I will let you make the final decision. I know you are the God-given leader. I know that after you have heard all my views, it is time to let you make the final decision. This way, you do not have to be afraid of my input. You can know it is only input and that you still hold the reins and get to make the final decision."

The Paragraph helps David take down his shield and not feel that he is getting coerced to take my opinion. It allows him to listen to my appeal, knowing he still gets to make the final decision.

David often wants my input and ideas. But honestly, the way I have presented them to him in the past has been too strong, and my opinion was often tainted with "You should choose my way." That is my tendency, for sure, to be heavy handed. But now, before we start to wrestle with an issue in which we disagree, I give him a version of The Paragraph.

David did agree to take my idea on advertising. But there are many times he has *not* taken my advice, and those are the difficult times. I admit that in the past, if I didn't get my way, I would occasionally try to press him up against the wall with my *educated* opinion. But as I grow in the Lord, I am doing a lot better in this area. Not perfect, but better. When David overrules and doesn't take my advice, I try to pray for my own heart to be submissive *and not angry*. I will continue to struggle with this until I die.

Respect is gigantic to men. Most husbands are reasonable, and if you treat them with huge respect, *they will listen* to your input. But women, there still comes a time when you have to lay down your appeal, even your most respectful and brilliant appeal, and let him decide. Again, this is the hardest part of Christian marriage, in my opinion, even though I have a kind and thoughtful husband.

Some of you may need to go to your husband and ask his forgiveness for your forceful personality and the way you have resisted his leadership. I hate asking forgiveness, too, so I understand, but it may be necessary to get your marriage cranking again.

Remember always to be the utmost respectful when you address your husband in a conflict. As recently as last week before we went out to dinner, David and I were discussing an issue in which we disagreed and that we both felt passionately about. I could tell that he was adamant about it, but I can tell you that *I felt just as adamant about it as he did*. We tabled it and went to dinner, but I truly felt like a cyclone had been twirling around in my brain over the matter. He told the couple we were eating with about the way we felt differently regarding the conflict. Then David said a surprising thing. "At least we were respectful to each other about it." That was really shocking, considering *what a hurricane my emotions were* when we discussed it. In earlier years, I would not have been so respectful. Always, always address your husband with the hugest of respect, even if your emotions feel like a tsunami. Never give in to releasing your emotional turmoil toward him.

DAY 3
The Beauty and Power of Empathy in Marriage

There are many things your husband wants from you that he will never ask for. We have discussed the *A* of Admiration. Men long for their wives to fill their tanks with admiration. We discussed sex last week and how a man wants an engaged partner who understands his great need in this area. Today, we will discuss empathy.

When another woman has a child who is sick, we are quick to run to her side with compassion and empathy. We understand the stress and sorrow of a sick child. When a woman has a breakup, and the man she loves leaves her, we understand this blow and are there to support her.

But we do not understand the pressures men face daily. Therefore, many of their struggles are met with indifference or (worse) advice to *buck up and move on.*

The area that I continually see women fail to give empathy in is in a man's occupation. Either the man is unhappy in his work, feels as if he is a failure in his work, or another of a thousand different situations. As I mentioned last week, men mainly think about work, money, and sex. A woman may feel strongly about her work, but in most marriages, it is nothing akin to how the man feels about his work. (Again, the 80/20 rule is true here, with only 80% of marriages being like this.) Men often define themselves as who they are by their work.

When husbands come home at night, we often want them to put work on the shelf and get involved with family life. And there's a time for that. But many wise wives let the first thirty minutes be a time when the husband gets to debrief and unload the pressures and trials of the day. Yes, you want to talk about little Johnny, your spat with your mother, and all your female issues. But he has his topics, too. Wise women learn to become excellent listeners who are also empathetic listeners. They soothe, they understand, they build up, and they express compassion.

Most wives will tell you that their husbands say the same thing over and over again about their work. It's as if the husband could come home and sit in the chair, and the wife could say, "Let me tell you about your day. You had issues with your boss. You had issues with your client. You had issues *x* and *y*, so let's move on and talk about me."

But that is not loving your husband at all. Maybe he struggles with the same thing at work, but your diligent attention to listening and then expressing sincere compassion and empathy for his struggles is a *huge* deposit into his tank. Don't try to talk him out of his struggles or (worse) ignore them.

You wouldn't believe the insensitive things wives say to their husbands. For example, "John, you say the same thing over and over again. When are you going to get past this? All men have to work hard and have trouble with their bosses. Can you get the kids washed up for dinner now?" That kind of insensitive remark will make a husband wish he were divorced. Really. One thing all men subconsciously want from their wives is understanding (You want that too, right? But you, the wise wife, don't demand it *but give it.)*

Your husband will relax and be refreshed in the presence of a wife who sits patiently, listens, tells him how hard that seems, is so proud of how he responds and endures, and is appreciative that he puts up with all that for the sake of her and the family. A wife who is understanding and compassionate to a man's struggles is a woman who finds a way *into a man's soul.* Quit being a know-it-all with all the answers. Of course, there are times when an idea that is fingertip dropped is helpful. But a wife must first demonstrate how she understands his trials and how she appreciates how he weathers the storm. You want emotional intimacy, right? You want him to listen closely to you and share his inmost self, right? Then you must learn to be an expert in the art of empathy. No man is going to open up and share himself if he is going to be met with constant advice, disappointment, or indifference.

We humans have so much to offer one another: empathy, deep listening, and expressing deep appreciation for another. A wise wife builds her house by making her husband feel he is understood and Superman at the same time.

He reciprocates by adoring her.

DAY 4
When Your Husband Doesn't Obey Scripture

I know you wanted a perfect husband, but there aren't any of those on this side of heaven. That means that you will have one who sins, either a lot or maybe just sometimes. He will indeed err.

Peter wrote a prescription so wives would know how to handle when a husband messes up. In fact, in 1 Peter 3, the Greek phrase says that if any husbands are *apeiqousin* (which the Greek Interlinear New Testament defines as "are-un-persuading" and "are-being-stubborn"), then wives have a certain way to respond in order to win or influence their husbands. Some translations translate *apeiqousin* to mean that husbands "don't obey the Word," and some translate it to mean they "don't believe the Word." But in either case, husbands are not acting right, and we need to know what to do. Peter gives us an idea.

Women want their husbands to straighten up, right? Peter says that husbands "may be won" (the Greek word is *kerdhqhswntai*). The idea is that husbands can be *influenced*. I like this. I want to know this strategy to win husbands. I'm ready to hear! Let it rip, Peter.

I will save you the Greek on the rest of this (but you nerds can look it up at Scripture4all.org). Peter says—ready?—that your husband may be won when—sure you're ready?—*he sees your purity and reverence.*

Uh, that's not what I was hoping for, Pete. I was hoping he would be won when he heard my brilliant oration or when I outlined my spectacular points! My purity and reverence? Gee. That's a crummy idea, Peter. What's up with that?

Nothing, nothing, nothing wins your husband like a heart that exhibits *purity and reverence*. This is God's prescription for handling husbands who "don't obey the word," who don't lead right, who don't respond right, and who don't live and love right. Those two qualities give a woman the power *to influence*.

The word *purity* means "innocent, modest, clean, and pure." The word translated *reverence* means (this is my own definition) "respect on speed." It is respect in all capital letters and then underlined. Women, we are so far from the biblical model of respecting our husbands.

Our clamoring, our condemning spirit, and our demand for high treatment will not help us win and influence our husbands. But a heart bathed in prayer, one growing in *purity and reverence,* will.

The two complaints I hear most often in marriage from women are these: "I don't feel loved" and "He doesn't lead well." Those are real problems and painful to women. But Peter says that husbands can be *won* by your purity and reverence. Don't expect to find that strategy on the cover of Oprah's magazine.

There is a throne in everyone's life; either you are running your life, or you are asking God to fill you with His Holy Spirit and asking him to run it. Those are your two choices. Every morning, give over the rule of your life to the One who created it. Pride, the lack of prayer, the lack of forgiveness toward others, and the desire to be puffed up show the carnal spirit. When we surrender and are filled with the Holy Spirit, God's Spirit fills us, and we are finally able to grow in these areas of *purity and reverence.* The woman who is filled with the Holy Spirit, *who has purity and reverence,* is the one who will influence others.

If you truly want to be pure and reverent and win your husband, then surrender to being led by the Spirit.

I must make an exclusion here. One wife I know has a husband who won't work, who watches porn, and who is verbally abusive. That is not merely annoying; that is evil. This advice is for wives with regular husbands. Please get professional help if your husband is abusive.

DAY 5, PART A
If You Are Having Trouble Accepting Your Biblical Role

If most of us are honest, we struggle with the role of being a biblical wife. Reading Isaiah 53 this morning, I was reminded again how "all we like sheep have gone astray; we have all turned to our own way." Doesn't that describe you and me perfectly as wives? Haven't we all turned to our own ways, turned to what we want, to what we think is a good way to be a wife, instead of what the Bible says about how wives are to think and act?

In your marriage, *turning to your own way* means you act how you want and that your husband is to be happy about it. But when I look at Scripture, I see how a wife is to treat her husband with reverence and that she is to get under her husband's authority. If Jesus didn't rise from the dead, then I would *never* go for this role of a biblical wife. I mean, there is no way I would let a man rule over me—unless I felt sure that the biblical account about Jesus is true. Honestly, whether I can live the calling of a biblical wife hinges on whether *I believe the resurrection of Jesus.* Did he come out of that grave? Because if he didn't, I'm not buying into the role of being a submissive, biblical wife.

I've just read the most amazing book called *Reliable Truth* by Richard E. Simmons III. It is a book about the validity of the Bible. I'm reminded again that—whoa—Christianity is *true.* Jesus walked on the earth, had disciples, and was arrested. The scaredy-cat disciples all fled, they saw the resurrected Christ, and then they became *unstoppable megaphones about him rising from the dead,* even in the face of torture and death. It's the truth. It is historical truth.

So as a woman, as a Christian wife, now you can live a life that is wildly different from what nonbelieving women live. You can obey the biblical calling of a wife. That means you can be *right* about an issue—when your husband is wrong—and not rub it in. You can praise your husband and lift him up as the patriarch of the family, making him king in front of the children, when no one is applauding you. You can hand him the scepter to lead, even though you are just as smart as he is. You can be quiet when you've given him a great idea and he then forgets to give you credit for it. You can be humble when he makes mistakes, with a 1 Peter 3 gentle and quiet spirit. You can be…well…godly!

Even if I *weren't* a believer, I would have to admit that families work better when the wife submits to the leadership of the husband. But still, I couldn't do it if I weren't a believer. If I weren't a believer, I *couldn't and wouldn't* submit to anyone. Why, that would be impossible for my proud ego to do!

But I am a believer. And so are you. And now, before the throne of heaven, we have to live in a way that pleases and honors the One who thought up the idea of marriage. And that means we wives adapt, submit, humble ourselves, and treat our husbands with reverence, regardless of their imperfect natures.

If you are struggling with this concept, I suggest you read *Reliable Truth* and remind yourself why you believe. Honestly, most struggles in marriage could be solved if spouses realize that their ultimate Mentor "did not come to be served, but to serve" (Matt. 20:28).

Many of us have fought letting our husbands lead, and understandably so. But have you noticed all the anger and self-pity that goes with that stance? Who wants to live like that? Once I bow my heart to God and give the Lord the scepter, then letting my husband lead and meeting his needs (without demanding that mine get met) not only is easier but also is the place of peace. *Oh, how I love to live in the place of peace,* not clamoring all the time to have things the way I think they should be. Being demanding is exhausting and miserable.

Living the role of a biblical wife is impossible if you are not clear on what you believe.

Are you struggling with your faith? We all do at times, but don't let this go on without addressing it. Two other amazing books to stir up your faith are *God's Not Dead* and *Man, Myth, Messiah*, both by Rice Broocks. Once a wife gets her faith firm, then she can get her role right. It is remarkable how she can then influence others—for good—in her realm. If you love your family, the best thing you can do for them is to be sure about why you believe. Then, live out your role as a discerning, meek, God-fearing wife.

DAY 5, PART B
A Story to Encourage You to Persevere

A wife told me last Christmas was one of the most memorable ones she has ever had. The family was gathered Christmas morning to open presents. Before they did so, the father wanted to tell the family what he appreciated about each person there. He discussed something about everyone in the room. Last, he got to his wife. Tears started rolling down the husband's cheeks as he told his family what his wife meant to him, how he adored her, and just how much he loved her. Friends, do you know what that is? This is the fulfillment of Proverbs 31:28–29, which says, "Her husband…praises her: 'Many women do noble things, but you surpass them all.'"

Stay the course. Focus on how you *give and love*, not on how *you're given to or how you're loved*. Someday, your husband will gather your children around the Christmas tree and tell them how blessed he is to have you as his wife.

The best three verses in the Bible on marriage, in my opinion, are 1 Corinthians 13:4–7.

Read these life-transforming verses:

Love is patient; love is kind; love is not envious or boastful or arrogant or rude. It does not insist on its own way; it is not irritable or resentful; it does not rejoice in wrongdoing, but rejoices in the truth. It bears all things, believes all things, hopes all things, endures all things.

That, my friend, is what the 8 A's are all about.

Prayer

God,

The Affection chapter last week (on sex) was really difficult. But the A of Authority this week is the hardest of all the A's.

I do not really like this lesson on Authority. But since you are Lord, I submit to Your order.

You know how hard this is for me, God. I have trouble even praying about it. Please soften my heart. Please pour your Holy Spirit into me, and make me want to obey in this area. I want to ignore the A of Authority. Yet, I realize, *it is the path of blessing* for my children and for me.

Grow my faith, God. As I get more firm on the fact that You rose from the dead, I can more easily get my heart and mind around the A of Authority, of submitting to one who is not smarter or wiser than me.

Lord, I do believe You are the Son of God. Therefore I will submit to You and Your command for me to submit to my husband. Help me with this most difficult of commands.

In Jesus's name,

Amen

WEEK 9

Assignments and Group Discussion Questions

1. Describe your prior thoughts and behavior regarding the A of Authority. What do you now see or understand that you did not before?

2. What has been your prior experience with appeals? What is your opinion about The Paragraph? Would that help your marriage? If not, what do you recommend?

3. How do you feel about purity and reverence being the God-ordained methods for winning your husband?

4. How is your faith? Would reading a good book on apologetics be helpful to you? Where specifically do you struggle?

WEEK 10

What to Do When Your Husband Fails or Has Adversity...and More

Contents

Day 1: What to Do When Your Husband Fails or Has Adversity

Day 2: Asking for What You Want in Your Marriage

Day 3: Improving Your Mood

Day 4, Part A: Another Important List to Start and Keep

Day 4, Part B: A Fabulous Parenting Resource

Day 5, Part A: Another Reminder about Expectations in Marriage

Day 5, Part B: How One Wife Endeavored to Bump. It. Up.

You are on your way to becoming a Marriage Champion. Bravo for you. Just as chess champions learn the nuances of how to play chess, we are learning the nuances of how to have a spectacular marriage. Your efforts will be rewarded!

Read chapter 10 in *Wife School* before you read the following lesson.

DAY 1
What to Do When Your Husband Fails or Has Adversity

Yesterday, attached to a Chinese tea bag, I read, "Kindness is always the answer." I laughed to myself, thinking how simple life can sometimes be. That brings us to chapter 10 in *Wife School* on the subject of *empathy and compassion* toward your husband when he fails or has adversity. In that situation, too, kindness is always the answer.

Judging by the way some women treat their husbands when the husbands fail, you'd think there were a Bible verse that read, "And if ye husband doesn't get it, let him have ye wrath." But that's not what the scriptures say. Instead, they command us to be compassionate. The two verses that come to mind are Ephesians 4:32, which says to "be kind to one another, tenderhearted," and Colossians 3:1, which says to "put on…compassion."

As you know, we often don't extend *our best* to our spouses. We want them to buck up, get it right, get with the program, and take it like men. Our husbands are dust, just like us, and they love tenderness and understanding, too.

Don't be so spent on the outside world that your family gets your leftovers. It is comical to see how women are nice to people whom they don't even really care about, yet they give their exhausted crumbs to the people they love the most (i.e., husband and kids). *Give your family your best*.

I love the verse "Bear one another's burdens" (Gal. 6:2). Remember, the *one another* who is the most important to you is that other person whom you woke up next to in your bed this morning.

DAY 2
Asking for What You Want in Your Marriage

The basic 8 A's have been thoroughly discussed now. You now know how to love a man in a language he can hear. This is the time to learn to ask your husband wisely for what you want and need. *Da-da! Trumpet, please*. We have been waiting for this moment.

We love our men by giving them the 8 A's, but that's not exactly how we want them to love us (yes, some of it, but not all of it). Remember that men say "I love you" by bringing home their paycheck and being sexually faithful. You want him to say "I love you" with words, gifts, romantic gestures, listening deeply, admiring you, being an awesome father and spiritual leader, and other types of high treatment (well, and doing the dishes).

Men have not been trained that women are different from them. Did you know that many men think women are sexually excited about seeing men's private parts because men are excited about seeing ours? When David and I were newly married, I remember reading a book that said that men's private parts excite women to the same extent that an elbow does. Men have trouble understanding this.

Anyhow…

Now you get to teach your husband what you want. This is a very slow method. But over time, you will be able to tell your husband everything you want and probably get most of it. First, some guidelines must be set. Read, star, and underline number one of the guidelines:

1. Be sure you are asking for godly things. I mean, don't manipulate and pressure him to buy you things he can't afford or ask for things you know aren't wholesome. You know what is good and what is not.

2. Be sure his tank is tip-top full of the 8 A's. When men feel loved by the 8 A's, they turn toward you and open to your influence, kind of how a flower turns to the sunlight.

3. No matter how much you give your husband the 8 A's, if you still give in to emotional turmoil or disrespectful behavior, you wipe the slate clean (well, really, put it in a deficit). No man can handle a disrespectful woman. Bury that woman. May she never breathe again.

4. Write down everything you want (I know the list is long) and prioritize it. You cannot ask for everything at once. Ask for the top one or two things. Try to keep your *number one thing that you want* in mind when you read the following guidelines.

5. You are admiring and appreciating your husband every day (right?), so he is used to this by now. Start the conversation by reminding him of something you really admire or how happy you are about something about him. Then, tell him that there is something you would really like. Then, just ask. Don't expect him to be overjoyed about this. He will probably not be. And don't take his negative response personally. Just thank him for listening, and go cook something yummy for him.

6. It is very important that you drop the subject and wait. Put your antennas up. If you see any behavior that is indicative of him *moving in that direction*, praise him. The following is a possible example of what you might say if your number one desire is that your husband spends more time at home with you and the kids: "Honey, I noticed that you got home at six thirty instead of seven tonight, and then you played with the kids! How happy that makes me. Did you see the children's bright faces? They adore your attention, and I am so appreciative because I know you have had a long, hard day." Then, if you can, *reward* him. (My husband says I have trained him as psychologists train rats in a maze.) Whatever reward you think of is fine. Reward him with extra sweetness, extra praise, extra attention, extra…hmm, just extra. You get it.

7. If he is a slow learner, do not fret. Most men are pretty slow when it comes to understanding women. Just rewind and do the whole ordeal again, telling him what a good husband he is. But as you said, you'd like *x*. Go back to number six. And repeat. Every time you see an inkling of this behavior, you tell him how happy it makes you, and you *reward* him.

Your husband is not a bumpkin if he doesn't get your issue quickly. Normal men usually don't understand their wives *until many years into the marriage*. I hate to use the word *all*, but definitely *most* men have to be trained by their wives. Don't bemoan that. *Just learn the art, and do it well.* You are no longer a normal wife; you are a Marriage Champion creating a marriage of the century. But it takes months and years to teach a man what a woman wants and how a woman thinks. Just be patient. The 8 A's will keep him turned toward you and *willing* to learn what's in your heart.

Your gentle and quiet spirit, coupled with the 8 A's, allows you to wedge yourself into your husband's heart. Men *long* to have wives like this. They eventually reciprocate in a gigantic way. They really do. Maybe not for months, but they eventually do.

Today's woman is so impatient. She wants the man to change by the weekend. Give up that ridiculous fantasy. No one changes that fast. I cannot tell you how many women I know who have persevered and turned frogs into princes (not perfect princes, but princes). These women have given and loved *when they were not given to or loved*. They endured for the long haul. The. Long. Long. Haul.

Just FYI, there is usually The One Thing in marriage that spouses have trouble giving each other. That is, there is *one major thing* that *you want* and *he doesn't want to give*, and vice versa. The One Thing can continue for years. The *best* marriages have The One Thing. Knowing this makes you not fret when you see The One Thing continue to rear its head in your marriage. When you are smacked again with your husband not giving you The One Thing, offer it to God and ask him to please work. Only God seems to be able to break through The One Thing. Just remember, *there is nothing wrong with your marriage*, even though there is The One Thing.

Pray. Overlook. Pray again. Deposit the 8 A's again. You focus on the zillion things your husband gets right, and you throw yourself on the Lord and beg him to help you in the area of The One Thing. But what you *don't do* is think there's something wrong with your marriage! You are both mere mortals. (If you think you have personally arrived spiritually, I challenge you to read the prayer at the end of this lesson which I copied from *The Valley of Vision*. You will see your true nature when you read the prayer.)

Women, you will not get *everything* you want from your husband. God won't let you be that satisfied on this side of heaven, because then you won't need God. But you can have an incredible, unbelievably satisfying, and godly marriage.

OK, got your list of what you want? Got your sweetness on? *Then it's time to ask.* He can't read your mind.

DAY 3
Improving Your Mood

In the article in week 2, day 1, "Changing Your Emotions," I gave an example to show that emotions come from thoughts. I will copy and paste three paragraphs from that section because you will need to review this knowledge base to proceed with the rest of this section:

> Imagine you are in an alley, it is midnight, and you are in the worst part of town. You are alone, and you hear garbage cans tip over and see shadows move across your path. What is your emotion? Fear, right? What if I told you that the truth is that you are perfectly safe, that there is no danger anywhere in the vicinity? Do you see that your previous emotion of fear followed your thoughts instead of following reality? It is of utmost importance that you understand that your emotion of fear followed your thoughts.
>
> Let's take another example. Imagine you are at a park with your four-year-old and your two-year-old (either children or grandchildren). The day is sunny and warm, and the children are delighted that they are floating their sailboats on the pond. The four-year-old brings you flowers and tells you how pretty you are. Then the two-year-old runs to you and kisses you on the cheek. What are your emotions? Joy and happiness, right? What if I then told you that the truth is that there was a kidnapper hiding behind the tree, waiting to grab one child while you were occupied with another? Do you see that your previous emotion of happiness followed your thoughts and not reality? Emotions follow thoughts, not reality!
>
> Do you see the gigantic implications of this? If we can learn that our emotions flow from our thoughts, then we can take responsibility for and choose to have good thoughts. The concept of thinking good thoughts is not my idea. Paul tells us in Philippians 4:8 what to think about (whatever is true, noble, right, pure, lovely, and admirable).

Most of us are wildly unaware of the constant parade of thoughts that march across our brains. A couple of days ago, I awoke to an encouraging email. I felt the immediate increase in my mood. I went into the kitchen to start breakfast. Before long, I was down. Hmmm! What was the deal? I retraced my thoughts. Sure enough, I was letting thoughts about a situation in which I am struggling go across the screen of my mind. Sad thoughts lead to sad emotions.

What has been tremendously helpful to realize is that most of us *have the same five or six thought patterns that bring us down*, not five or six hundred. Many of you have read *The Screwtape Letters* by C. S. Lewis. It is a fictional story of what demons' strategies are in the spiritual realms to keep humans from following *the Enemy* (God). At one point in the story, one demon is instructed to get a certain human's file. In that file are the typical patterns that always *trip up* that certain human. In other words, each of us has patterns that will trip us up.

This will take some work, but it will be tremendously positive if you can identify the five or six areas of thought that repeatedly get you down. Maybe the area that gets you down is finances, a rude boss, in-laws, a difficult child, a health issue, a relationship with your family of origin, problems with a close friend, or maybe one of a zillion other things. For sure, you have your *files*, the things that *repeatedly trip you up* and upset you. It is vastly helpful if you can *listen in* on your thoughts and write down the areas in your Turquoise Journal that repeatedly pull you down. Then, you can devise strategies to refute those negative thought patterns.

I don't want to blame anyone, but—sorry to say this!—you probably think a lot like your parents. One of my sons said something very discouraging and wrong the other day. I said to him, "Oh, I'm so sorry you think like that. You got that from me. That's how I thought while you were growing up and I didn't know any better then. Now I know how to think correctly about that." This son has my previous bad negative pattern, and he will have to learn to overcome it, just like some of you.

Truly believing the Word is the absolute best medicine for a happy heart, knowing that the One who created the universe from nothing, and who created you, is listening and cares for you. That, my friend, is the ultimate prescription for conquering discouragement. If you are not rock solid on your faith, please google "Ahmanson Lecture Series: Apologetics." It is a series of five lectures at Rick Warren's church—Rick is the author of *The Purpose Driven Life*—in 2012. They gathered five top apologetic speakers from around the world in one weekend. It is of the utmost importance that you know why you believe. You will not be able to trust God unless you truly believe that He's powerful, able, and caring.

A very helpful practice that has freed many people from continually being discouraged over the same issues is to write the problem on the left side of a piece of paper. On the right side, write possible *positive* explanations or substitute thoughts. For example, maybe you struggle with in-laws. Possible positive thoughts might be as follows: "All people have some struggles. I'm glad my struggle is with in-laws and not my parents," or, "Obstacles are not insurmountable, and there are many ways I might improve this situation if I am proactive and learn about it. Many women have learned to handle tough in-laws through the ages. Although I can't change my in-laws, I can research and learn how others have learned to respond to difficult in-laws."

Another example might be that you are having trouble with finances. On the right, you could write down the following: "This is a common struggle for many couples. I will learn about finances, and we can change our situation with knowledge and effort. Learning to handle finances is something many people have to wrestle with, and it is not rocket science. I can learn this."

For a last example, maybe your problem is your weight, and you are very discouraged. On the right, you write the following: "I am of (at least) average intelligence, and many average people have learned how to lose weight and keep it off. I will give myself to learning how people have done that. Although I have failed for years, I can still learn how to do this. I feel discouraged by my prior failure, but failure is a path to learning *what doesn't work*. Yes, I have tried, but I have not tried enough. I will not quit until I learn and master the secrets. They are out there. I must find them." (*Skinny School: Where Women Learn the Secrets to Finally Get Thin Forever* can teach you how to think about food and eating. In addition, the *Skinny School Study Guide* will help cement your new mind-set about eating.)

Do you see the hope in all of those responses? The helplessness and hopelessness you feel about your problem is not true! There is hope beyond belief for almost everything to change. Do not let discouragement beat you up. Instead, be *wildly proactive* about solving and learning how to conquer your problems!

I love the book *Jesus Calling*. One reason is because that book reminds me over and over that God says, "For I know the plans I have for you, plans to prosper you and not to harm you, plans to give you hope and a future" (Jer. 29:11). God wants us to seek him with our whole heart, and He is listening and loves us. (Matt. 7:11 says, "If you, then, though you are evil, know how to give good gifts to your children, how much more will your Father in the heavens give good things to those who ask him.")

Another helpful thought to me is that in the unseen world, God has legions of angels ready to do his bidding. Friends, we must be women of prayer. This is not an option if we are to fight discouragement. My life verse is 2 Corinthians 10:4: "The weapons we fight with are not the weapons of the world. On the contrary, they have divine power to demolish strongholds."

As you know, I like to research my problems, looking to the ends of the earth for answers. *But there comes a time when I have to quarantine those thoughts and put them on the shelf in heaven*, where I know God will work on my problems in my behalf. If I let the problems continue to roll around in my brain, I can get very discouraged because *emotions come from thoughts.*

Especially when I wake up in the morning, my problems and the WMD (What's Missing and Disappointing) can come rolling in. You have to *fight*. I have positive things that I start thinking about (and coffee helps). ASAP, I get in the Word. I know you know this, but the Word is living. Living! God dwells in his Word. He refreshes your soul as you soak in His thoughts. Prayer is indispensable for everything.

We have discussed the Turquoise Journal and its benefit on your mind because it bathes your mind with positive thoughts about your husband. In addition to the Turquoise Journal, I advise women also to keep multiple lists of items they are grateful for, things they are looking forward to, the strength set that God gave them, the areas which give them joy to think about, etc. One man told me that he had a *happy place* in his mind, and it was thinking about his favorite basketball team. That wouldn't work for me, for sure, but I have my own lists of happy places that I know will lift me up and *out of my ruminating* about my problems. We're depressed when we continually think about what is *missing and what is disappointing* in our lives. We have got to grow discipline in what we continually allow ourselves to think about.

Another positive thing you can do to improve your mood is to read inspirational books. I love to read old authors such as Andrew Murray, Francis Roberts, etc., who inspire me to think about how God is using my trials for good. Currently, I'm obsessed with books and DVDs on apologetics (Norman Geisler, Rice Broocks, Creation.com resources such as Jonathan Sarfati's materials, etc.). It's hard to be discouraged when you're reading arguments for the existence of God and the historical reliability of the New Testament documents.

Don't neglect feeding your brain *positive* thoughts.

When negative events happen, we can let the negative event *begin to take over what we think about*. Be intentional with what you think about. Pay attention to the parade of thoughts that constantly march across your brain. As Paul commanded in Philippians 4:8, *choose to think about* whatever is true, noble, right, pure, lovely, etc., because emotions flow from thoughts. Insist on looking *for positive explanations to upsetting circumstances.*

Another activity that improves mood is having friends/mentors with whom you can take your mask off and be accepted. God made us community creatures. Meeting with a small group of godly women who encourage you and share your burdens is unbelievably healing and helpful in growing a good mood. The acceptance of a group like this and the fellowship they provide are powerful for your mind. Loneliness is a downer. We were not created to live alone, and we will definitely be discouraged if we do.

Having someone listen to you unties your knots. Quit living by yourself and figuring things out by yourself. Ask for help. 1 Corinthians 10:13 says, "No testing has overtaken you that is not common to everyone." Other women *feel exactly the same way* that you do. Make time to meet in person with godly, encouraging women. (The phone is not the same thing.)

Hebrews 10:25 is often used by church leaders to tell us to go to church, but I believe it has more meaning than that. The verse reads as "not neglecting to meet together, as is the habit of some, but encouraging one another." We have to *meet together to encourage each other.* The average Sunday morning worship service does not allow much time for meeting together and encouraging each other. You will need to find a Sunday School class or a small group to have these fellowship needs met. Your mood is very affected by your sincere, authentic, fellowship with others.

You know that fatigue can negatively affect your moods. But did you know that research now shows that sugar and refined carbs are terrible for your *mood*? The women in my *Skinny School* groups say they have regained their sanity by ditching sugar and refined carbs and trading those idiots for protein, good fats, and veggies. Quit eating junk!

Being *disappointed* in life is a natural, normal human occurrence, but *being discouraged* must be battled. I have listed several methods to fight discouragement and low moods. You have a lot of control over if you are discouraged or not. It's a discipline and course in itself to learn to *conquer discouragement*. Learning how to think and what to think about is imperative to conquer low-mood issues. You do not have to continue to wallow in the lowlands of discouragement.

Jesus is coming someday on a white horse to rescue you, but no human is coming on a white horse to rescue you today. You are responsible for what you think about.

DAY 4, PART A
Another Important List to Start and Keep

A few years ago, when I started keeping my own personal Turquoise Journal of my husband's sweet and kind remarks/acts, I also started lists for each of our six children. Oh, how I wish I had done this since their births!

A few days ago, I was mad at a child because of a couple of things he'd said/done. There definitely was tension between us. I reread a 2011 list I had written for that child. I *never* would have remembered the sweet things on the list that that child said/did if I had not written them down. On the list was how he stood up to a teacher who was compromising some Christian values, how he thanked me for something about me that I truly cared about, how he apologized, how he asked my opinion about something that mattered to me, how he sat with me instead of his friends at a funeral so I wouldn't be alone, how he received correction on a matter, and how he realized a big mistake he was making in an important area and took massive strives to correct it. The best one was how, during an argument, he said, "I really care about you deep down" (since he certainly wasn't acting that way at the moment).

You have to record their sweet things. You will forget. What a joy to go back and read the amazing words/actions my husband and kids have said/done. (I don't record their offenses but hope to forget those.)

Needless to say, after reading that short list from 2011, all my anger/annoyance was immediately gone, and the goodwill toward that child was immediately back. (Emotions are from thoughts, remember?) Don't neglect filling out your lists in your Turquoise Journal (and your other lists). It is imperative you record the good stuff that happens so you can stir up your happy thoughts, because *emotions come from thoughts*! You have much power over the emotional climate you live in.

DAY 4, PART B
A Fabulous Parenting Resource

Many of you came from solid, healthy Christian families. Therefore, many of you learned parenting from your family of origin, which is the best way to learn it. But many of you did not have the ideal family of origin, so this resource recommendation will especially greatly benefit you.

You know I am a book hound. I would rather have a new good book than new clothes or any other new thing. So when we started having kids (thirty-two years ago), I devoured the Christian books on parenting. Every time a new one came out, I bought it. During Mother's Day Out when my children were little, I often sat in a cemetery or park and read. When I offer the next advice, know that I have read many of the Christian parenting books of the past twenty-five years. Some were awesome, for sure. Some, to be honest, were horrible. I still own most of them, and many are like old friends.

My daughter just had a baby, and I found my old baby management book, *Preparation for Parenting* by the Ezzos in my attic. The book has now been replaced by the newer version, called *On Becoming Baby Wise* although I much prefer the older one.

About thirteen years ago, someone put me on to an organization called Love and Logic (LoveAndLogic.com). The founders are Christians, but they do not cater exclusively to a Christian audience. They teach parents—as well as teachers—how to *handle discipline*. To tell you how valuable their material is, I can only say that if I could do five things from the past differently, one of them would be that I would have had this material when my first child was born. It *teaches your children by natural consequences and keeps the softness in the relationship.* Love and Logic teaches parents how to handle kids "with parents' hands tied behind their back." The anger, the arguing, the yelling—all are gone.

You *can't* learn this whole mind-set by listening to one Love and Logic CD series or by reading one book. It is opposite to your natural inclinations, and you need to listen and re-listen to many of their resources. This material is nothing short of miraculous as far as disciplining kids, in my opinion. But to think you will master this material easily is absurd. It is more akin to learning to speak French. So don't listen to a CD and say, "This doesn't work." It is a mind-set and worth hours of listening and learning the thinking. The CD set on teenage parenting completely reversed some parenting mistakes I was making.

What children end up doing when you parent with Love and Logic is *learning to think about the upcoming consequences.* They make mistakes, but that is OK because we want children to make mistakes when they are *young,* not when they are adults.

Of course, *you are going to teach your children the Bible, Christian character, and to love the Lord.* That's who you are at your core. And I strongly recommend you read all the great Christian parenting books out there. But this material will change your parenting style, will allow you and your husband to get on the same page regarding parenting, and *get the anger out of parenting.* I wish I'd had it earlier. I would have saved myself a lot of frustration.

Love and Logic is to handling the *discipline in parenting* what Dave Ramsey is to *understanding money!* Parenting and finances are two of the biggest stresses in marriage. Learn these areas like an expert. Stop any of the other foolishness that you are doing, and learn about the important things that will affect your marriage and family! The resources are out there; all it takes is your willingness and your time.

When my husband and I started implementing the principles of Love and Logic, it took six months or so to see the results (we had teens at the time, but Love and Logic has material for every age). The softness and fun returned to the parenting relationship. Parenting became a joy again instead of a never-ending battle and burden.

I don't endorse many products. But if I could give stars to this material, I'd give it six stars out of five.

You need to disciple/mentor your child to know and serve the Lord. The Love and Logic material, though, will help you handle many of the practical areas of discipline with your kids.

DAY 5, PART A
Another Reminder about Expectations in Marriage

Let me remind you again how the expectations of marriage in this century are wildly different from other time periods. TV, movies, and novels have given us unrealistic pictures of romantic marriage. You know I love marriage, but honestly, *it is gallons of work.* It is overlooking, depositing into your husband's tank (when yours is empty), and overlooking some more. Once we get the false expectations removed (that there is this romantic, into-the-sunset relationship that others are experiencing), we can see that we have a normal relationship, one in which two sinners are sharing space in close quarters.

Friends, I have gazed inside some of the best families on the face of the planet, and guess what? They *also* are two sinners living together, pricking each other with their porcupine needles. There are *no* romantic comedy marriages in existence. None. Yes, there are some fantastic marriages out there, but what that means is that they've learned to handle conflict, say they're sorry, overlook, forgive again, and deposit into each other's tanks. Mark this down: no marriages with kids and finances and jobs and life are smoothly sailing into the sunset. Zero. If your friends are bragging that their marriages are perfect, they are lying.

Quit beating yourself up because your marriage takes a lot of work. All great marriages do! You will be annoyed again and again, and so will your husband. Forgiving and overlooking are maybe the most important skills in a marriage. Quit wishing for Camelot. It doesn't exist.

DAY 5, PART B
How One Wife Endeavored to Bump. It. Up.

In week 8, I wrote a section entitled "Bump. It. Up." Below is an excerpt from an email I just received by a precious, young godly wife and mother. She is pretty, savvy, and articulate. Enjoy her email, in which she explains how she endeavored to Bump. It. Up. (This is used with her permission.)

A couple of months ago, I looked at my underwear and bras and cringed. Beige, boring bras and faded, boring underwear. So, I went to [the store] and scoured the clearance section and found some new bras and panties that were fun colors and materials. I unveiled these on our trip to [the city] to celebrate [an event] last month. Needless to say, they were a big hit. Seeing his reaction made me realize that it doesn't take a lot of money (if you shop smart!) to add a lot of fun. Now, I'll send him coded texts hinting at what I'm wearing so he'll have something fun to think about during the day. I've never thought about the dancing before, but I just might have to try that too! Eek! ;)

I remind you again: Bump. It. Up. Husbands love it.

Prayer

Lately in my quiet time, I have been reading and using prayers from *The Valley of Vision, A Collection of Puritan Prayers and Devotions.* For our prayer this week, I have copied and pasted the prayer from page 74.

> Lord,
>
> I can scarce open my eyes but I envy those above me, or despise those below me.
>
> I covet honour and riches of the mighty, and am proud and unmerciful to the rags of others;
>
> If I behold beauty it is a bait to lust, or see deformity, it stirs up loathing and disdain;
>
> How soon do slanders, vain jests, and wanton speeches creep into my heart!
>
> Am I comely? What fuel for pride!
>
> Am I deformed? What an occasion for repining!
>
> Am I gifted? I lust after applause!
>
> Am I unlearned? How I despise what I have not!
>
> Am I in authority? How prone to abuse my trust, make will my law, exclude others' enjoyments, serve my own interests and policy!
>
> Am I inferior? How much I grudge others' pre-eminence!
>
> Am I rich? How exalted I become!
>
> Thou knowest that all these are snares by my corruptions, and that my greatest snare is myself.
>
> Yet what canst thou expect of dust but levity, of corruption but defilement?
>
> Keep me ever mindful of my natural state, but let me not forget my heavenly title, or the grace that can deal with every sin.
>
> In Jesus's name,
>
> Amen.

Assignments and Group Discussion Questions

1. How would you describe your level of empathy and compassion in your relationship with your husband?

2. What are your thoughts about "asking for what you want in your marriage?" How would you describe your prior method, and how do you plan on tweaking that?

3. Do you often have struggles with a negative mood? Have you always understood that emotions come from thoughts, or is this a new thought for you? How do you plan to improve your mood?

4. Day 4 encouraged you to start lists of your children's delightful words and thoughts. How are you doing with your Turquoise Journal assignments in recording your husband's strengths and virtues?

5. Have you applied yourself to learn parenting, or are you simply hoping to do the best you can? What are your thoughts about parenting in the way your parents did it?

6. Have you come to grips with how the modern American woman has unrealistic expectations of a perpetual, romantic love story for a marriage instead of doing the work of overlooking and depositing the 8 A's?

WEEK 11

How to View Your Husband's Work from His Perspective ...and More

Contents

Day 1: Will My Husband Ever Reciprocate?
Day 2: A Discussion about Charm, Beauty, and Fearing the Lord
Day 3: Three Qualities that Predict Addiction
Day 4: Learn to Not Be Offended
Day 5, Part A: Another Quick Thought on When Others Fail
Day 5, Part B: A Tirade on Health

Overcoming previous programming in your mindset is extremely difficult to do. But repetition is the key to learning. Do not be discouraged with yourself if you still see evidence of contentious behavior and feel you have so much to change. God loves to give "beauty for ashes" (Is. 61:3). Stay with it. Endure. Persevere. "Let us not become weary in doing good, for at the proper time we will reap a harvest if we do not give up" (Gal. 6:9).

Read chapter 11 in *Wife School* before you read the following lesson.

DAY 1
Will My Husband Ever Reciprocate?

A sweet lady from Bible study said, "We must realize and accept that *some* husbands will never reciprocate, even though we fill them with the 8 A's." There are always the *extremely* rare exceptions. But honestly, I think that the overwhelming, gigantic majority of men *eventually reciprocate*. Let's discuss why.

I was up very early this morning and noticed the gorgeous sunrise. What splendor! "Oh, God! What beauty!" I said. A young couple I know has some happy, chubby-cheeked toddlers I recently saw at church. "How adorable!" I thought. I felt compelled to tell the mother. In addition, I am reminded of how I recently walked into a beautifully decorated room, and my tendency was to *praise and comment on its beauty*.

That's because humans are designed to want to *praise* beauty and goodness. We don't conjure it up; it is a natural response in humans to artistry.

As women live the 8 A's coupled with a 1 Peter 3 gentle and quiet spirit, husbands eventually notice the beauty and goodness. Therefore, *their tendency is to praise it.* Some husbands are more vocal than others, but most husbands, in time, will notice and comment.

Women ask me over and over again, "How long will this take if I truly change how I act toward him?" The answer is always, "It depends. How much emotional turmoil have you brought into the marriage and for how long?" Newlyweds can self-correct pretty quickly. Those who have been married longer have deeper grooves in the brain with their previous unloving patterns, and these take longer to override.

I received an email this week from a young woman who told me her husband admitted that he had been considering leaving her before "she changed." Her marriage did not take very long to heal, as she had been married only a few years. To override a harsh pattern of fifteen years will take longer than these mere 22 weeks in the study of *Wife School*. But it is doable.

The degree of the emotional turmoil is a factor in how long it takes to turn around your marriage. Severe sarcasm, breaches of trust, and repeated hurtful remarks make deep grooves in the brain. I do believe the change can occur, but these marriages need an extra dose of perseverance to convince your husband that the change is sincere and permanent.

I, like you, want easy answers to fix life. But there are none. Life has pain. Life has problems. Life has challenges. You decide if you are going to throw yourself on the Lord and have him meet your needs and therefore you can be a lush, fruitful garden that others may come and pick your fruit (John 15). Your beautiful, fruitful garden will please the One who created you and will draw the hearts of those who eat your fruit.

Find contentment with the portion you now have. (Learning contentment is a course in itself, and we will further explore this topic in future lessons.) Quit demanding that your portion is not enough, and do the work to make things better while accepting *what is.* You know women who incessantly whine, have self-pity, and complain. Don't be like that. Be that uncommon woman with the gracious spirit. Proverbs 11:16 says, "A kind-hearted woman gains honor." Kind hearted? That word in itself is a rebuke to many of us. Take responsibility for your own nourishment, and then give lavishly to others from an overflow from your prayer life. We are women of prayer, or we are women of angst.

Solomon tells us that a kind-hearted, gracious woman will gain honor. Just like the gorgeous sunrise, or the adorable fat-cheeked baby, this rare nature in a woman elicits praise for its beauty. But give up looking for it;

give up demanding it. Focus on your luscious fruit to give away. Someday, when you are not expecting it, this will happen:

"Her children arise and call her blessed; her husband also, and he praises her: 'Many women do noble things, but you surpass them all'" (Prov. 31:28–29). Her husband and children arise and bless her, not because she is brilliant, charming, or gorgeous. They bless her because she is a *godly, gracious giver*, meeting *their* needs instead of demanding that she be coddled all the time. Strive for godliness, not cleverness.

You and I don't want to be self-absorbed and critical women. But that is our natural tendency, my friend. And it gets worse as you age because the losses accumulate. That is why so many middle-aged women become alcoholics, become addicted to sugar, or have problems with spending. They want to medicate the pain of the accumulated losses.

We must fight our natural tendencies to focus on What is Missing and Disappointing (the WMDs). We must become grateful, focusing on the good that is in our life. That is why I am repeatedly adamant about filling out your lists in your Turquoise Journal. That is a tool to fight discouragement and to fight self-pity.

Maybe your husband is not reciprocating today. Overlook that. Focus on how you love and give to others, not on how you are loved and given to. It's a sowing and reaping world, my friend. But the reaping comes much later than the sowing. Your husband will (most, most, most likely) eventually reciprocate, but try to take *looking for it* off your plate. This is the man you were given to love. Do your assignment well. When you least expect it, the rain will come.

DAY 2
A Discussion about Charm, Beauty, and Fearing the Lord

Today we will discuss three attributes from Proverbs 31—charm, beauty, and fearing the Lord—and how they relate.

When I was in my thirties, I was with some older women, and one of the successful and attractive women was talking. She was discussing another woman who was recently widowed. "She'll be married again soon because she's charming with men."

I sort of knew what she meant, but I was curious. "What does that mean specifically?"

She laughed. "You know, she asks their opinions, gets them to talk about themselves, strokes their egos…*She just makes them feel wonderful about themselves.*"

I remember the light going off. I thought, "Hmm, that's a formula for being charming with men." (As you know, many of the 8 A's teach you to be *charming* with your husband. And that is not a bad thing!)

But I knew the woman she was talking about, and she certainly did not exhibit godly character. That was *not* a person I wanted to pattern myself after at all. I realized then that charm and good social skills can often be a mask for an ugly, small, self-centered soul.

Next, let's discuss beauty. There are two ditches women fall into regarding beauty. One ditch is to be obsessed about beauty. We hear Christian speakers warn of these dangers all the time. The Apostle Peter warns us to not focus on outward beauty as much as acquiring a gentle and quiet spirit (1 Pet. 3).

The other ditch is not to focus on beauty at all, much to the disappointment of many husbands. Men derive pleasure from looking at their attractive spouses. Dr. Adrian Rogers once said, "Some people say it's a sin to wear makeup. I think it's a sin for some women *not* to."

We know it's all right to invest some effort into beauty. The Proverbs 31 woman was said to dress in fine linen and purple. Esther was given twelve months of beauty treatments before she was taken to the king (Esther 2:12). Why, God chose to make three of the main Old Testament women beautiful: Sarah, Rachel, and Esther. But how much can we think about and invest in the area of beauty, and when does it get too much? We all want to know, *where is the line*?

When my mother was growing up in the 1930s in rural Missouri, her mother insisted that she get braces for her crooked teeth. Many of the surrounding neighbors criticized this because they thought it was vain and focused too much on the exterior. We all laugh at that now, as we feel sorry for young children who are not able to afford braces. Braces are accepted and expected in our current culture.

Standards change. What the culture criticizes in one generation is acceptable in another. This doesn't help us much with deciding *what is acceptable*.

Obviously, God is not opposed to beauty in a woman. But we are to have the priority *of having a focus on inner beauty*.

There's something interesting in what King Lemuel's mother wrote to him when she was giving him advice on whom to select as a wife in Proverbs 31. She says, "Charm is deceitful, and beauty is vain."

What does that mean? Does she mean don't marry someone who is charming? Don't marry someone who is beautiful? You have to know what comes next to appreciate what she is trying to say. What comes next is "but a woman who fears the Lord is to be praised." It's OK to be charming with your husband. But *without fearing the Lord*, charm can be deceitful and manipulative. And it is fine to be beautiful. But a woman who desperately endeavors to be beautiful *without fearing the Lord* can be vain and often self-absorbed. Charm and beauty can both be cover-ups for shallowness and selfishness.

Be charming with your husband. For sure, it's fine to buy some cream to get rid of the crow's-feet around your eyes. (I love when Sally Field in *Steel Magnolias* says, "Honey, time marches on and eventually you realize it is marchin' across your face.") But the most fabulous, important attribute in a woman is that *she fears the Lord*. A woman who fears the Lord knows He is watching and knows He is in control. She lives in His presence, living with kindness and integrity. That's the *mindset* that wins over charm and beauty every time.

At the time of this writing, we have four unmarried sons (one is married), and I know all four of those unmarried boys want to marry someone who is beautiful and charming. But the best advice I could give them is to marry someone *who fears the Lord*.

Look lovely for your husband, and certainly treat him with charm. But a man is truly blessed when his wife *fears the Lord*.

DAY 3
Three Qualities that Predict Addiction

I love studying anything associated with the human personality, and a fascinating topic is addiction. Did you know that there are certain personality traits that are associated with addiction? The three qualities that are found in almost all addicts are *insecurity*, *grandiosity* (expecting high treatment and getting offended when they don't get it), and *resentment*. Let's talk about these three weaknesses. If you know this is a problem for you, you can take strides to help heal the problem.

Let's discuss insecurity first. People who are insecure are always walking around with their antennas up, looking to see how other people treat them. Honestly, other people are not thinking much about us, so it would be easy to feel insecure and overlooked much of the time. When people fail to acknowledge you, invite you, speak to you, return your email, call or text you back, talk nicely to you, or include you, it's easy to interpret that as "They don't like or respect me." Those thoughts are hurtful, and hurtful thoughts beget hurtful emotions that we then want to medicate. (Remember the alley and park examples that demonstrate that emotions come from thoughts? See Week 10, Day 3.)

Instead, we are to know *we are accepted in the Beloved* (Eph. 1:6). We are wretches by nature, but the penalty for that sin has been paid, and we are now free to enjoy who we are and to enjoy life. We don't have to be perfect; we simply have to walk in the Spirit, listening to the still, small Voice saying, "This is the path, walk ye in it" (Is. 30:21). We no longer have to envy or despise. We are OK, and so are others.

As far as the issue of grandiosity, people with addictions often feel slighted by how much attention others *don't* give them and by the *lack of* special and high treatment they receive from their families, friends, fellow church members, or even store clerks.

If there is one theme in the Bible, it is to have humility. It is to lay down getting treated like a big shot (Haman in the book of Esther is a great negative example). We are called to serve others, not to impress them or to receive service from them. When we focus on how others are perceiving us or how we are being treated, we punch our insecurity and grandiosity buttons. These feelings are uncomfortable. Therefore, the desire to medicate (addictions) arises.

The third mega-theme in addiction is resentment. We especially resent people whom we expected to be there for us: parents, siblings, close friends, in-laws, etc. I can think of two women right now who said mean things about me. But because I didn't have expectations from them to truly care for me, their words didn't hurt (as much). But there are people whom I counted on and thought they should be there for me. When they weren't, it was easy to feel resentful toward them. (It is helpful here to think of who has offended you.)

Giving up resentment and forgiving others, as you know, is commanded over and over again in Scripture. But we often linger and fail to do this, especially when we continue to be in a relationship with them and when they continue to hurt and disappoint us.

Resentment is now correlated with all kinds of disease. Our bodies were not created to harbor resentment. When we do, we have physical issues with our bodies. "'Up to 90 percent of the doctor visits in the USA may be triggered by a stress-related illness,' says the Centers for Disease Control and Prevention." (From an April 6, 2005 article on Mercola.com.)

I don't have all the answers, but I know that your resentment toward whomever is harming you. It is harming your health, it gives you a proclivity toward addictive behavior, and it is not a good example for your children (because your heart is the schoolroom for your children). Give it up. If it comes back, give it up again. Get some professional Christian counseling if you cannot give up your resentment by yourself.

If we could conquer our insecurity, our grandiosity (pride), and our resentments, we would grow exponentially. Not an easy thing to do, I admit. Prayer is always your first go-to answer.

DAY 4
Learn Not to Be Offended

Very close to resentment is being offended. However, we can learn not to be offended (or at least grow in being *less* offended). Addicts are regularly and ridiculously offended (it triggers the insecurity and grandiosity buttons).

Outside of Christian circles, much is written on healthy human functioning and learning *not to be offended* is often at the top of those lists. When an offense comes your way, try to be steam and let it pass through instead of being like a brick wall, in which the offense hits with a thud. Yes, you acknowledge the offense in your mind, but you choose to overlook, to let it pass through. Years ago, a Bible teacher used to say to *OLAT*, or "OverLook A Transgression" (Prov. 19:11).

Overlooking or not being offended is not an easy thing to do, especially if you have grown up being criticized a lot or were treated harshly as a youth. But you can begin to grow in this healthy way by seeing how Jesus responded when mistreated. Jesus forgave his offenders and said to return a blessing for an insult. Some standard!

Let's see what this would look like if you are offended. Let's say someone has criticized you (or your child) in a harsh and hurtful way. That would ruffle your feathers, right? Tell God how unfair you think it is, how harsh it was, how mean it was, etc. Then, it's time to get God's perspective on the offense.

Jesus was certainly not given high treatment or understood. It is not our tendency to bless those who mistreat us (Rom. 12:14), but we are called to do this. It is not our natural inclination to give up revenge (such as slandering them) in exchange for peacemaking (Rom. 12:17–20) when we have been mistreated. We don't want to live out Ephesians 4:2 "with all humility and gentleness, with patience, bearing with one another in love." But that is God's method for dealing with offenses. Overlook and forgive, and do it seventy times seventy.

One day, I was walking with my wise friend Karen, and she told me about a situation in which a man had said and done something negative to her. I was getting upset hearing about it, thinking how offended I would be. But not her. She OLATs all the time. If you sin against her, she forgives. I remember how struck I was with her perspective.

Something God is teaching me that I still struggle with is to move toward the person who offends me. This can be a family member, a friend, a church member, or even a waitress. If I am offended, then I am to move toward that person with kindness. Obviously, I don't have feelings that make me want to do this. I am merely attempting to return a blessing for an insult or good for evil, which is what we are called to do. Yes, it's uncomfortable, but whoever said that life was always supposed to be comfortable? (Thinking that life is always supposed to be comfortable is another erroneous thinking pattern of addicts.) Letting our feelings primarily dictate how we live is idiotic.

To conclude our discussion on insecurity, grandiosity, resentment, and being offended, let's discuss if your husband struggles with these issues. The advice is not the same as if you struggle. Remember, we have double standards. We treat ourselves one way but treat our husbands another. If your husband struggles here, do not be the Holy Spirit and tell him what you've learned, how you're growing in this, and what he needs to do differently. The response to an insecure man is to fill his tank with evidence of his strengths and godly virtues. The healing that takes place when a wife focuses on her husband's good qualities is unsurpassed. We all need spouses who overlook, who forgive, who see the best in us, and tell us. Now, don't expect this from your earthly husband, but expect it from your Heavenly Husband. Get full of God, and then *give it to your spouse*. If, by chance, your husband gives you grace, admiration, forgiveness, or kindness in return, then—what should you do?—write it in your Turquoise Journal! (Did you guess correctly? Good! I knew you would.)

DAY 5, PART A
Another Quick Thought on When Others Fail

In Week 10, Day 1, we discussed having empathy and compassion for your husband when he fails. I quickly and briefly want to build on that theme.

At a basketball game, one of our boys was given a technical foul for being disrespectful to a referee. I sat stunned in the stands. The pride in my son that he would be disrespectful was upsetting. And in addition, he did it in front of all these people I know and care about. Why, how embarrassing and what a terrible testimony.

But as I talked with several other moms, they showered me with grace, giving me examples of when their children had embarrassed them and reminded me that all our kids are sinners, too. This example of acceptance and grace toward me reminded me that this is how I am to be to others: helping others find grace when they experience failure, showering others with understanding, throwing out the judgmental attitudes I have when others fail.

Be a vessel of grace to others when they fail instead of a self-righteous Pharisee who thinks she has it all together. We sinners need to forgive other sinners (Matt. 18:21–35).

DAY 5, PART B
A Tirade on Health

Aw, now I get to get on my soapbox and stomp around a little. I get feisty talking about this subject. I am not a nutritionist or a doctor or anything scientific at all, only an avid health reader. There is obviously a lot of scam information out there, and the challenge is finding the right information. If you study something voraciously, though, the secrets will eventually rise to the top. Health is a subject that I am extremely interested in, as are many of you. I offer this section only to stir you up to think about your family's health. I certainly do not set myself up as any kind of expert at all. I am sure that I do not have all the right information in this area. But, like you, I am a learner.

The Bible doesn't talk about eating healthy because it was not an issue in biblical times. Processed food didn't exist. The soil was rich and nutrient dense, and thus the food supply was pure and whole.

However, even the Bible talks to the farmer in Exodus 23:11 and says, "[B]ut the seventh year you shall let it [the land] rest and lie fallow." In this century, we know how important this is for the soil to "lie fallow" (unused) so the soil can rebuild itself with nutrients (of course, you would be hard pressed to find many farmers who do this).

It is scary what is happening to our food supply. Some corporations couldn't care less if you are healthy. In fact, they make money when you are not. You can't trust the government or big businesses to care about your health (some people do care, but just not all). You must learn this area and take responsibility for learning about food.

Many foods are now becoming genetically modified (GMOs). These are very dangerous foods and cause all sorts of problems in the human body. I won't even buy corn at the local grocery anymore because the corn supply is so tainted with GMOs. I go to the health food store and make sure it says non-GMO.

God created your amazing body and also created amazing food to nourish it completely. But we eat things God didn't create. Our conventional beef is from cows that are grain-fed instead of how God designed them to be grass-fed. The grain-fed cows are often given hormones and antibodies so they will grow faster and thus are more financially rewarding. But grain-fed beef causes inflammation in the human body. Make the effort to secure grass-fed beef.

Much farm-raised seafood is high in mercury. (I say *much* because there are some honest and caring companies out there trying to give you a healthy product.) You want to buy wild-caught seafood, as how God originally made the fish to live. (Although, with recent oil spills, I like to buy fish from the northern waters.)

Most of us are vitamin D deficient (the sunshine vitamin), and then we lather chemical-laden sunscreen all over us to keep the sun out. Vitamin D deficiency is worth studying because it wreaks havoc all over your body.

You should also check out the chemicals in your makeup. Some of these chemicals have been linked to cancer.

Then there is the issue of sugar. Try counting the sugar grams you eat in a day. It will blow your mind. You are not supposed to eat more than twenty-five sugar grams a day. Excessive sugar is terrible for your body. There is hardly a disease that is not influenced by excessive sugar.

Have you ever studied the subject of aspartame, the sweetener in your Diet Coke? Do you have any idea how much havoc that toxin does to your body? I drank the toxic stuff for years, so I still may have to pay a price for that.

I could go on and on about pesticides and soil that is depleted in nutrients and yada yada.

This is a tirade to try to alarm you that you must not ignore this subject. One of my favorite health heroes is Dr. Joseph Mercola of Mercola.com. He is often criticized because he quit his medical practice to write a daily blog and now sells supplements. (That doesn't bother me at all. He has to make a living, too, and he is educating millions on how to be healthy.) If you will read Mercola's blog daily, your understanding of health will skyrocket in a year.

Be ready to be shocked at what you read about vaccines. I have two brothers who are MDs, and I love doctors. But we have to be wise and carefully examine the evidence about vaccines. Especially read the June 6, 2017, article entitled "New Studies Reveal Vaccine Harm" on Mercola.com, as well as the July 2, 2017, article entitled "Critical Vaccine Studies: 400 Important Scientific Papers Parents and Pediatricians Need to Be Aware Of."

An article appeared on Mercola.com on January 15, 2014, called "Banned to Horses…But Allowed on Your Dinner Plate." Here is an excerpt:

> The beta-agonist drug Zilmax has been used to promote muscle growth in American-grown cattle since 2007. Within the first two years, the number of euthanized cattle shot up by 175 percent. FDA records show that reported side effects of Zilmax include stomach ulcers, brain lesions, blindness, lethargy and lameness, bloody nose, respiratory problems, heart failure, lost hooves, and sudden death.

You have only one body. It has to last your whole lifetime. Be intentional in how you take care of it. You cannot serve God if you are in the grave.

If God didn't make the food (or make all the ingredients in it), don't eat it. Check out what processed food you are eating, and intentionally wean yourself and your family from junk. The women in my *Skinny School* classes call this food Trash Food because that's what it is—trash. A friend talked to me years ago about opening a fast-food restaurant (one of the unhealthy ones). Really, I would have moral issues doing that, selling something to people when it was not good for them, just to make a profit.

Many experts say that you are fine if you eat well 90 percent of the time. But *try* to eat 100% healthy every day. Why fool around with food that is bad for you? (There are other pleasures in life besides sugar and carbs!) Try to learn about food, and move toward a more natural, wholesome diet.

I have been dabbling in learning about health and nutrition for almost thirty years, and I still feel as if I don't know anything. One thing we do know: God made whole food to nourish our bodies. We best pay attention.

One thing that is very sad (and I think Satan is having a celebration with this) is that although the Church is where we learn about eternal salvation found only in Jesus, the modern Church is in darkness and duped about health. I pray that God will help the Church understand and see the huge problem that it is ignoring. We are spiritual/mental/physical beings, and we cannot ignore any area. I offer this information with sadness, not anger. I want to be part of the solution, not condemning anyone or anything.

OK, back to your regularly scheduled programming. The tirade is over, for now.

One More Thought

This is an aside, but who you hang around will influence you in the most magnanimous of ways. David and I were eating with some friends, and a couple of us were joking about the new spouse our current spouse would marry if we died. We were teasing somewhat, but honestly, I was a little concerned that the new spouse would come in and take the "inheritance that rightly belonged to my children and use it for her children." (I feel like a wretch even admitting this conversation.) The gracious friend with me said, "Oh, I would want the new spouse to be able to use some of the money to help her children. I'm sure her children would need help, too." A lovely and humble heart in another person is the best teaching device ever. Whom you hang around is gigantic in forming how you think. Search out and pursue some godly women!

Prayer

For our prayer this week, I want to copy and paste Psalm 100. I learned this Scripture by memory when I was 11 years old in a neighborhood Vacation Bible School. The huge truths found in these few, concise sentences still serve as a compass on how to live.

Psalm 100

Make a joyful noise unto the Lord, all ye lands.

Serve the Lord with gladness: come before His presence with singing.

Know ye that the Lord He is God: it is He that hath made us, and not we ourselves; we are His people, and the sheep of His pasture.

Enter into His gates with thanksgiving, and into His courts with praise: be thankful unto Him, and bless His name. For the Lord is good; His mercy is everlasting; and His truth endureth to all generations.

In Jesus's name,

Amen.

Assignments and Group Discussion Questions

1. Where are you in your thinking as far as "how much you expect your husband to reciprocate?" What do you need to remember that would be helpful to you?

2. Have you ever thought about the fact that charm and beauty can be a mask for shallowness and selfishness? What are your thoughts in this area? What is God saying to you?

3. Do you feel you struggle with any three of the attributes of addiction (insecurity, grandiosity, and resentment)? If so, what are your plans to grow?

4. How would you describe yourself as far as being *easily* or *not easily* offended?

5. How would you describe your response to others when they fail?

6. Were you offended by my tirade on health? Was this new information, old information, annoying information, or unwanted information?

WEEK 12

Regrets, Femininity, In-laws, Contentment... and More

Contents

Day 1: If You Struggle with Regrets
Day 2: Your Husband Wants a Womanly Woman
Day 3: Are You Causing Turmoil in Your Husband's Family?
Day 4: Helping Your Husband Grow Spiritually
Day 5, Part A: Beginning Thoughts on Acquiring Contentment
Day 5, Part B: When Husbands Let Down Their Guard

Chapter 12 in *Wife School* is called *How to Correct Your Husband*. Another title could be *The Art of Telling Your Husband What He Needs to Hear without Offending Him*. This chapter is crucial to read and reread until you learn how to discuss negative things with your husband in a wise fashion. Next week's chapter is about *word pictures*, which is a continuation of this week's lesson. I suggest you take as much time as needed to learn these tremendously important wife skills.

I almost named *Wife School, The Art of Being A Wife*, because that is what this course really is, a study in the rare and magnificent art of being a fantastic wife. You are well on your way to being that Marriage Champion!

Lesson 12 in *Wife School* is self-explanatory so I took this week to discuss some other important topics.

DAY 1
If You Struggle with Regrets

At a family meal in a restaurant over the holidays, our adult children were gathered and my husband, David, asked their advice on what would be a good ice-breaker question to a group of people that didn't know each other. Of course, before the group gave serious answers, they all gave their funny answers. Our son-in-law was especially funny. His suggestions for an ice-breaker was, "If you were going to take a medication to overcome one of your personality issues, what medication would it be?" He also offered, "What is your biggest lifelong regret? Tell us all about it in detail."

We all hooted over those questions because the thought of asking such incredibly invasive questions to a group of people who didn't know each other was so absurd. Sharing your greatest personal regrets in life strikes at the very core of your privacy and pain. We don't want others to know our greatest regrets and mistakes. But sadly, many of us continue to let regrets ravage our own personal peace.

The healthy approach is, of course, "Let bygones be bygones." But few of us do that.

Years ago, one friend told me that before she came to Christ, she had had three abortions. I'm not sure what you regret, but I can't imagine anything that is more painful than realizing that you chose to take the life of your own child. Now this woman has three lovely children, but the pain of ridding her body of those earlier fetuses continued to vehemently attack her. Eventually, she joined a healing group of other mothers who had had abortions. This group had a candlelight service in which they honored their aborted children and received forgiveness from God for their mistake. This woman continues to be occasionally harassed by the devil for her past sin, but every time, she goes to God and is reminded that she is forgiven. Then, she purposely decides to think about something else. This is how we must approach regrets. Regrets can eat you alive if you don't know the healing balm of the forgiveness of Jesus.

An example with less intensity is my grandmother, who was a farmer's wife, and lived through the Depression. When some inexpensive neighboring land became available to purchase, she and her husband declined. Then, the farmland rose astronomically in price. For years—and I mean thirty years!—I heard, "If only we had bought that land!" The regret of not taking advantage of the opportunity to obtain financial independence—when she could have—continued to haunt her.

Another older female relative used to bemoan, "If only I had gone to college" and another woman lamented, "If only I had decided to have more children." The list goes on and on with regrets which plague women.

The Apostle Paul had some regrets. He killed Christians before he was converted. What a horrible memory to endure. But Paul says something that I have to say over and over to myself, and that is, "forgetting what lies behind and reaching forward to what lies ahead" (Philippians 3:13).

For sure, we must learn from our regrets, but there is a time when we must receive forgiveness, put the regret behind us, and not let it continue to wash over our brains. Since it is true that what you think about determines your mood (you know that, right?), *repeatedly pondering regrets* (not counting, of course, mining them for their learning experience) is a tool of the Enemy.

God takes all of your and my mistakes and regrets and weaves them into this awesome, beautiful tapestry for good because "…we know that for those who love God all things work together for good" (Romans 8:28). I think of the train wrecks of my earlier relationships, and how God used that to motivate me to learn about relationships. Some of my earlier relationship skills are comical to think about. David was warned by one of his friends before we got married that I was going to be a handful. One girl in middle school class was not allowed to hang out with me because her Christian mother said I was a bad influence on her. Just because you *had* a prior failure doesn't mean you *are* a failure. God takes our weaknesses and gives us beauty for ashes. "… His compassions never fail. They are new every morning" (Lamentations 3:22-23). Who can believe that? We are such wretches, yet His compassions never fail. Just the best news ever! Although we don't deserve it, we are forgiven and now, God has plans to bless us in spite of our failures.

Give up letting your regrets beat you up and give up wasting time thinking about them. God is using them, even though you wish you had done differently. Isaiah 55:8 says, "For my thoughts are not your thoughts, neither are your ways my ways," declares the LORD.

When you give up your unproductive and untrue thought patterns, such as regret, you begin to enjoy your freedom in the Lord. Enjoy that He has plans to prosper you. Enjoy that the hairs on your head are counted. Enjoy this day because the grass withers and the flowers fade and your days are numbered. Quit wasting your life with negative emotional thought patterns such as regret. Instead, focus on the delightful surprise around the river bend. "For I know the plans I have for you," declares the LORD, "plans to prosper you and not to harm you, plans to give you hope and a future" (Jeremiah 29:11).

We all have regrets. We all make mistakes. Learn from them. Confess and repent of any sin. Then receive forgiveness and move on. God has much more for you to do.

DAY 2
Your Husband Wants a Womanly Woman

I know a young single woman who is extremely gifted in her profession. She has degrees from here to China. She's pretty, charming, bright, and godly. In fact, she's absolutely adorable. But she has had trouble finding Mr. Right. Although she is a rock star in her career, she has not quite learned the art of being a womanly woman. Men still want a womanly woman in their romantic relationship, one in which he feels manly. Let's discuss what this means.

It is wonderful for women to be amazing at their jobs. One example is a young wife who I know that can outwork and out-produce all the men at her office. However, she has had to learn to leave her combat boots at the door. When she gets home, she turns into a Cinderella, and puts her tiger personality in its cage.

This isn't phony. You can have different aspects to your personality. You just have to remember that men like womanly women. Even if you are the CEO at work, bossing everyone around, you are to have a gentle and quiet spirit at home.

God made men to desire womanly women. You aren't going to change that, just like you are not going to change what time the sun comes up. Being mad about this doesn't change it from being true. So be smart. Be a soft and sweet woman around your husband. Yes, be a dynamo at giving direction and orders on your job, at running your house, at your home business, at running the events in which you are in charge, etc. But your husband doesn't want you being a dynamo *in running him*. He wants you to hand him the scepter and follow. This is difficult for all women, but especially difficult for you dynamos.

I think it's a great time to be alive for women. We can enjoy using our gifts as well as enjoy having our heart's desire, which is a wonderful marriage and home. In marriage, we will always have to watch our powerful and controlling natures. Men don't like it. They never have, they never will. Use your intelligence and energy for good. Don't check your brains at the door when you get home; just check your combat boots.

Your husband wants to be married to Cinderella, not G.I. Joe.

DAY 3
Are You Causing Turmoil in Your Husband's Family?

A while back, we met a missionary couple who have four married sons. The husband told us that the oldest two boys are fourteen months apart and were inseparable growing up, the best of best friends. However, after they got married, their wives developed a personality clash. The two boys that were previously best friends hardly speak anymore.

Having five sons, this story grieved me. But knowing how wives influence husbands, I can easily see how this happened. Another friend of mine was very close to her only son. When he got engaged, somehow my friend ruffled the feathers of the new daughter-in-law and now the son barely communicates with his mom.

Women, it is incredibly selfish of us to steal our husband's heart from his family-of-origin, just because we don't like something about them. But I see it all the time! The new bride realizes the power she now wields over her new husband so she drops hints and discusses his family's dysfunction (as if hers didn't have any). Since husbands are ridiculously influenced by wives, they often cut ties or radically change their prior relationship with their family of origin.

If your husband loved his family before you arrived, then your job is to find a way to fit in. I didn't say "they need to find a way to fit in with you." I said, you need to find a way to fit in with them. How dreadful for you to be a stir stick in your husband's family. Even if they are weird, are lazy, are too outspoken, are shallow, are greedy, are not Christians, are Christians, or are anything else. This is the man you were given to love and he loves his family of origin. Fit in.

If his mother or sisters are hard, then give extra. If your new sister-in-law gossips about you, then model Christ by overlooking, forgiving, foregoing, and returning good for evil.

All in-law situations are laced with dynamite. Suddenly, these weird and different people are your family. Of course that's difficult. But you have all the power. You are the one who influences their son. Why, he's not going to cross the only person in the world from whom he gets legitimate sex.

But you're not a brat, right? You're not ugly like that, right? You love and give to his cracked-up family because that is what love looks like (see 1 Corinthians 13 for a definition of love). Yes, they are dysfunctional wretches. But so are you. And so am I.

Guess what? Even though your husband's family drives him bonkers, he loves them. And it honors him when you love them, forgive them, overlook their idiotic idiosyncrasies and hang-ups.

Your husband's family may be rude to you and then, yes, ask your husband to defend you and stick up for you. But don't withdraw from them. Don't hold a grudge against them. Set some good boundaries in your life (see Week 7, Day 5 for more on in-laws) but be a peacemaker. That's your calling.

I read a story once about some soldiers who were in the bunkhouse and were making fun of a Christian soldier. One particularly mean soldier said some really ugly things to the Christian soldier and then threw his boot at him and hit him in the head. The soldiers all went to bed and the next morning, the mean soldier woke up to see his boots at the side of his bed, polished. With tears, he went to the Christian soldier, and said, "What is it in you that makes you able to act like this when you are mistreated?"

Friend, it is Christ in us who can love others when we are mistreated. Love your husband by forgiving his crazy relatives, his selfish relatives, his rude relatives, his stupid and mean relatives, his relatives who don't get it and think they are always right. This is when we are most like Jesus, when we forego and forgive others.

I didn't say it was easy. I said it was Christ-like.

If you are one of the lucky and rare women who married into a family that respects you and is semi-normal, then…(do what?)…write it in your Turquoise Journal and rejoice!

DAY 4
Helping Your Husband Grow Spiritually

Today we will discuss several ideas to help your husband grow spiritually. The first idea is to remember that we all become like the people we hang around. Therefore naturally, spouses have more influence on each other than anyone else.

We don't fool the ones we live with. You may fool your friends or the folks at church, but your husband knows the real you. He knows what you read before you go to bed; he knows what you watch on TV. He knows what excites you and what upsets you. The number one piece of advice to help your husband grow spiritually is to be the person you want him to be (spiritually). If you want him to be a man of prayer, first be a woman of prayer. If you want him to be honest, be incredibly honest yourself. Often women want a quality or attribute from a man and then they are not like that. Being the person (spiritually) you want him to be, however, doesn't mean hitting him over the head about him being a spiritual leader. That's not how Scripture suggests that we influence our husbands. Instead, study 1 Peter 3 and learn to influence your husband with your pure and reverent behavior. Your behavior *is louder than your words.*

Secondly, if you want to help your husband grow spiritually, find some godly qualities about your husband and praise them. Is he honest? Is he faithful? Is he responsible? Loyal? Women fuss about the towels not being hung up and then ignore the fact that their husbands are the kind of men who if they were in a foxhole, would sacrifice themselves to protect others. Think about his virtue. If he makes an insightful comment about the sermon, tell him how much it pleases you that he thinks hard about Scriptural truths. If he stands up to a wrong, tell him how protected you feel by his character. If you look for character, you will find it. His weaknesses have had your focus and now that you are concentrating on something different (his virtue), his strengths will appear.

Thirdly, encourage your husband to form friendships with other godly men. The church has tried many ideas to form community and still, the basic Sunday School class seems to work extremely well. Small groups and other ideas are awesome, but many men with jobs and families can't add one more night a week to be out, so the traditional Sunday School class (when a nursery is available) works for many couples.

Let's discuss what to do if your husband is engaged in something you think is unwholesome. If your husband watches some trash TV (or trash internet comedy), do not criticize him. You simply say "I'd rather not watch that show" and go find something else to do in another room. He will know how you feel. You don't want to be a judgmental Pharisee but you also don't want to endorse something you feel is sinful. If you are walking with the Lord and meeting his 8 A's, he will be drawn to you and slowly, your ability to influence him will increase. Many men have been plucked from sinful activities by the example of a godly, humble, reverent wife (again see 1 Peter 3) who meets his needs rather than from a nagging Pharisaical wife. Let your godliness call him up. (This advice is not for women whose husbands are abusive or addicted to porn, alcohol, or drugs. Please find a godly counselor to help you if this is your unfortunate situation.)

Many women forget the most obvious and important strategy: prayer. Daily, cover every aspect of your husband in prayer. One book that I recommend on prayer is called *Secrets of the Secret Place* by Bob Sorge. Learn how to storm the gates of heaven with prayer. I am currently again reading *The Soul Winner* by Charles Spurgeon. In a chapter entitled, *How to Raise the Dead*, Spurgeon speaks to young preachers about how to help others become born again. The part on prayer in this chapter makes me want to carve out hours each day to wrestle with the God who hears, who cares, and who is able. If you are not a praying wife, then you are not a godly wife. Don't ignore your first duty in life!

Although your husband is not where you want him to be right now, there is much hope for tremendous change in a man when a woman gives the 8 A's, gets rid of her emotional turmoil, develops a gentle and quiet spirit, and walks with the Lord. You are on the fifty year plan!

DAY 5, PART A
Beginning Thoughts on Acquiring Contentment

In Week 10, Day 3, we discussed some ideas to improve your mood. Hopefully, by now, you are taking responsibility for the thoughts that float across the screen of your mind, knowing that *thoughts about* circumstances—not circumstances—cause emotions. It is a continual battle to gird up the loins of your mind, and you must fight diligently.

The mind, as you know, tends to be like gravity, which means it has a downhill, negative bias. I mean, we notice the red ink on exam papers, and we notice what's wrong with ourselves as well as others. We have to make a huge effort to reverse this trend. If you can train your mind to cast off negative thought patterns and to substitute Philippians 4:8 thoughts (whatever is true, honorable, just, pure, etc.), then you can actually change the emotional climate you live in. Navy Seals, as well as elite athletes, engage in mental training. There is much you can do to overcome a scattered, emotional, negative mindset.

We've discussed worry and leaving your issues on the shelf in heaven after they have been thoroughly prayed through. We've discussed regrets (this week, Day 1). Today I want to begin a discussion on contentment.

Many years ago, David had an associate named Alvin. One day Alvin came to work and said, "I may have some problems, but the Lord gave me a contented wife." When David repeated that remark to me later that night, I remember thinking, "How is that possible? How could she be content?" She didn't have the wealth, the lifestyle, or many of the other things that I thought were absolutely crucial for happiness and contentment. (You can see I was pretty immature.) But she had that rare jewel of contentment, something I was still light years away from understanding at the time.

I find that women are in two ditches as far as contentment. Let's discuss both and then hopefully, find something positive space in between.

Ditch one, and the most common ditch, is the woman who complains, complains, and complains, without much prayer. She manipulates, moves, corrals, and re-orders. Then complains some more. Whether it's her children's lives, her church, her friends, or her own life, this woman is disappointed with the scenery and lets everyone around know.

Ditch two seems very spiritual, but this woman just says, "Well, I want it to be all of the Lord." Therefore, she takes no action to improve her life. Women, God feeds the birds, but He doesn't put the worms in the nests! To be honest, this woman is *lazy*. We are to pray with gusto, listen for His still, small voice, and then we are to proactively move forward. The New Testament is full of Spirit-driven effort. Paul says in 1 Timothy 4:10, "That is why we labor and strive, because we have put our hope in the living God…"

So what is the balance? The balance is to be a prayer warrior, asking God all the time, all the time, what to do, what to do, and then waiting in prayer to hear His marching orders. Yes, we are to search for wise answers as if they were silver. But after you have prayed like the persistent widow and exhausted hunting for wise answers, put your problems on the shelf in heaven. You can't let your mind continually think about your problems. Put the yappy puppies in the basement. Thinking about what is missing and disappointing all the time is a surefire recipe for depression because *feelings always follow thoughts*. At some point, you have to surrender to *what is* while pleading with God to change things.

Paul says he is content with food and clothing. Ha, that's a joke right? He means great food, awesome clothes, good schools, a beautiful house, lots of free time, and a great social network. Surely that's what he meant to say. That's certainly the standard I see. (I forgot to mention slimness and youthfulness. Those are necessary, too, right?)

One man told me that his wife gets up singing like a little bird every morning. The smile on his face told me how much pleasure he derives from her happy heart. If you think about it, you know that one person's mood affects everyone else's in the house. So if you are happy and content, trusting God to do you good, you pull others up. If you are discontent and sullen, discouraged and doubting God, you do the opposite. Your contented and peaceful heart is one of the most important gifts you give to your family. What a blessing to your family for you to have tranquility and an inner happiness. I'm talking about a deep peace because the Lord of the universe is carrying your burdens. He knows, He cares, and when He thinks the time is right, He is able.

I would like to mention the sullen, downcast woman who nevertheless, endures. This is not a woman that blesses anyone. No, the woman that blesses others "laughs at the days to come" because she has spent time in the presence of the Almighty. This woman has godly energy and a loveliness that is youthful, no matter what her age.

If you have ever been in one of my groups, I talk repeatedly about Deruchette, the heroine of the novel, *Toilers of the Sea*, by Victor Hugo. He writes of Deruchette, "Her presence lights the home; her approach is like a cheerful warmth; she passes by and we are content; she stays awhile and we are happy. Is it not a thing of divine to have a smile which, none know how, has the power to lighten the weight of that enormous chain that all the living in common drag behind them? Deruchette possessed this smile; we may say that this smile was Deruchette herself."

Hugo continues, "There is in this world no function more important than that of being charming—to shed joy around, to cast light upon dark days, to be the golden thread of our destiny and the very spirit of grace and harmony. Is this not to render a service?"

On a heavenly resume, can you put that you have the "power to cast light on dark days?" Do you ever read in the current women magazines that to be beautiful, you need to have the "power to lighten the weight of that enormous chain that all the living in common drag behind them?" No, but these are the descriptions of the truly beautiful women in our lives, the contented ones, the ones who live close to the heart of Jesus, know Him, trust Him, and obey Him.

David and I know a young woman like this. She walks into the room and her energy radiates, fills, and lightens the spirits of all present. We have a sentence we have said to her for years when she leaves, and it also is a quote from Victor Hugo: "She stays awhile and we are happy."

Contentment is a rare jewel, a rare commodity. What marvelous beauty!

There is not a formula for contentment, but the best balanced advice I can come up with is to be content with *what is* (knowing that God hears, cares, and is working all things for good) while all the time, prayerfully pursuing how to fix what isn't right.

Paul says he learned contentment. You can't get this in a day, any more than you can learn Japanese in a day. But start. Work in your Turquoise Journal. Make a list of your areas of discontent. Learn to persevere in prayer so that God carries your burdens. List ways you may solve your problems and pray over the list. Rest and leave your burdens on the shelf in heaven, even as you are taking proactive, Spirit-led actions toward solving your issues. Psalm 121:4 says, "… He who watches over Israel will neither slumber nor sleep." God is aware of your issues. Rest and wait on Him to give you peace and direction. Then rise up and be wildly proactive in the direction He leads in solving your problems.

Contentment is accepting *what is* right now but it is does not prohibit you from looking for answers.

DAY 5, PART B
When Husbands Let Down Their Guard

Eating sushi with a rather high-strung young married man, I asked him if his wife soothed him. He looked at me as if he had never thought about that question. But the answer that came forth was yes, she greatly soothed him. Men are drawn to women who are able to make them feel calm.

As you become a better listener, more empathetic, and more encouraging, your husband will let down his guard to you. You will hear him say, "I have so much stress. I have my job, the money, my responsibilities at church, and da-da-da." At this point, so many wives erroneously rush in with answers: "All men have that, Joe. If you remember, I have the kids, the house, your mother…."

When men let down their guard, be ready to throw pillows around them. Let them unwind to you. For a man to be vulnerable and let you see his internal stress and pain, you are paving a highway into his heart. One man said he came home each night and then his wife "put him back together." That's a good thing. Don't begrudge the work of putting your husband back together with listening, soothing, and encouragement. It is one of the most beautiful gifts we humans give to each other. When men are having hard times, or just a stressful day, be there to say, "I'm sorry you have to handle that. It's impressive how you handle so much responsibility." If you have a brilliant idea how to fix his issue, don't rush in and tell him now. What he needs is reassurance that he is man enough, smart enough, and strong enough to handle his problems.

Of course later, at the right time, you can finger-tip drop, "Maybe you already thought of this, but I was wondering if..." Remember, if he takes your suggestion, never claim rights to the idea. It is now *his* idea. Woman was created for the man, and when you make your husband successful, you ride on his coat tails. You do not need praise for being the source of his brilliant ideas. Honestly, he will forget you gave him the idea so you need to forget it, too. If you focus on making your husband happy and successful (sowing), then when you are not expecting it, the little buds will burst forth from the soil and before you know it, you will enter the harvest (reaping). Women waste so much time and energy being offended and wanting admiration/ appreciation/ credit themselves. That's how small people live. Be a person with a big heart and focus on how you are blessing others.

Women are eventually rewarded for all their efforts by something that is ridiculously satisfying. Before too long, a woman with a gentle and quiet spirit who makes mega-deposits of the 8 A's into her husband's tank will notice her husband's desire to please her, her husband's true concern for her well-being, and her husband's willingness to be influenced by her. No diamond necklace comes close to that reward. Learn this art of being a woman. When he lets his guard down, that is an opportunity for you to tie strings around your hearts.

Prayer

Dear God,

Truly, I want to be a contented Christian. I admire others who walk with You with joy and peace. I seem to have difficulty doing that.

I admit I often whine and fuss when things don't go my way, instead of looking to You for answers and resting in You. Help me learn that delicate art of resting in You while searching passionately for answers, and then waiting on You to direct me.

God, I admit that I do not always guard my thoughts. Therefore, I can sometimes let in negative thoughts filled with regrets and self-pity. Remind me to insist on not letting regrets and self-pity have any place in my life! Strengthen me to find rest in You and then to be a fruitful garden where others may come and find nourishment.

Help me know how to love my husband. Help me know what he specifically wants and needs. And then help me not focus on how he loves me, but to focus on how I love him.

And God, as far as my husband's family, they are…well…difficult! Actually, maybe they are normal, but they are certainly difficult for me to handle. May I forgive, forgo, and overlook as much as possible. Then if necessary, may I set appropriate boundaries. Help me in this. Give me the ability to love these strange people that are now my family. Help me understand them and then give me love for these unruly creatures that are called in-laws. May I be a woman that others can't explain without understanding how Jesus changes lives.

In His name,

Amen

Assignments and Group Discussion Questions

1. What is your previous pattern when you needed to correct your husband? Are you now able to tell him difficult things without offending him?

2. How would you describe your struggle with regrets? Explain.

3. Do you struggle with the concept that men want womenly women? What are your thoughts?

4. Are you causing turmoil in your husband's family?

5. How have you attempted to help your husband grow spiritually in the past?

6. How would you describe yourself as far as being a contented woman?

7. Does your husband let down his guard with you? What are your thoughts on how you should respond when he does?

WEEK 13

If Your Husband Doesn't Celebrate Your Special Days Well, If You Don't Feel Loved by Your Husband....and More

Contents

Day 1: How Husbands Feel about Your Birthday, Anniversary, and Other Holidays
Day 2: Examining the Choices in Educating Your Children
Day 3: If You Don't Feel Loved by Your Husband
Day 4: Bump. It. Up. Story #2 (and a Word to 20%-ers)
Day 5: A Superior Wife Skill

Chapter 13 in *Wife School* is called *How to Explain Anything to Your Husband*. It is actually a chapter about word pictures. Word pictures take time to think of, but are tremendously effective in communicating something your husband has trouble grasping. Save them for your top one or two issues, though. Word pictures are annoying and ineffective if used too often.

Your marriage is now changing and this will affect future generations, as well as those around you. Not to mention how amazing it is to have a soul-stirring marriage!

We will take this week to study some other important subjects to many women.

DAY 1
How Husbands Feel About Your Birthday, Anniversary, and Other Holidays

The Valentine's Day before David and I got engaged, he called to tell me that he was going to the Memphis University Tigers basketball game with his dad. I will not print my response to that here, but let's just say that he was *wildly* unaware of how important that day was to me.

After my sister-in-law married my brother, her birthday rolled around and he had not gotten the memo about "how to celebrate the birthday of a wife." I'm not sure what she said to him about her birthday, but to me, she said she wanted a card (mushy), a present (wrapped), a cake (with candles), Happy Birthday sung to her, to be taken out to dinner, and a parade. For years, we have texted each other on our birthdays, and said, "Hope you get a parade."

Of course, we are silly and kidding, but maybe—if the number of emails that I receive about how husbands hurt wives by forgetting their special days indicates anything—then there is definitely something here to talk about.

Why? Because women have this ridiculous notion that *how others treat us on our birthday (Valentine's Day, etc.) shows how much they care about us*. But, actually, the real truth is, *others treat us on our birthday/holidays as they have been trained to* and not necessarily according to how much they love us.

Women, we have to give our husbands a break. They tell us they love us by being sexually faithful, by bringing home their paycheck, and countless other dutiful ways. They do not understand this desire to be treated as royalty on our birthdays/special days.

To be honest, *it is a burden for them.* Many men have financial pressure to just pay the bills and now, he's expected to drop a wad on this woman in order to express affection. It's not his idea of a good time. If you are having financial issues, please give your husband some slack. Help your husband navigate this day by giving him some ideas that are not expensive but are meaningful to you. (Only give him ideas if you are sure he wants your ideas. Some husbands see this as pushy.) Maybe he could write you a poem if he's bent in that direction. Give him some ideas that are not too difficult for him to pull off.

Recently I heard of a wife emailing her husband a link and a picture of a necklace she wanted for one of her special days. Then she emailed again and said to ignore the first email because this email now had the link to the necklace she wants. Then she sent him a third email, changing the necklace and the subsequent link again. Wives, most men don't have the patience for this.

Another wife, in contrast, was asked by her husband what she wanted for one of her special days. She sent him a text, telling him about a bracelet, and at the end, she wrote, "but whatever you give me, I'm sure I'll be happy with it." Which wife do you think is probably easier to live with? Which wife probably wears her husband out? These are small things, but small things add up. Try not to be so high maintenance. Try to be content and grateful for small things, not demanding and always manipulating, trying to get everything to work out just right for you.

We have to say here, again, that most men are not good at celebrating our special days. They are just not. Do you see the ridiculousness of getting mad at a first grader who doesn't understand algebra? Men that have been married a while to women who give them the 8 A's eventually begin to understand the need to show up for special days. But honestly, this can take years. You might have a mountain of a man, but he doesn't know that you love lace, roses, and to get gussied up. You have to realize over and over again that the creature who loves football, work, and sex is not put together like you. So, we give him a break. Eventually, we softly tell him what we'd like, *and then when he still doesn't get it,* we give him another break. We don't expect kids to get fractions and decimals easily and we don't expect husbands to understand the heart of a woman easily. We give them grace, stay in the game, and know that wise wives eventually influence husbands.

What women want their husbands to do is…ready for this?…is to *read their minds.* That's right. They want their husbands to know them so deeply that they read their mind and know what they want. They want their husband to find a way to adequately express to them that they are adored, known, understood, and cherished. There are some men out there like this. There are some men who have a knack for this, but honestly, it is pretty rare. What I have found to be helpful is for women to help their husbands *by asking for something on their special days that is not too difficult for their husbands to do.* The best advice is to realize that celebrating your special days in a way that excites and pleases you is again, a big burden for them. Over the years, you will be able to tell your husband what you want. Men improve tremendously in this area after years.

Of course, there are ditches that women fall into when they react to their husband's non-celebratory behavior. Let's look at two ditches.

Ditch One when husbands fail to adequately celebrate The Big Five (birthdays, anniversaries, Christmas, Valentine's Day, and Mother's Day) is to give the husband the silent treatment. The wife thinks, "Why, if he doesn't love me more than this, he certainly won't be getting any great treatment from me." The simmering begins.

Ditch Two is an emotional turmoil outbreak. Usually, it is about something else, though, because we hate to harp that others don't celebrate our day more. So we find something else that is *legitimate* that the husband did wrong and let him have it for that when in fact, it is a punishment for failing to celebrate "us" better.

What I've found over the years is that if women repeatedly and faithfully write down in their Turquoise Journals their husband's sweet gestures along with his self-sacrifice to the family, they begin to understand that this is how he expresses his love. To him, it is not about flowers and presents. Retailers have blown up these holidays to make money, and now, husbands must scramble to ring bells and jump through hoops or women are dissatisfied. Re-read in your Turquoise Journal all the sweetness your husband brings to your family, and let go of wanting a circus and a parade for your special days. Whatever he gives, it is enough for now.

One more remark on this subject: Facebook and the beautiful pictures of roses and the huge boxes of chocolates that some husbands give wives don't help you feel loved when your husband works late on Valentine's Day and you eat leftovers. When I see some grand gesture that another husband does to his wife, I realize that that husband has his set of weaknesses, too, and the flowers, although nice, do not speak of a perfect husband. They speak of a husband who is *smart in this area.* Try not to envy others. There is pathology in every marriage. If your husband is faithful and hard-working, accept him, pour in the 8 A's, and give him a few years to learn to celebrate holidays in a manner he can handle. Give up wanting high treatment all the time. It is an unhealthy symptom of addiction, if you remember (see Week 11, Day 3).

I do want to say again that he cannot read your mind. You have to fingertip tell him what is in your heart. But then also remember, that you can only ask for the top one to two things in your heart. If gift-giving is not in the top things, I suggest letting it go. The poor guy is trying to understand you, and it is ridiculously difficult for him. Be dutiful in focusing on what he brings to the marriage. Do not decide how much your husband loves you by how he celebrates your special days. Instead, be grateful for his many acts of self-sacrifice and dutiful giving to the family. Romance is nice, but it can take years to train a man how to do it as it is not programmed into his DNA (unless it is the mating season as he has extra hormone support at that time).

If your husband goes without new golf clubs or drives an old used car so your kids can have braces, then *that is true love.* Write that down in your TJ and be grateful for his faithfulness. Don't let the culture decide if your husband loves you. *His faithful actions say he does.*

(See story #2 in Week 13, Day 4 (Bump. It. Up.) for an idea of what to give your husband for Valentine's Day this year.)

DAY 2
Examining the Choices in Educating Your Children

What a gigantic and often, heart-wrenching decision it is for Christian parents to decide how to educate their kids. Public school? Private school? Home school? If there is a subject that strikes angst into the heart of Christian parents, it is, "How are we going to educate our children?"

At a Sunday School event over twenty years ago, Dr. Adrian Rogers was asked this question, "What is the best way to educate children?" Being a homeschooler at the time, I thought there was only one path and I was doing it.

But Dr. Rogers didn't agree. He thought all three avenues might be God's will. He said it was up to each family to hear from God and of course, now I agree.

Let's discuss the pros and cons of the different education systems. Obviously, you will have to discern what God's will is for your family. The following discussion is only offered as *input* to your thinking. What I do want to acknowledge, though, is that godly kids come out of all three educational systems. Also, some kids with… eh…issues…come out of every system. Finding God's will for your family will be *your* job.

First, let's talk about homeschooling. Having total control over a child's environment and his influences can be a phenomenal method for rearing kids. If a family feels called by God to do this, I have seen quite fabulous results. One thing I repeatedly notice is the creativity in these kids. Not being a victim of the system, they often develop an outside-the-box approach, which is quite refreshing. Of course, there is an obvious benefit that you do not have the competing forces of opposing value systems. The problem is, of course, *how tired Mom gets.* If Mom is teaching all day, and then expected to run kids to ballet and soccer as well as keep up with the house and meals, you will often find one exhausted mom. When it is time to take off the Teacher Hat and put on the Mom Hat, she is often without energy to do so. Obviously, the more kids a family has, the harder homeschooling is. One of the girls in one of my very first groups over 25 years ago, Jessie, has 13 kids and has homeschooled them all. They are one amazing family!

Secondly, let's discuss the private school. This is a favorite choice for many. Some faithful Christians certainly come from this system. Many of these schools have dedicated teachers who feel a calling to Christian education and who will positively influence your children. Then, also, you have the advantage of your children socializing with children of Christian families. But, as you know, there is a financial output for any private school and this is a huge hindrance for many. Some people simply cannot afford this choice.

The third choice is public schools. Many of my friends from two decades ago would have screamed if you told them their children would have to go to public school. My husband was a lawyer for Home School Legal Defense for seven years, and we were immersed in a homeschool culture that bashed public education, and many times, rightfully so. However, some people *cannot* homeschool and *cannot* afford private schools. That is a tough situation, my friend. A young couple we know just moved to another city for the sole reason that the public schools *were good* in that city. Definitely moving to a school district with the best public schools is a wise choice if you are going this route. David and I have godly friends who chose public education twenty years ago. The parents were incredibly involved in everything at the school, and their three kids all turned out exceptionally well with a deep love for the Lord. In some ways, when Christian kids go to public school, the parents *step it up*, knowing that they must learn and confront the lies of evolution and the pagan worldview. (Creation.com has an amazing DVD on the false lies of evolution called the *Achilles Heel of Evolution*.)

In the Old Testament, I do not see much regarding education except Deuteronomy 6, which calls the parents to train up the children for God. Ultimately, it is the parent's responsibility to be sure their children know what they need to know.

The Bible commentator, Matthew Henry, writing on Galatians 3, said that school masters were servants who led the children (whom they had care of) to school. So we know *going to school* is okay. Paul was said to be tutored by Gamaliel which again says, you don't have to be homeschooled. Timothy learned from his mother and grandmother, but that was *spiritual* truths, not necessarily education as we now know it. The Scripture, as I see it, is not adamantly clear about how to educate your children, only adamant that we train our children spiritually. I know many Christians go beserk at the thought of sending their child to public school, but honestly, many Christians have done it with success. They just make sure that the influencing factors at home *are stronger* than those outside the home.

I do not have answers for you in this area. Actually, I am concerned for the education of my grandchildren. Each system has its pros and cons. I know how much wear and tear homeschooling is on the mom (especially if there are many children). I also realize the dangers of the public school, as well as the cost of the private school. Prayerfully, prayerfully, handle this decision. In the end, God seems to have apples fall from apple trees. Your children will be a lot like you, a chip off the old block, regardless of where you send them to school.

At this point in our family's journey, the one child still at home is enrolled in a public school, but he went to private school for years (and was homeschooled some, too). Our daughter says she is probably going to homeschool for the first few years and then, she doesn't know after that. She is thinking of moving to a school district where the public schools are good, if they cannot handle the private school tuition or if she does not think she can continue to homeschool. One of our sons thinks that the public schools in his town are fine, and many people in his church are sending their kids to the town's public schools and are happy about it. (*Written later: This son has now married and his new precious wife says she is homeschooling their future children, so we shall see.)

I am not giving you answers *or even direction*. I am with you in the seriousness of the issue, as well as the heaviness that I know many of you are experiencing.

We haven't even touched the issues of learning disabilities, medical issues, and immature or problem behavior that makes these choices even more difficult. You love your kids and you want what's best for them. You are to be applauded for that. Education is a gigantic and difficult decision.

One of my favorite think-tank friends told me about a woman who was working ridiculous hours and was almost never home, just so her kids could go to private school. That wouldn't work for me. Again, I do not know what God is telling you. But if you can move to a school district that is acceptable, it seems better to me to go to public school than for mom to be gone all day. Homeschooling works for some families, but not for all. Each family must decide. May God reveal His will to you and may all your children be blessed.

What I have observed after many years, is that most of the time (certainly not all), the huge factors in rearing kids for the Lord is not what school they go to, but how much the parents love and obey the Lord, how spiritually and emotionally healthy the parents are, and (choke on this one) if the mother submits with a happy heart to the father, thereby creating peace in the home. But then, of course, *God operates outside this box however He wishes.* The race does not always go to the swift.

If I had to do it over, knowing what I know now, I would do many things differently. (Remember last week's lesson on regrets? I have had to take my own advice here.) There is one piece of advice that I always know is the right choice: obey God and daily seek His face.

DAY 3
If You Don't Feel Loved By Your Husband

Many women are disappointed with the fact that their husbands don't know how to love them in a language that they (the wife) can hear. Many women do not understand that a husband has to be taught to love you, just like a four-year-old has to be taught to read. He does not come into the marriage understanding your longing for intimacy, tenderness, deep sharing, and romance. He does not understand your desire to feel his appreciation for your unique gifts and beauty. We have to remember *that there is an order in teaching him how to love you.* Just like you don't learn algebra until you understand multiplication and fractions first, you can't teach a husband to love you until you first understand his needs and fill his tank with the 8 A's.

This order of the woman going *first* seems to be where women get hung up. God made women to be the influencers and He decreed that "wise women build their homes and foolish women tear theirs down." This is the way God created the marriage, with the woman being the influencer. Wise women know they can't change the time that the tides come in and that they cannot change nature, *only adapt* to universal truths. Demanding that the relationship is 50/50 may sound right, but you will constantly be disappointed since he has no clue what your 50 looks like.

Your husband is wildly different from you and you must repeatedly remind yourself that he wants different things than you do. What is important to him is not the same as what is important to you. This man thinks about his job, money, and sex. You think about your children, your home, your health (weight/looks), relationships, emotional intimacy and closeness, and the list of what you have to do. Women expect to come into the marriage and then both spouses *give the same effort toward the things that* she *wants*. She doesn't realize that he basically doesn't care about many of the things on her list. After the initial hormones of the engagement die down, she realizes that she is married to a man who does not think about or care about what she does—at all! Why, he is interested in his own goals, not hers!

What a disappointment marriage is now! She thought there would be roses, candlelight, and deep sharing in which she would feel like the most beautiful, adored woman on the planet. He, on the other hand, thought there would be sex and someone to applaud him while he made his mark on the world. Oh dear.

Once we accept and understand a man, that he is wired radically different, we can begin to minister to this creature. As we progress in *Wife School*, we understand that our husband needs constant encouragement about who he is. He also needs recurring, engaging sex, and he needs a deep understanding from you of the struggles and pressures he faces daily with his job/calling. As women, we are engineered to perfectly supply these needs.

We listen deeply, admire, appreciate, and soothe. When the beast comes out in the husband, we step it up, and soothe even more. The comfort and faithfulness we exhibit to our husbands is like a deep healing balm to a wound. How a man longs for a woman who refuses to see him through his failures, *but insists on seeing him through his virtues.* This man's soul is attached to the soul of his wife.

Women are full of emotional tension, just like men are full of sexual tension. Much of her emotional tension is a negative tension toward her husband because he does not love her well and he does not understand her.

If a newlywed wife won her husband's heart by meeting his needs and then giving him a pass on *knowing her* until she has an opportunity to teach him (*years needed*), then marriage in Christianity would turn around. When the wife has the husband's heart open to her, she gently influences it, not demanding that things change today. He is learning Chinese (how to love a wife) and it will take a few years.

After his needs are met, *a man's shield falls off his heart.* He begins to trust you and to want to please you. Then you slowly ask for your legitimate needs in a sweet way. I'm sure there are some hard-hearted, thick-brained men who don't respond to this, but I have *never seen one.* Men respond to this, as plants respond to sunlight, good soil, and water. But most women don't want to pay the price of persevering. They want to unleash their emotional tension and they want to feel loved today.

I hear story after story of husbands turning and opening to their wives' hearts as husbands begin to feel admired and their 8 A's are met. If your husband is still not responding, then stop and think if you are still bringing emotional turmoil into his life. Are you meeting his 8 A's? Do you have a gentle and quiet spirit that God has bathed with Himself, so that it is a calming influence, instead of a stirring and disruptive influence? God made woman to be the influencer and if she wisely builds her home, she will reap the benefits.

What power you have. What influence you wield. But it's not in demanding or blasting him with his inadequacies. It's in your kindness, your comfort, and your goodness.

If you don't feel loved by your husband, back up, re-organize, get your needs met in the Lord, meet his needs, and when his tank is full, ask for the top one or two things you want/need. I know there's a list of thirty, but ask for the top one or two things. Praise him to the hilltop when you see any evidence of him responding. Live like this for years. Know that he will not get it the first, second, or even third attempts in which you try to explain things to him. Really, maybe not even after the first twenty attempts by you. But eventually, a man with his soul needs met, will respond to his wife. Mark this down: you won't even recognize a man in five years as the same man if he has had the 8 A's poured into him by a loving and sweet wife. It is quite the miracle. Love never fails. Men are created to want to please their wives. *However, wives have not understood the playbook.*

Word pictures (chapter 13 in *Wife School*) are magnificent for explaining foreign concepts to husbands. Use them wisely, but sparingly.

DAY 4
Bump. It. Up. Story #2
(And a Word to You 20%-ers)

My, my, so many of you are certainly rockin' Bump. It. Up. I'm so proud of you!

One of the cutest, sweetest girls in my classes decided to Bump. It. Up. To appreciate this story, you have to know that she is working full-time and having trouble finding time for herself. You also need to know that sex is not one of her top needs, desires, or anything of the sort. However, knowing how important sex is to her husband, she decided to give him a little surprise.

He was gone for this certain day and she was home. She decided to make him a nice meal. In addition, she put on her *little outfit,* along with thigh high stockings, high heels, and an apron. *Oh my goodness* is all I can say.

What I thought was so extra adorable about this story is that this girl is having trouble finding time for herself. As I said, her top need is certainly *not* sex. But this isn't about her. This is about loving her husband in a language he can hear. This is love that seeks to minister to another in a way that is meaningful *to them*. This is unselfish love.

I talk to many women who read sections like this one and they are hurt because they are in the 20 % and they feel like they beg their husbands for sex. Women, there is nothing wrong with you if your sex drive is higher than your husband's. All marriages have incompatibilities, and you will have to work on this one in your marriage. But I want you to hear again that *if 20 % of marriages are like this* (and they are), then *nothing is wrong with you*. Nothing. Do not get offended by your husband's lower sex drive. This is not about your desirability as a woman or about his manhood. (Read chapter 32 in *Wife School*.)

DAY 5
A Superior Wife Skill

Imagine you are the CEO of a huge non-profit business. Whether you keep the doors open or not depends on the contributions of your supporters. Let's suppose that you are in a board meeting, and your biggest contributor, Mr. Smith, says something like, "I think we should have hot dogs and french fries at our events, to make everyone feel comfortable and more at home."

You are abashed. Shocked. What a terrible idea that is. Number one, you are trying to get your folks to eat healthy, and number two, there is neither time nor manpower for this idea, etc. But you don't start laughing at him. And you certainly don't say, "Mr. Smith, that is absolutely looney. Stupid. That will never work and is a terrible idea."

No, instead you say, "Hot dogs? French fries? Let's think about that, Mr. Smith. I realize that you are trying to grow community and for everyone to get to know each other a little better. I certainly love that goal! Let's consider hot dogs and French fries. I am so glad you are giving ideas!"

Then, when the topic comes up again, and Mr. Smith is excited about his hot dog event, you say, "Well, I don't know for sure. Have you decided who would buy the hot dogs and serve them?" He will tell you how easy it all will be. Then you say, "Well, I'm not sure. I want to sleep on it some more, Mr. Smith." He is beginning to see that you are not *all in*. Yet, you have been respectful and instead, have listened thoroughly to everything he has had to say.

Can you imagine the difference in marriages if wives treated their husbands with this kind of respect and courtesy? What wives often say to a husband's ridiculous idea is, "You've got to be joking. You're joking, right? Please tell me you're joking." Some wives respond to husband's suggestions with what is equal to throwing a cold glass of water in his face. Why can't you treat your husband with this kind of fingertip kindness and respect?

"Well," you say, "that's a lot of work. I want to let loose in the marriage and be the real me."

That's fine, and I want you to be authentic. But don't be mean and authentic. Don't be rude and authentic. Speak the truth *in love*, with delicate kindness, always guarding his ego. This is how you would treat anyone who was important and your husband is the most important person in the entire world as far as you are concerned.

Do the work and pay the price of handling your husband with kid gloves. You will get to say everything you want; just maybe not as directly and not as quickly. Wise women build their houses *by controlling their tongues.*

The amount of affection a man has for his wife is very tied to how she makes him feel. Remember that. It will change your marriage.

Prayer

Lord,

Just being honest, God, I still wrestle with not being understood by my husband. I still wrestle with not feeling loved in the way I thought I would be when I took my vows. I mean, presents and poems and candlelight are in my heart, not cars and tools and electric bills.

I am sticking with this, Lord. I believe your Word that says a wise woman builds her home. I believe your Word that says a gracious woman attains honor. I trust 1 Peter 3 that says that a disobedient husband can be won with a gentle and quiet spirit. I continue to choose against my natural inclinations, Lord. I continue to do what is right, *not what is easy.*

Forgive my self-pity. Forgive my pride. Forgive my judgmental spirit. Forgive my fear and my worry. Please grow a calm spirit in me that builds others up, that doesn't envy, that doesn't slander, that doesn't seek to win the applause of men, but rather, to serve. I have a long way to go, but I've got Your Word. I've got Your Spirit. I can stay the course.

Thank you for calling me out of darkness into Your marvelous light…the light of seeing how to have an awesome marriage. I'm not a Marriage Champion yet, but I do feel like I'm on my way. May my marriage be a picture of You, the husband, and Your bride, the Church.

Please bless and protect my home, my marriage, and my children. Oh, how I love them all.

In Jesus name I pray,

Amen

WEEK 13

Assignments and Group Discussion Questions

1. What kind of expectations do you have for holidays, such as Valentine's Day? What can you do to take pressure off your husband, but at the same time, sweetly communicate what's in your heart?

2. Has the issue of education been a source of friction in your life? What are your thoughts about education? What are your husband's?

3. How are you doing with understanding that your husband says "I love you" differently than the romantic notions we have come to expect? What are your plans to teach him in a language that *you* can hear, while all the time, patiently knowing that this is a difficult subject for him?

4. If you are in the 80%, how have you been doing with Bump. It. Up? If you are in the 20%, how are you doing with accepting that this is normal in many marriages?

5. If your husband gives you a terrible idea, how are you doing with letting him know gently that you are not *all in*?

6. Are you aware that the amount of affection a man has for his wife is very tied to how she makes him feel? Are you therefore extremely guarded with your words of correction and disapproval?

WEEK 14

Affairs, Feeling Misunderstood, Feeling Mistreated...and More

Contents

Day 1: Safeguarding Against Affairs

Day 2: When Your Husband Doesn't Understand You

Day 3: When You Have Been Mistreated

Day 4, Part A: Talking behind Your Husband's Back

Day 4, Part B: Throw Your Husband a Homerun Pitch

Day 5: What Makes Wives Happy in the Marriage

Chapter 14 in *Wife School* is called *What To Do When Your Husband Mistreats You*. I recommend rereading this chapter until these skills are second nature to you.

DAY 1
Safeguarding Against Affairs

Affairs are happening everywhere. I hardly go a week without hearing about someone who has had an affair and now the marriage is in crisis. Couples can forgive a lot, but this breach of trust seems to be the one that draws a line in the sand and is the most difficult marriage violation from which to recover. I know couples *do* recover (all things are possible with God), but if you can prevent your marriage from experiencing this horror, it is wise to think about how you might do that.

Years ago I heard a radio Christian personality say that the best insurance against an affair is *intimacy* in the marriage. When I heard that, I thought, "Right on. We should be *emotionally* close. Woohoo!" But what I didn't realize then is that intimacy for women looks *different* than intimacy for men. What this radio speaker should have said was that the best insurance against an affair was *that the needs of each spouse are met in the marriage,* which of course, leads to intimacy.

You have already studied in *Wife School* the needs that humans experience on a deep level, such as to be deeply listened to, to be affirmed, to receive attention, to be understood, to have kindness expressed toward one, and to have someone show they care with actions as well as words. *These human relationship needs cross every culture and every generation and stand at the very foundation of close relationships.* These gifts tie heart-strings around your spouse's heart and yours, which helps guard against affairs.

Obviously, the temptation to have sex outside of marriage is easier to resist if those needs are met *in* the marriage. You are learning many relationship skills and I'm sure your marriage is getting better all the time. However, the temptation to have sex outside the marriage *still exists*, even with great marriages, because we are *dust*. You have to be exceedingly wise here. There is no substitute for doing the work of loving your husband with the 8 A's, but a little discussion with your husband about affairs doesn't hurt either. Let me explain.

Many people who have had affairs and have seen their marriages blow up, will later say, "If only I had known the consequences…" It's sad to see how many people *fall* into an affair without realizing what consequences would follow. To them at the time, it's just a slip or an accident. To help prevent this *accident* from *accidentally happening* (although there is no iron-clad guarantee), I have repeatedly talked to David about the subject of affairs during our marriage. If he or I slip, it will not be because we were not informed of the heartache or consequences.

The inevitable subject of affairs comes up regularly as we hear about couples in which one spouse has cheated. I say to David something like, "How that would break my heart if you had an affair. I would be paralyzed with such a hurt. I don't know how I would get over it. Can you imagine if *I had an affair? Can you imagine how much that would hurt you if I did that to you"* I can picture my sweet husband right now, sadly shaking his head, as he pictures me having an affair, and how that horrendous breach of trust would undo him.

I don't stop there. I continue with things like, "I heard he came home and his wife was in the bed with his best friend. Can you imagine how hurtful that would be if you came home and your spouse was in your own bed with a friend? How do you navigate that kind of hurt? How do you recover?" I leave these word pictures in his mind, making him think about how devastating an affair would be to him…or to me.

Friends, *I want him to see how devastated he would feel* if I had an affair, so he would get in his heart how devastated I would be *if he had one.* We probably have had some version of this conversation ten or more times in the last 30 years. *I don't want an affair to creep up on us.* That's why early in the marriage, we agreed that David would never hire or work closely with a woman that was in the *temptation* category. Having a woman around in the temptation category is like trying to be on a diet and being surrounded by key lime pie and brownies all day long. Zig Ziglar used to say that kids did drugs exactly proportionately to how often they were *offered* drugs. *Multiple exposures to temptation predict a fall.* Keep the brownies out of the house if you are dieting and try to keep the hot mamas out of your husband's daily work life. It's a temptation your husband doesn't need to battle if it can be avoided (and this is not always possible, of course).

Men who have tanks full of the 8 A's and who are understood, cared for, and respected at home have much more concrete in their "Just Say No" boxes. Fill him with the 8 A's, talk to him about what it would feel like if either of you had an affair, and discuss his situation concerning working alone with hot mamas. If your husband travels with an attractive woman, and has multiple opportunities to be alone with her, *that is a volcanic explosion waiting to happen.* Head that one off, friends. *In any situation* where a man and woman are alone (unless she is thirty years *older* than he is), chemistry will occur and sparks will fly. *That is how the human body reacts to a person of the opposite sex.* We are engineered to have chemistry. A wedding ring does not change that chemistry. You have to be wise and take precaution that you or your husband are not repeatedly and extensively alone with members of the opposite sex.

Dr. Adrian Rogers used to say don't give a woman a ride unless she is over 80 or under 8. He understood the nature of a man. No one is immune to this temptation. Don't be offended that your husband is sexually attracted to other women. *This is how God made men.* Of course he is called to keep himself pure, but it is helpful if wives understand what is going on below the surface in your husband's body. To be honest, you have to admit that you are still attracted to men who make you feel wanted and beautiful.

Let's wise up. Let's make some decisions so we don't accidentally get led like *an ox going to slaughter* (Proverbs 7:22).

Affairs wreck a marriage. Affairs break hearts. Attempt to protect your marriage from this awful occurrence.

We all have regrets. We all make mistakes. If you or your husband have already failed in this area, there is *beauty for ashes* with the Lord. I am thinking of a beautiful woman I know right now that experienced this horror years ago and has one of the most lovely and giving hearts I know. Even though her marriage took a hard hit when this happened, God *is restoring her marriage* after this land-mine explosion. Don't give up if this has happened to you. You can recover, too.

The book of Proverbs is a gift to humans from God to tell us how to receive blessings (the path of the righteous) and how to avoid curses (the path of wicked). God didn't leave us without instructions on how to live. You've got to go after the wisdom though. *It doesn't come knock on your door.* A very basic tenet in *Wife School* is, "God feeds the birds, but doesn't put the worms in the nest." Prov. 2:1-5 can be summed up as, "Look for (wisdom) as for silver." Wise up on this whole situation with your husband and his huge sexual desire. He is a M.A.N. and you need to strongly consider the temptation he faces daily.

I heard a non-Christian say, "Men need many women for one need, and women need one man for many needs." As sinful as that thought may be, there is some truth in that sentence because in their flesh, *men do desire multiple partners.* The fact that your husband is sexually faithful is enormous!! Gigantic!! Stupendous!! Write it down, circle it, and star it. Sometimes women don't appreciate the huge gift that faithfulness is from a man.

We were at an event recently and an up-front Christian man was checking out a woman's legs. Okay, he's a man. I'll give him a pass. Then, at the next event, he was checking out some other women who were dressed immodestly. (He would die if he knew I was watching his eyes.) If your husband makes an effort to guard his eyes, you might say to him, "I know how men long to look at women's bodies. And it so honors me the way you try to guard your eyes. I know how difficult this is for men, and I appreciate it so much that you try to fight the battle. Thank you." Try to acknowledge and appreciate the effort he makes to fight this normal temptation that men face. You need to know that if your husband is in the 80%, *he's eaten up with sexual desire a lot of the time.* Thank him for his sexual faithfulness. Thank him for guarding his eyes. Thank him for fighting the good fight. Don't take his faithfulness for granted. Appreciate it!! Applaud it! Reward it!!

Do not think you are immune to this problem and that your precious husband would never do this. When I was in my twenties, one of Memphis' finest female Bible teachers said this about a young preacher: "He's the catch of the century." Knowing this young man, I agreed. He was godly, handsome, winsome, and an inspired teacher of the Word. Guess what happened to him? He married and went into the ministry. As a pastor, he started counseling. Then, he had an affair with one of the women from his church that he counseled. Friends, this is as common as March winds and April showers. Don't take your husband for granted in this area.

All through the Scripture, God seems to have a special problem with the sin of sexual immorality, in which category, of course, adultery falls. I mean, why does this sin rip apart the hearts of spouses? I have thought about this a lot, and if I may, I'd like to go out on a limb and tell you my opinion why God hates sexual immorality so much.

If marriage is a picture of Christ and His bride, the Church, then *sex inside the marriage is a picture of something very wonderful.* I'm not sure what, but that kind of fusing, that kind of oneness is a picture of something very spiritual. Is it being born again? Is sex in marriage a picture of how we are to constantly unite with the Lord and walk with Him, being grafted into the Vine? Is it a picture of when we will be one with the Lord in heaven? Again, this is only my opinion and my speculations. But I think adultery or sex outside the marriage is a picture of apostasy. It is a picture of us leaving our supreme Lover, and going off to other lower-case gods. It is a picture of us turning our backs on God and becoming disloyal to Him. I know there are scholars who have better educated opinions than I, but I offer this to you to see the severity of adultery. It is not a spill or an accident than you can get a mop and bucket and just clean up. It is lifetime devastation to many marriages unless the Lord brings monumental healing (which of course, He can and does). Do your best to make sure it doesn't happen in *your* marriage.

Hebrews 3:14 says, "Let marriage be held in honor among all, and let the marriage bed be undefiled, for God will judge the sexually immoral and adulterous."

DAY 2
When Your Husband Doesn't Understand You

When women and men's brains were hooked up to a computer to measure their internal response after they heard a sad story, almost six times as many neurons were affected in women's brains as compared to men's. That scientific fact can help your marriage.

God made women with neurons that respond to emotional situations. Think about how you understand your children and your friends. We often bash our husbands because "they don't get it" and that they don't have feelings like they *should*. (Again, only 80% of couples are like this and 20% are opposite, so no worries if your marriage is in the 20% and you are the unemotional one.)

In general, God created men to respond less strongly to emotional stimuli. If your husband doesn't understand how important something emotionally is to you, *it's because he has one sixth less neurons firing about the same event.* How that helps us give him a break. How that helps us not be disappointed that he does not understand and respond with the intensity we feel the situation deserves. It makes us see that just as we have to teach children the multiplication facts, *we have to teach our husbands how to understand our emotional natures.*

When you feel yourself becoming disappointed because of his less-than-perfect emotional response to a situation, remember that you appreciate the way he can be logical about many decisions that impact your family. I have learned that when I am stirred up by my twirly-swirly female thought life, my fewer-neurons-flaring husband can often bring clarity to the situation that I, at first, miss.

When a husband doesn't emotionally respond like a wife does, wise women adopt another perspective on the situation. First, these women focus on what is good about their husband (by re-reading their TJ lists). They tell their husbands that they appreciate "how he knows how long things will take, that he understands if the logistics are right, or that he understands the manpower needed to sustain a long-term goal." They tell their husbands how they appreciate the less-emotional brain because he can often see through what is clouded by her emotions. God made men and women to balance each other in this area. They each pull the other one to a more sane norm.

Of course, since we are all self-deceived sinners, we think our way is the *right* way (husbands and wives both think this). We think he is a dope for thinking like he does and he thinks we are ridiculously emotional. (Just a warning here: If you treat a man like you think he's a dope, I can guarantee that he will soon want out of the marriage. He may be trapped or he may have Christian values that won't let him escape, but I am telling you *that he will want out.* No man can tolerate a woman that makes him feel stupid.)

Your husband *will not get* some pretty important emotional feelings that you have (feelings about relationships, children, the home, etc.). Over time, you can gently teach him that this is how women respond. Be prepared for him to not get it for a long time. Tell him again, gently, and then, probably twenty to fifty to a hundred more times. In marriage, it's okay for us to take years to deeply understand each other.

One young girl told me that when she explained to her husband how she felt about one of her issues, the husband said, "I don't think you should feel that way. After all, it was only x, not y. Shouldn't you give it to the Lord and let it be over? How often are we going to have to talk about this?"

She explained to me *the utter disappointment* in that this was the man that she was given to love, and how he *completely didn't get her heart.* One of the main expectations we have from our husbands is to be understood, right? And when his 5/6 less neurons don't flare like ours do, we feel totally misunderstood. And unloved. And unhappy.

A friend's husband recently wrote her a poem on her fiftieth birthday. The poem had five stanzas, one for each major concern in her life: her children, her health, her work, her ministry, etc. In the humorous poem, though, was the deep understanding that he knew who she was and how she felt. She told me that he could not have written this poem ten years ago, much less twenty. He *gets* her now at this deep level because she has persevered with teaching him how she feels, never bashing him. Because she has his open heart and has had it for years, *eventually he understood her.* Young wives, right now your husband is *nothing like he will be* after years of you treating him with understanding, the 8 A's, and a godly spirit. He will eventually get you, even if he has 1/6 as many neurons flying as you. You just have to stay in the game, keep attempting to teach him without anger or disgust, and keep playing the playbook. Love never fails.

On a side note, men do love and appreciate the way women can feel deeply. Men think your childlike emotions are adorable, as long as they are positive and sweet. The way you are tender with little children, the way you are kind to old people, the way you are sad about a dead puppy…it is all very womanly and beautiful. It's the negative, upset, cross words that come from negative emotions that slay a husband.

Not too many things are more satisfying than a marriage where you feel understood, loved, and protected. But as you smart students in *Wife School* now know, *most men don't come into the marriage knowing how to do any of that.* A wise woman builds her house, and she has the long-sightedness to build her marriage with great relational skills and great character. She knows that Season 1 is for sowing and Season 2 is for reaping. She records her husband's sweetness, and becomes very grateful for all he *does get right*, while she continues to persevere in teaching him her heart. Beautiful, absolutely, beautiful results happen down the road!

DAY 3
When You Have Been Mistreated

Over and over again, I have tried to stress the importance of O-LAT-ing (Over Looking A Transgression, Proverbs 19:11) in a close relationship. Mature people overlook and forego; immature people get offended easily and are always demanding their rights.

But with that said, there comes a time when we need to "speak the truth in love" when we have been sinned against in a significant way. The following two examples are not from marriage, but from the workplace.

A friend of mine is a masseuse. Another masseuse took a couple of her clients and scheduled them for herself. Obviously, the first masseuse was extremely upset. Another example of being mistreated concerns a saleswoman in an antique jewelry store. One rare item was on hold for a recurring customer of hers. The rule in the store is if you want to sell an item that another salesperson has on hold, you have to first call the salesperson who is holding the item so they can offer it to their customer first. The owner had a customer who wanted to buy the item, so she just sold it, without first calling the salesperson who had it on hold. The original salesperson was furious with the owner.

We are called to speak the truth in love when people sin against us. Not bashing them, cussing them, or condemning them. But as unemotionally as possible, confronting them in love. This conflict is not fun or easy and most of us hate it.

But what about your husband? What if he sins against you? Your first go-to behavior is to forego, if you can. But sometimes, a discussion must be held. An example would be if he spends a large sum of money on something without consulting you, or if he has lunch alone with another female, or if he speaks disrespectfully to you, or a trillion other examples.

Talking to your husband in a calm voice is imperative. Even though he has sinned against you, you must still remain respectful. You can tell him in a calm voice that you were hurt, that you were grieved, that it upset you. Don't go into a hissy, a meltdown, or a "no way, buddy" voice. Don't become the mother, correcting the bad little boy in a stern, lecturing voice.

Conflict is uncomfortable and we certainly will have conflict in our marriages. If you are focusing on the 8 A's, then you have built up deposits and the relationship can withstand the respectful confrontation.

One husband quit his job and came home and said they were moving back to his hometown where his parents lived. They were going to move in with his parents until he could get a job, get back on his feet, etc. When I heard this story, I wanted to scream, so I can imagine how the wife felt.

The wife didn't like it (obviously) and she got out her fire hose, letting the emotional turmoil rip. This couple is now divorced (of course, many other issues were involved). I completely understood the rage this woman felt when her husband sinned against her by not consulting her on such a major decision. But what if she had responded with a sane approach, trying to figure things out, without the emotional tsunami? Wise women get hit with pies in the face, too, but they don't drop to emotional hysteria and anger. If your husband brings home the slap-in-the-face news, don't go berserk. Of course you have to confront and discuss the situation, but keep your cool. Keep your anger from saying those things that you will later regret.

One friend of mine told me that her husband, the owner of a business, gave all his employees a raise, but didn't take one for himself, since it had been a lean year. This wife had been scraping and pinching pennies to get by, and was appalled by this decision from her husband. She blasted him, telling him how inconsiderate of him that was to *her*. She said, "Why didn't you consider me and how I've had to sacrifice?!" She admitted her tone was dripping with venom. In her words, she said she *blasted* him. She told me that her tirade took months to heal. She said the damage her tongue did in three minutes was like when the hurricane ripped through the houses in New Orleans. Utter destruction. Friends, you are not free to randomly unload. You must communicate in a wise way, because unloading has terrible consequences for your husband's affection for you.

"A gentle answer turns away wrath" (Proverbs 15:1). I'm sorry if your husband is insensitive and inconsiderate, but honestly, it's not that infrequently that I hear these stories. If you can be calm, guard your tongue, and discuss the issue without hysteria, you can often avoid an oncoming train wreck. Speak the truth, but in love.

One time during a terrible disagreement between David and me, we went to the bedroom away from the kids to see if we could solve it. I started the conversation with, "We are both terribly upset with the other one. We are as mad as we have ever been. But no one is going anywhere. We both know we are not divorcing. We will work this out somehow. We both really care about the other one."

David immediately calmed down. But do you want to hear something funny? I remember saying all that, but I don't remember what the fight was about! What seems horrible to you at the moment will fade, but how you treat each other will not fade. Don't let an intense situation make you give in to emotional hysteria. Instead, speak the truth in love.

Bill and Cathy Ivey once taught a brilliant course on marriage and I distinctly remember one thing they said. It was this: "You have to go through conflict to get to intimacy." I like that. I like that it is the norm to have conflict in marriage, because we certainly have had our share. But remember, during the storm of conflict, carefully watch your words and tone. Mean and hurtful words are hard to forgive. Don't say them. Just don't.

It is important to buy some time in these radically upsetting and surprising moments—until you can get your thoughts together. One way is to gently shake your head and calmly say, "I am tremendously upset by this" while you wither with sadness and grief (not anger). Then you can add something like, "I don't see how this is going to work for me." Again, it is important that you speak from sadness and grief, not anger. Use sentences like these for times when you receive pies in the face. Remain calm. Remain sane. Buy a little time until you can get your head together. However, know that you are not a rag doll that he bought at the toy store that takes unquestioned orders. Yes, he is the leader of the family, but ordering you around without any input is emotionally abusive. And of course, he can never hit you or physically intimidate you. (Oh my word, do I even need to say that? You need to get help from your pastor or a Christian counselor if your husband ever attempts to do that.)

I constantly warn against using word pictures too often, but the time to use them is when he mistreats you. A woman with dignity is humble, but she does not allow herself to be mistreated.

If you are rocking the 8 A's with a godly, gentle, and quiet spirit, and your husband is insensitive to your need/desires, you can say, "I'm sure you don't realize this, but when you said (or did) x, it really hurt me. I was very grieved by that." Sweetly, you tell him. Softly, you tell him. Not like a boss, who would sit down, man-to-man, and say, "Joe, some things need to change around here." No, you are a woman, so act like a woman.

If he lights up around another woman at a party, then say, "I'm sure you didn't mean to hurt me like this, but tonight at the party, when Heather was talking to you, you got all excited. I felt so hurt by that. *(Word picture coming here...) I know it would hurt you if I got all excited talking to* (name someone he doesn't like)." When men hear word pictures like this, they get it. They understand. Learn to do word pictures exceptionally well and save them for your biggies.

Your husband can't mistreat you. But communicate with a spirit of grief, not anger. Tell him you are hurt. Remain in a womanly mode, not a commander-mode. Men respond to women much better than to drill sergeants.

And btw, husbands mistreat wives all the time. The *best husbands mistreat wives* and have to be corrected. Don't let this upset you too much. Just know that you have the skills to tell him without damaging the relationship.

Men are sinners. They mess up. Tell them, but tell them softly. And be sure their tanks are loaded to the max when you do.

In Chapter 14 in *Wife School*, the Genie instructs Jessica when and how to use "The Big Guns" and the "Mother May I?" technique. Please re-read that section for review.

Let's talk briefly about people other than your husband that mistreat you. If you have someone in your life who continually interrogates, criticizes, demands, or pushes you, you will have to learn the skill of speaking the truth in love. When these people pull their stuff, ask them politely not do that, and if they don't abide by your wishes, tell them you are busy and will have to talk later. People do not get to mistreat you repeatedly. They do not get continual access to you just because they want it. You can withdraw and set appropriate boundaries, calling or visiting less. One woman told me that her mother would not quit giving her advice, telling her what to do about her kids, her health, her finances, and criticizing her severely. The young woman tried and tried to speak the truth in love, but nothing worked with this mother. So after years, the daughter had to eventually change the relationship and try to talk about subjects such as the weather and Super Bowl quarterbacks. This is not desirable, but when we attempt to speak the truth in love with extended family members or co-workers or whoever, and they refuse to listen or get it, backing it up with appropriate boundaries is the only solution as you cannot get out of the relationship with them.

It can be difficult to navigate inconsiderate parents/in-laws/co-workers. Honor them, and treat them respectfully, but don't feel you have to tell them everything or always be available. If you speak the truth in love, and it is not heard, you can eventually—again, as in the game Mother, May I?— take two giant steps backward.

None of us like conflict. We all desire the fantasy of living on a tropical island with flowers, sunshine, love, and happiness. But actually we are broken people handling broken people. No one ever said it was going to be easy. In fact, in John 16:33, Jesus said, "In this world, you will have tribulation." Don't be surprised at how difficult life can sometimes be. Handling the crummy stuff—being mistreated—is part of it.

DAY 4, PART A
Talking behind Your Husband's Back

One thing you should never do is talk about your husband behind his back in a negative way. Always pretend he is there, listening, when you talk about him. He is your primary relationship, and should receive your most fierce and devoted loyalty. Your family of origin or your best friends, no matter how wonderful those relationships are, are second as far as to whom you owe loyalty. There are some girls I know who have very godly mothers, and when they go to their mothers for advice, their mothers always tell them some form of "deny yourself and give to your husband." *This section is not written to those girls.* This is written to the girls who go and babble off to their mothers/sisters about something the husband does wrong and then the family of origin all offer some version of "how horrible/ how terrible/ I wish he were different." Unless your mother is one of the few who always directs you back to the Lord and always directs you back to being the giver/lover in your marriage, then you may need to resist the urge to tell your mom everything. I know that's hard for some of you to do. But you will forgive and forget as far as your husband's transgressions but it is likely that your mother/sister will have more difficulty doing that. Be very selective in anything you say about your husband that is negative.

Your husband is your first relationship and again, it is disloyal to him for you to talk behind his back. Talk to him directly. Or talk to a wise Christian counselor or to a trustworthy, older godly woman if you need help (and there are certainly times you will). Never talk bad about your husband to a (gasp!) group. If you will think about it, his reputation is yours. Why would you want to air your dirty laundry for others to hear and see? You and your husband are one and you are telling everyone *your* issues when you talk about your husband.

DAY 4, PART B
Throw Your Husband a Homerun Pitch

This summer Donna and David Libby came over to visit David and me. My husband, David, knew the Libby's before he knew me, so they all have a strong friendship. The four of us sat in the den, enjoying each other's company. The Libbys have been married for over 40 years. I watched a real Marriage Pro, that day, although if you knew humble, demure Donna, she would definitely deny that title.

She was telling a story, and then she said to her husband (both husbands are named David), "David, why don't you tell the rest?" He jumps in and happily finishes the story. Then later in the conversation, she says (to her husband), "David, tell David and Julie about x." He jumps in again and happily goes down the trail.

FYI, Donna is not new to these advanced wife skills. When I was a newlywed, I called Donna because I barely knew how to cook and she was an expert. I said, "How do you cook eggs?" Her answer was, "Just the way he likes them." We have laughed for thirty years over that great marriage advice: *Just the way he likes them.*

So next time you're with your husband's parents, give your husband a homerun pitch. Say, "Honey, tell them about that promotion/ award you got at work." And if he leaves out that there were 300 other men in the contest, throw that in. Praising your husband in public is a wonderful thing to do. (Just be careful not to do this too much in front of your friends. It comes off as braggy and obnoxious.) Do it in front of his parents or in front of the kids. When your kids are assembled, say to your husband, "Tell the kids about that big case you're involved in…" or "Tell the kids about that great lesson you taught last Sunday in Sunday School." Throw your husband some homerun pitches.

When a discussion is going on with a group of people, turn to your husband and say, "What is your opinion about this subject?" We all love to give our opinions and your husband is no different.

If you are thinking, "Well, what about me? No one throws me homerun pitches," then go back and re-read your prior *Wife School* lessons. You should now be able to slap your own wrist when you hear that *self-pity thinking*. These advanced lessons are for those who have nailed the 8 A's and are ready to move on. Of course you are not ever going to be perfect, but recognizing your wrong thoughts is one gigantic step in the Marriage Champion direction.

DAY 5
What Makes Wives Happy in the Marriage

John Gottman, a secular marriage counselor, said that a woman is satisfied in the marriage according to *how much her husband allows her to influence him*. Think about that. That's a pretty insightful statement…and a very helpful statement. We do not want to be just concubines, maids, and babysitters. We want to be "bone of his bones" (Genesis 2:23) and share a closeness where we operate as one flesh (Mark 10:8). We want to influence our husbands.

Wife School teaches you to gain influence with your husband. The 8 A's and a gentle and quiet spirit begin to break down the shield that covers your husband's heart.

Let's discuss the influence you have on your husband.

It is true that men are to hear from God and get their marching orders from Him. But even the wisest man on the planet, Solomon, *could not resist the influence of his wives.* In a perfect environment, the Garden, Adam could not resist the influence of Eve ("Honey, eat this"). Bowing to a wife's *negative influence* is definitely not good, but of course, having a wife with *godly influence* is a fantastic benefit to a man (for example, Esther). I am assuming that you are influencing your husband in a godly direction.

Wise wives will learn to influence their husbands *for good*. I cannot make your heart good; only *you* can repent of your greed, sloth, worldliness, self-pity, lusts, pride, and other sins (to name a few of my major areas of struggle). But I can teach you how to gain influence with your husband. And more influence means more happiness for you in your marriage.

Only the Holy Spirit can let you know if you are influencing your husband for good or for harm. Proverbs 31:12 says about the virtuous wife, "She brings him good, not harm, all the days of her life". Are you bringing your husband good?

Prayer

Lord,

I get rather weary sometimes, with so much responsibility, so much giving to do, and so many people who pull on me. I feel like the Psalmist in Psalm 63 that says, "…earnestly I seek you; my soul thirsts for you; my flesh faints for you, as in a dry and weary land where there is no water". That's how I feel, Lord, *as in a dry and weary land where there is no water.*

I'm not sure what I need. Maybe I need a good night's sleep. Maybe I need a friend to truly listen to me and encourage me. Maybe I need a touch from You, saying You understand and You care. All I know is that I'm weary.

Fill this empty tank up one more time, Lord. It drains so easily. May I focus on the joys I do have, instead of the obvious holes in my life. May it be true that "You have put more joy in my heart than they have when their grain and wine abound" (Psalm 4:7).

In Jesus name,

Amen

Assignments and Group Discussion Questions

1. Have you and your husband ever discussed affairs?

2. Does it help you to know that your husband has 1/6 fewer neurons flying about emotional issues? Does this help you give him a break?

3. No one wants to be mistreated. What were your thoughts about this section?

4. Do you have a personal rule that you never talk behind your husband's back?

5. Are you good at throwing your husband a homerun pitch?

6. How would you describe your ability to influence your husband at this stage in your marriage? Have you examined your heart before the Lord to see what kind of influence you are to him?

WEEK 15

Boredom in Marriage, Contentment, a Happy Heart....and More

Contents

Day 1: If You Are Bored with Your Marriage

Day 2: Learning Contentment in Hard Circumstances

Day 3: More on Learning to Have a Happy Heart

Day 4: The Awfulness of a Despondent Spirit

Day 5, Part A: The 2-Day Rule

Day 5, Part B: If Your Husband is Not Responding to the 8 A's

Yesterday at a women's meeting, I was asked what I thought was a woman's biggest problem in marriage. My answer was that she was contentious versus having a gentle and quiet spirit (which is the same as having a happy heart). Most of this week's lesson addresses a woman's deepest problem, her heart.

Chapter 15 in *Wife School* is about parenting, but we will discuss other topics in this week's study guide lesson.

DAY 1
If You Are Bored with Your Marriage

Boredom in your marriage is not about *not having* enough exciting activities to do together in your marriage. If you are currently bored in your marriage, what is really going on is that your husband does not get you, is not interested in what you are interested in, does not pay attention to you, listen well to you, understand you, or pursue your heart. When women are bored with their marriages, it is about *not having enough friendship and emotional intimacy in the marriage.*

I found a photo on the internet where the husband was engrossed in playing video games and the tag line was, "Is this marriage bad enough to leave?" He wasn't doing anything terrible; he simply was in his own world and didn't respond to his wife's need to be understood, listened to, and given attention and affection. Women crave emotional intimacy and closeness. However, most men understand emotional intimacy about the same as how you and I understand quantum physics.

I am not saying that it is okay for men to not understand their wives, but I want you to know that it is *normal*. Men have not been *taught* how women need many and continual demonstrations of love and affection, as well as emotional release (talking and being deeply listened to) to the same degree that men need sexual release. This was recently illustrated to me by the number of Christian husbands I know that just ignored Valentine's Day. Ignored! Women love Valentine's Day and men hardly even know the day exists (unless again, a mother or a wife has trained them). Your husband has not been trained how to ask your opinion, how to encourage and affirm you, and how to care for and comfort you on a deep emotional level. For women to be deeply fulfilled in a relationship, men must eventually be taught these skills.

Teaching husbands to be emotionally intimate with their wives should be compared to teaching kids math from grade 1 (addition) to grade 10 (geometry). It is a course. It builds on other principles. You don't teach second graders calculus. But, after 10 years of math, you can teach kids calculus. Women, we have to understand that men do not have a clue about what we want as far as emotional intimacy. It's so ridiculous to discipline kids for not getting linear equations at eight years old. Yet, we do that to our husbands. We don't want to take the time to teach them how we feel and what we want. We expect them to know. That is absurd. The vast majority of men don't know. He will want to please you, though, and will be willing to be taught, if you are filling him to the brim with the 8 A's.

Make your list of what you want. Systematically, ask for the top one to two things, but accept what he gives for now. In the meantime, enjoy the intimacy of sisters, best friends, and God.

You don't have to teach cats to chase mice and you don't have to teach men to want sex. But *you have to teach men how to love you in a language you can hear*. After they learn how to have emotional intimacy with you, you will not feel bored in your marriage anymore.

Learn to do marriage as one would learn to play chess. There are skills that enable one to consistently win. Teaching your husband how to understand you and meet your needs will definitely prevent your marriage from getting boring. But of course, this is a lot of work and takes a truckload of patience.

Consider getting some of your intimacy needs met from other female relationships so you do not pull on your husband so much in this area. Years ago I read that marriage is only to be about 25% of our relationship plate. (Where do people get these numbers?) Anyhow, when I read that, I remember thinking how my relationship with my husband was about 85% of my relationship plate. The problem with that is, of course, *you have a lot of expectations* from someone if they are 85% of your relationship plate. Since then, I have intentionally grown other relationships. But still, the fact remains that I expect a lot from David, which frequently makes it difficult for him. I don't think David will ever be *only* 25% of my plate, but when he is 85%, he is bound to fail. One human can't give that much to another. I have some awesome friends (no sisters, dang it) in which I enjoy deep, intimate conversations. But now I have a grown daughter and a precious daughter-in-law with whom I have very satisfying relationships. The challenge to me remains not to expect David to be Superman in filling my emotional intimacy tank. He is wonderful and generous, and that is enough. Superman expectations cause us to be disappointed and contentious. Be on the lookout for how much emotional intimacy you expect from your husband. Women are notorious for wanting their husband to fill most of the relationship plate. Your husband will be worn out if he is your only close relationship.

Bottom line, *we are to work on our demanding hearts in prayer with the Lord.* We are to be filled with the Spirit, and that comes from getting off the throne of our lives and putting God on the throne. We choose to be content with the portion we've been given while praying for (and working for) what is still not right (which at this point might be that your husband still does not reciprocate the depth of relationship you want).

Let's look at the life of Hannah for help with contentment. Contentment is often a woman's most pressing need when she is bored with her marriage.

DAY 2
Learning Contentment in Hard Circumstances

All of us right now have issues in our lives that we'd rather not have. Sickness, issues with kids, infertility, marriage struggles, job problems, depression, weight issues, loneliness, no money, no free time, rude in-laws, difficult extended family members, and inattentive friends are just a few of the many concerns women have. We all have things we want to change.

In the Old Testament, Hannah had some *very* difficult circumstances. She was in a polygamous marriage and had to put up with *mean* Peninnah, another one of Elkanah's wives. On top of that, she was infertile, an extremely painful burden for women to bear. Many commentators say how nice and comforting Elkanah was to her, offering her a double portion of food to show his love. Obviously, *those commentators were men.* Yes, Elkanah was a dutiful man, who regularly went to worship. But to me, Elkanah was a typical man who did not understand women.

He says to Hannah, "Am I not better to thee than ten sons?" If I were Hannah, I would have *wanted* to say, "Elkanah, a double portion of food is *not* what I want. And you are *not* better to me than ten sons." (This might be why God picked Hannah and not me to be the mother of the great prophet, Samuel.) Anyhow, I don't think Elkanah was any great relational genius who listened well. Hannah is aching from grief over infertility and Mr. I'm-Enough wants her to be satisfied with his awesomeness. Give us a break, Elkanah. I know you meant well, but you don't get women, that's for sure. So let's add "a husband who doesn't understand women" to Hannah's list of woes.

(I am sorry if you think I am being harsh toward Elkanah. I think it is comical that God captured the repeated hurt that women experience in marriage and male commentators miss it. If you have been in *Wife*

School very long, you know that I love men and admire their courage to face the harsh work place, their strength to protect their families, and their responsible natures that seek to provide. Women, not men, (and women's tendencies to emotional turmoil) are whom I repeatedly reprimand. However, a man being emotionally dense is equal to a woman being dense about a man's gargantuan appetite for sex (as well as being dense to a man's need to be accepted 'as is' without continual advice on how to improve). This is the recurring clash of the sexes throughout the ages. I am only illuminating Elkanah's failure here, but you understand that I equally understand our failure as women in the male/female relationship. Correct?)

Now to continue with our topic of contentment… Hannah has something magnificent for us to learn in the midst of difficult circumstances such as dealing with her husband's mean additional wife (can you imagine?), infertility, and a husband who doesn't understand her (see 1 Samuel 1-2). The magnificent behavior that Hannah models for us is *her prayer life.* Prayer is where we can find peace amidst our unwanted circumstances. It is through prayer than God gives us the *peace that passes understanding* as He gives us His very presence! In Hannah's case, her heart was ripped apart with grief, but it was not demonstrated in emotional turmoil to her husband and *she did not blame him.* Her grief, disappointment, and requests were offered to God in prayer. What we find in Hannah is that in the midst of her pain, she still has a spirit of trust, patience, and devotion. Now that's a lovely woman and a woman to model ourselves after!

God answered Hannah's prayer. If you will read her prayer in 1 Samuel 2:1-10, you will find striking similarities to Mary's prayer in Luke 1:46-55 after Mary was told that as a teenager, she would be pregnant out of wedlock. These two women are reverent, grateful, and had moldable hearts in the midst of extremely difficult situations. How interesting that God selected such lovely, godly mothers for Samuel and for Jesus!

Prayer is the greatest work any of us can do, and maybe, the most difficult. Make this your year that you learn to pray and that you *do* pray. Carve out time every morning and pray the Psalms back to God. Until we become women of prayer, our hearts will clamor with discontentment. *Take your heart to God and learn to wrestle in prayer until you become the gentle and quiet spirit that is a blessing to God and to all around.* Make your first job every day to get your soul happy in the Lord. Of course, you will have disappointment. Jesus said, "In this world, you will have trouble" (John 16:33). But learn to be a woman who can live above circumstances, who is able to be nourishment for others because she is full of the Holy Spirit, and she has rolled her burdens onto the Lord (Psalm 55:22).

The normal downhill stream for most women is to focus on what is *missing and what is disappointing.* You must put energy toward overcoming this natural negative system and this normal pull of gravity in your life. Prayer, your Turquoise Journal lists, and disciplining your mind to think Philippians 4:8 thoughts (controlling that parade that marches across the screen of your mind) are good starting places.

DAY 3
More on Learning to Have a Happy Heart

We have discussed having a happy heart many times before and will continue to discuss this subject, as this is quite a challenge for most women.

Paul says he *learned* to be content (Philippians 4:11). I think Paul is talking about the choice to accept his hardships and portion as from God. I remember a girl in one of my groups who was struggling with discontentment before she had kids. She then had a baby and even though she loved her baby, she still struggled with being discontent. The second child came, and she was devastated with this new workload. It wasn't until her third baby (three babies under three) that she learned contentment. *Contentment is not as much about circumstances as it is about letting go of who rules your life.*

Paul goes on to say that if we have food and clothes (1 Timothy 6:8), we are to be content. Paul is not saying to *not* diligently pursue your God-given goals, to lie down passively, and do nothing. Here is that delicate dance, that wobbly balance, where you accept God's hardships and portion, yet seek legitimate means to overcome your problems and pursue your goals.

The secret in doing this is to, in one hand, be content today with the lot you have been given. But also, hold in the other hand, the pressing forward of your calling. Finding the balance of "accepting what is today" with "how much do I pursue answers and to what extent"…is difficult and tricky for all of us to comprehend. Yes, you must learn to be content and accept *what is*, while still, peacefully battling and pursuing *what isn't*.

In Exodus 17, the Israelites grumbled because they had no water and their grumbling was upsetting to God. It blows my mind that God was upset with them for grumbling over no water. They were wandering with no homes and now, they had no water and still God was upset with their grumbling. *(That's some high standard, Lord.)* Yes, the Israelites had big issues. But they were to come to God and trust Him to provide and not grumble. Of course it was okay to ask God for water and of course it's okay for you and me to seek answers to our problems. But God looks at our hearts and we are not to *clamor and grumble, but instead trust His promises*. (He has given us irrefutable evidence in creation that He exists. Have you ever studied the uber-complex language and code that exists in DNA, as well as the eyewitness accounts of the resurrection and the reliability of the New Testament documents?). Somehow, we are to learn to be content with our difficult situations because he is God, and yet, *with quiet hearts,* seek answers. What maturity and godliness this balance demands!

I think of a lovely woman I know who has had major heartache with her family's health, broken financial dreams, major issues with adult children such as divorce, and more. Yet, in talking with her, you would never know. Her spirit stays soft and happy. Yes, she is seeking answers, but her heart is not demanding.

Then I think of another woman who has had some issues with her children but otherwise, has had the life of a princess. She constantly takes the conversation *to how horrible and terrible she has it*. She has definitely not learned contentment. Somehow, someway, we are to wrestle our hearts down, accepting that life includes hardship! Life is not a Thanksgiving Day Macy's parade. What we do is look at others' best two seconds of their day (which they post on Facebook) and then we look at their adorable Pinterest lives, and we feel "less than." What a ridiculous standard to try to obtain.

When I was young, an older non-Christian woman told me that "some people really do have Cinderella lives." I believed her, and thought my life stunk. But one thing counseling others has done for me is to teach me to realize *that circumstances are not the predictor of who has a lovely heart.* Some of the women with the best circumstances are the biggest whiners and some of the women in the hardest places are the most lovely.

I know your life is not perfect. I know you are wrestling with your in-laws, your friends, your weight, your finances, your time, your health, your church, your husband, your children, aging, etc. I know. I promise, I understand. But learn contentment during it all. *Figure out how to get your heart* under *and still be a lovely garden to invite others into for shade and nurturing.* Nothing is worse than a complaining, grumbling "Oh-my-life-is-terrible" woman. Become grateful for what you have, but also, legitimately/actively try to fix that which is wrong, and then put your problems on the shelf in heaven while you laugh at the days to come. Become a delightful woman, even in the midst of suffering and hardship! No one can do that for you. Your husband can't. Your pastor can't. You must decide that this is who you are going to be and ask God to make you this kind of woman.

Learning to have a happy heart is one of the most important lessons in a woman's life. Your heart is on open display for everyone in your home. You cannot hide anger, disappointment, or bitterness from those you live with. Clean out your heart. Finding contentment and developing a happy heart is non-negotiable. Paul had to learn contentment, so I'm pretty sure that means the rest of us do as well.

Over and over again, I hear men talk about the beauty of their wives' gentle and quiet spirits. Men seem to rejoice in their wives' softness, goodness, and kindness more than almost any other attributes (well, let's not forget the 7th A of Affection). What a delight a soft heart is to a man. A woman can be absolutely, stunningly gorgeous, but if she has a grumbling and discontent heart, it negates all her beauty. Men are attracted to happy women. These women sparkle. They twinkle. Work on your heart. But remember it is the impossible frontier to conquer without the Lord.

DAY 4
The Awfulness of a Despondent Spirit

I cannot stress how awful a despondent spirit in a wife is to a husband. A despondent, sad spirit robs energy from others. It is very difficult for you to fill your family's tanks when you are continually down. If heaviness pervades your spirit, it is a very serious issue.

Some women just seem to get the gene of resilience. I am thinking of a woman who has had a child with cancer, a husband with an illness which necessitates that she work full-time, children with learning issues, and still has the most selfless and joyful spirit. Then, I have seen women with money, beauty, time, and family still whine and waddle through their discouragement. Some women have learned to have a happy heart by what they saw in their mothers growing up (that's your goal for your daughters, right?) It is really impossible to say exactly why some people have such resilience to heavy trials and others break under much smaller trials.

Said another way, I'm not sure why God gave some women strong minds and the ability to overcome hardship while other women received a proclivity to become severely discouraged. But I do know that *you can learn to have a strong mind,* and you can take responsibility for growing and developing a mind that is disciplined, unwilling to be offended, refuses to fall into the pit of self-pity, and refuses to blame others. No matter what childhood you had and what genes you were given, there are many skills you can learn to overcome a despondent heart.

One skill that we repeatedly discuss is the discipline of making time to bathe your mind with Scripture and prayer. Another essential in growing a strong mind is to fellowship frequently with other strong believers. If you are given to discouragement, this is especially important.

Another outstanding and helpful insight is that you have control over what thoughts you allow to parade across the screen of your mind. Focusing on what is missing and what is disappointing is a surefire method to have a despondent spirit. Instead, learn to kick out negative thoughts by instead, *choosing to think* positive thoughts. I like to have many *Philippians 4:8 pages* in my Turquoise Journal. This is where I keep lists, such as, "The Gifts That God Has Given Me" (giving away our gifts gives us joy). I also have a page called "My Life

Purpose" where I write what I perceive God is telling me about my purpose here on earth. This helps me not sweat the small stuff. I write down all of my trials and across from each one, I write down an encouraging word from the Lord on how to think about this trial. I have lists of God-given goals and of course, gratefulness lists. Included are lists of sweet things my husband and children have done/said, etc. Bathing your mind daily with positive thoughts is the key to overcoming the habit of thinking depressing thoughts. Learn to encourage your own heart in the Lord. Reread the alley/park examples (Week 2, Day 1) until you learn to take full responsibility for the parade of thoughts that march across your brain.

Stoic Marcus Aurelius claimed, "If you are distressed by anything external, the pain is not due to the thing itself *but to your own estimate of it;* and this you have the power to revoke at any moment." Did you understand that? It's not what happens to you; it's *what you think about what happens* that determines your emotions. A few years ago, a woman I didn't know criticized me severely (and I mean severely) because she did not like the choices I made regarding handling some issues with our family's pets. I remember thinking, "Ha, she's a crazy. That doesn't bother me." And then later that day, one of my sons said a small, negative thing to me, and I became un-glued. I said to myself, "I guess I'm not a good mother." It's not what was said; *it's the value I personally attached to each circumstance.* What I told myself was "the crazy lady's remarks don't matter" and I told myself "my son's remarks are uber-important." Do you see how your self-talk determines your emotions? *It's the value you attach to situations that drive your emotions.* Realize that you have the power to watch the parade of thoughts march across the screen of your mind, and then, take mature action to refute your own thoughts. I used to say to myself, "That woman doesn't like me very much because she didn't call." Now I say to myself, "That woman must be very busy because she didn't call." Try to frame situations in the best possible light. Repeatedly explaining things to yourself from a negative perspective can make you a despondent person.

Your life experience is based on the thoughts you have. Learn to control your thoughts. Navy Seals study mental training. Elite athletes engage in mental training. So why not you? Why don't you take responsibility for learning how to think like a positive, giving, happy, godly woman?

*Since I wrote this article years ago, I have written Happy School *and the* Happy School Study Guide. *With this study, women who struggled with depression for decades have found a path out. It's all about your thoughts and learning how to Move into Another Room in Your Brain.*

DAY 5, PART A
The 2-Day Rule

I don't like unneeded, mindless rules. But here is a rule that has saved me many regrets. It's called the *2-Day Rule* and it goes like this: If a woman is upset with her husband about anything, give it two days to settle. If after two days—and much prayer—she still feels like she needs to confront the situation with her husband, she may. But only after two days.

What happens in those two days is that if we will pray, God will download His perspective into us. Two days is enough distance that the emotional sting of something has dwindled. When a lawyer presents his case to the judge, the judge often delays in making a decision because he wants to think about it. He takes the issue *under advisement,* which means he will think about it and get back to you. What grief you will save your marriage if you will simply *zip it up* and take the issue *under advisement.* I am shocked that what seems like an 8-out-of-10 issue when it happens becomes a 4-out-of-10 issue if I give it 2 days.

Try it. It's a cool way to buy yourself some self-control…and save a lot of unnecessary conflict in your marriage.

DAY 5, PART B
If Your Husband is Not Responding to the 8 A's

I want to address the women that feel they are trying to give their husbands the 8 A's, but he is still distant or is holding back from turning toward them. Let me offer a couple possible reasons this might be going on.

It is possible that your husband is still afraid you might return to the *emotionally tumultuous* days of the past. If you brought your husband great emotional turmoil in the past, it would be beneficial to have a discussion that goes something like this: "Honey, I know I brought you a lot of emotional turmoil in the past, but I now realize what I was doing, and I'm trying to change. Have you noticed? Is there something I'm still doing in which I have a blind spot? My goal is to understand you and make you happy."

Most human beings will soften to that kind of sentence *if it is sincere.* In the past when you asked your husband why he was distant, then slammed him when he told you, he will be reluctant to tell you again. For Pete's sake, if he tells you something hard to hear, don't get defensive. Listen without getting emotional. Men hate to be honest and have a direct conversation, only for you to break down in tears. Try to listen objectively and humbly to what you've done wrong. *This is very difficult for women.* Women want to respond, "Well, if you treated me like you loved me, I wouldn't do that."

But humility demands that we go first and change. Humility demands that we not insist on getting high treatment, but give it to others. Before he will really open to your new change, you may have to hear some hard things, and humbly accept them. *This is a fork in your marriage.* Will you be humble? Will you go first and change, even though he is not being humble? This again is where the "wise woman builds." She builds her house with humility and with meekness, which is not demanding that she is "right."

Again, as we've discussed before, what I'm talking about are those same two qualities that Jesus used to describe himself in Matthew 11:29, "gentle and humble in heart" (the word *gentle* means the same as *meek*, which is yielding your rights). And again, these are the same two qualities that Peter discusses in 1 Peter 3, *a gentle and quiet spirit.* These two crowning qualities are imperative for a woman to master. If a woman can live out those two virtues, miracles happen in a marriage. But these virtues are for women who are ready to get off the throne of her own life and put Jesus on it. No woman can live with humility and meekness in her own strength.

Understanding marriage is not rocket science. But doing it well is difficult to do.

If your husband is not responding to the 8 A's, is it possible that you are still trying to run the show? Are you still trying to get him to serve you versus truly serving him? Are you still wallowing in self-pity? Men do eventually respond to a gentle and quiet spirit (1 Peter 3 says that husbands "may be won"). Ponder this. Pray over this. And get off that throne and give it to the Lord. You are doing a crummy job running your life, anyhow, aren't you? Let Someone who sees the path ahead run your life.

A second reason your husband may not be responding to the 8 A's is if he is involved in a deep sin, such as porn. He will feel very guilty if he is doing this and will probably want to blame you for things that are not really your fault. But know that the first step in helping him is not to blast him, but to respond to him with a gentle and quiet spirit. God uses wives such as this to draw their husbands *up and out* of their sin *all the time*. (We become like the people we hang around, remember?) You are not the Holy Spirit in your husband's life, but God will use your godliness and goodness (not your harsh words of reprimand) to prick your husband's conscience. There will be a time when you will need to speak the truth in love about a husband's sin, but husbands know if you are really trying to love them or if you are only trying to admonish them because you are personally annoyed. You can't fool your husband with your motives.

Time after time, I hear how a man comes out of a deep sin area and how he attributes his wife's love, acceptance, and perseverance as the keys to his deliverance. This is not fun, to be the godly rock. *We want our husbands to be this for us.* But this is our call, to be godly, gentle, and humble, even if our husbands are not. Soak in 1 Peter 3. This was written for women who have husbands that are disobedient. Our tendencies are to get bitter, and then to be sarcastic and critical. Here is your work, friend: change yourself in prayer! How impossible it is to return good for evil without God's enablement!

The wise wife builds her house, but houses are not built in a weekend. They take months and years to build. Remember, "The rain fell, and the floods came, and the winds blew and beat on that house, but it did not fall, because it had been founded on the rock" (Matthew 7:25). Do not get discouraged when there are storms. Prayer is where you will find your peace that passes understanding. Women who persevere will find the pot of gold at the end of the rainbow. *There is no substitute for perseverance in hard times.* This is where you will see what you are really made of. Pray and then put your hurt on the shelf in heaven, where He that watches Israel neither slumbers nor sleeps. Then live above your circumstances because God listens to the cries of His children and in His time, gathers His forces.

To keep yourself from getting discouraged, repeatedly camp out in Jeremiah 29:11: "For I know the plans I have for you," declares the Lord, "plans to prosper you and not to harm you, plans to give you hope and a future. Then you will call on Me and come and pray to Me, and I will listen to you. You will seek Me and find Me when you seek Me with all your heart. I will be found by you," declares the Lord, "and will bring you back from captivity."

Wise women build their houses, but there will be thunderstorms during the building process. You, though, the wise wife, are armed with the Word and prayer, the double sticks of dynamite that blast the Enemy's stronghold.

Note to Reader

The beauty of a woman who is filled with God is one of the most beautiful creations in all the world. No mountain, no ocean, or no sunset can compare with that beauty. May God make us all women filled with His Spirit. God tells us directly in 1 Peter 3 that "Rather, it should be that of your inner self, the unfading beauty of a gentle and quiet spirit, which is of great worth in God's sight." You can be of great worth in God's sight.

David and I have co-authored, *Husband School: Where Men Learn the Secrets of Making Wives Happy.* We wrote this book so it would explain to husbands what wives want. But please don't ask your husband to read it until you are rockin' the 8 A's.

Prayer

God,

When I think about contentment, I realize there is a lot of ugly smut hidden in my heart that I try so hard to cover up. I don't want anyone to know about my self-pity, about my desire to be up front and applauded, and about my secret greed. I want everyone to see me as the "put-together-Christian." You and I know the truth about who I really am.

Lord, you know how I expect other people to be perfect and not mess up, or else they get a tongue lashing (either directly or behind their back). But when *I* mess up, I want lots of grace from others, lots of understanding. I'm such a contradiction!

This sin in my heart is deep. When I see how it is truly all about "me and mine," I doubly know it grieves you. I'm supposed to love my neighbor as myself and I can't even do that correctly to my friends!

So, Lord, I want to bring these ugly parts of me out into the light of Your presence. I want You to show me how You feel about them. I want You to give me the motivation to change. Fill me with Yourself. Christ in me, there's the hope.

Take my heart and plow it as a farmer plows the earth in the spring. Then water me with Your Word and grow some beautiful fruit. I am really helpless and pathetic unless You show up. But You said You would. You said if I draw near to You, You will draw near to me. I don't have to be discouraged about this heap of filth inside my heart. I can believe that You are drawing near and will begin the demolition. It is certainly needed.

I go back to my day's work now. I receive Your forgiveness, which of course, I don't deserve. I will put my burdens on a shelf in heaven as I calmly go about trying to solve my problems, with Your Spirit leading me. I will put on a happy heart, knowing that at any second, You could call upon legions of angels to help me. I will walk in the truth that You love me and have good planned for me, even though it feels hidden at the moment. I trust You, God. The evidence You have demonstrated in creation shows me that You exist. I believe.

In Jesus name,

Amen

Assignments and Group Discussion Questions

1. Do you understand that boredom in a marriage is really about that your husband does not get you, he is not interested in what you are interested in, he does not pay attention to you, listen well to you, understand you, or pursue your heart? How do you feel about having to teach your husband those skills? What percent of your relationship plate is your husband? How could you grow other relationships to get your intimacy needs met while you wait on your husband to learn to do better in this area?

2. How does Hannah's contentment compare to yours? What is God saying to you in this area of contentment?

3. Would you say your heart is *under* and that it is a lovely garden to invite others into for shade and nurturing? Why or why not? How are you doing with whining and self-pity?

4. Do you have a despondent spirit or are you more the resilient type? Do you have a tendency to focus on what is missing and on what is disappointing? How can you change that?

5. How are you doing with standing apart from the parade that marches across your brain and taking responsibility to instead, think Philippians 4:8 thoughts?

6. What are your thoughts about the 2-Day Rule? Would that work for you?

7. If your husband is not responding to the 8 A's, are you willing to ask him if you have a blind spot?

8. The Bible says that storms will come, but the house built on the rock will stand. How are you building your house on the Rock?

WEEK 16

In-laws, Incompatibility, Kids, Disappointment ...and More

Contents

Day 1: More on Difficult In-laws

Day 2, Part A: How to Discuss Conflict and Areas of Incompatibility in Your Marriage

Day 2, Part B: Yes, Kids Are a Lot of Work (Research that Documents Season 1 and Season 2)

Day 3, Part A: The Spiritual Leadership of Your Husband...Revisited

Day 3, Part B: Something Husbands Like

Day 4: Handling Your "Disappointing Thing"

Day 5, Part A: A Difficult but Necessary Discipline to Master

Day 5, Part B: Are You Having Difficulty with Your Faith and Subsequently, Your Role as a Woman?

Chapter 16 in *Wife School* is called *What to Do When Your Husband Has a Bad Idea*. I love this chapter as women often get so bent out of shape over their husband's impractical ideas. There is a better way to handle husbands than to jump down their throats when you disagree, right? You, *Mrs. Wife School student,* now know this.

DAY 1
More on Difficult In-Laws

Years ago, a 19-year-old woman married a 21-year old man. Because they were both very young, the parents of the bride (who were Christians and very good parents) were exceptionally protective. In fact, at one time, the girl's parents jumped on the young man for something they did not find appropriate about him. Obviously, this is not the best way to start a relationship with the new husband of your daughter.

However, something strange occurred. Because of this young man's high emotional intelligence, he did the unusual. *He pursued his wife's parents.* He took them out to dinner. He brought his mother-in-law flowers. He forgave their offensive comment and moved *toward* them. He won them. Now, thirty years later (this is a true story) those in-laws *adore* this son-in-law. Instead of getting offended and starting down a course of "we don't get along," the wise husband decided that he would make huge, bold deposits and *win* his in-laws.

This is brilliant, I tell you. Spectacular. It's rare and lovely to the max. What if we lived like that in our extended families? What if we loved the difficult in-laws instead of getting offended and pulling back? What if we forgave, overlooked, pursued, and moved toward them with love?

This is why this family is now one of the top families that I respect in the world. This is how they live, with humility, letting the offenses of others "pass through." Of course your in-laws are going to do things differently, say the wrong things, and have different values. But they are now your family and it's up to you, the wise woman, to smooth out the bumps and try to learn to get along.

A friend recently told me that after 20 years, her mother-in-law still makes derogatory cracks toward her. I asked her how she handled that. She said, "I hear the remarks, but I let them go. My mother-in-law's not going to change and if I get bitter, that would only *tarnish my soul.* My husband loves his mother (even though she drives him crazy sometimes, too). We set appropriate boundaries with how much we see her and talk to her, but *we are careful to be very dutiful to her and honor her.* I know what a blessing it is to my husband for me to get along with his cantankerous mom. When she criticizes me and I let it go instead of confronting it, my husband is very appreciative."

Some of you are thinking, "What about speaking the truth in love and confronting that mother-in-law for her inappropriate behavior?" Yes, maybe sometimes this is necessary. Sometimes it is wise for your husband to talk with her. But often, confronting mothers-in-law about their inappropriate behavior does not work. If you have a humble mother-in-law that will receive your thoughts and opinions, then greatly rejoice. However, it is *common* for older women to have trouble taking correction from their daughters-in-law. (This is a wake-up notice to all of us who are now in this second stage of life). Therefore, if your mother-in-law always thinks she knows how to best live life, then your "speaking the truth in love" will fall on deaf ears. You and your husband will have to pray about this and ask God for wisdom to know if you should confront or to continue to overlook and forgive.

Wise women know that the in-law situation can be filled with tension, but they also know that it is *a gift to their husbands* to not only try to get along, but to *demonstrate love toward* his family. *You do not have to feel a certain way to respond with goodness to others.* Responding to your husband's family with goodness is about the virtue *in you*, about returning good for evil, about you being a Christ-follower. The norm is to complain and stomp your foot; the godly response is to forgive and overlook.

I want to say again that establishing appropriate boundaries is necessary if an in-law is repeatedly verbally abusive and unpleasant. Nevertheless, if you can, forgiving and moving toward difficult in-laws is a *higher* response. This is about you and your desire to honor God with a humble life. It's fabulous, but it's rare. It is how the woman lives whose worth is far above rubies.

DAY 2, PART A
How to Discuss Conflict and Areas of Incompatibility in Your Marriage

A few lessons ago, we discussed incompatibility in marriage. For example, some of us are cleanies and married to messies. Some of us are spenders and are married to savers. Some spouses like practical jokes and funny jabs while others want home to be a safe place. Spouses differ in how much time they think they should invest in hobbies, in work, and in the family. These are values and areas of incompatibility, not necessarily sinful areas (although women often think these areas are sinful on their husband's part).

Being incompatible in your marriage in many areas is not a deal breaker. Yes, it's easier if you share the same values and interests, but spouses can learn to have compassion and understanding in areas of incompatibility.

Let's discuss what happens if you and your husband have a disagreement over an area where you don't share the same value or opinion. This area continually pricks and upsets you. Let's take the example of spending verses saving, as this area is a major source of conflict in many marriages. Pretend the husband in this example is the saver and the wife is the spender. You can start the conversation with something like this, "As you know, honey, we feel differently about money. Let me see if I understand your perspective correctly." Then you attempt to explain to him how he feels. He will correct you if you say something that is not right. That's fine. Be humble and teachable. Listen well until you demonstrate that you *understand his perspective* perfectly.

For example, you might say something like, "Honey, because you know we will have some heavy expenses with education and orthodontics in the near future, you feel that spending money on anything which is not absolutely necessary is wrong. Am I correct? Having large expenditures looming in the future puts a lot of stress on you, too. Is this how you feel?"

After your husband feels completely heard and says, "Yes, that is how I feel," then you say, "Now, would you please listen to how I feel?" How amazing it is that after others feel heard and understood, they will *then* be willing to listen to your perspective. Stephen Covey calls this principle, *Seek first to understand.* This is not a new thought, though. James 1:19 says, "Everyone should be quick to listen, slow to speak…"

Now that you have accurately articulated your husband's perspective, give your perspective. For an illustration, let's assume that you want to spend a little money on a vacation to make family memories. If he responds to your perspective with, "Well, that's stupid and wrong," don't get offended. You simply have more teaching to do. You can say, "Honey, this is an area of preference about money and I want to see if we can negotiate and come to an agreement." He can bark all he wants but stay sweet and calm and say, "I hope that you will consider my perspective". If you stay sweet and are always depositing the magic 8 A's, this man's bark will soften, I promise. It's okay for you to say, "I want you to understand and consider my opinion just because you love me." Most husbands will soften to that in time (maybe not today). They know they shouldn't demand that you feel exactly like them about everything. When their tanks are full, they are usually willing to hear your perspective (of course, this is assuming that you have thrown emotional turmoil out of your house and into the deepest part of the Pacific Ocean). Having a godly, giving, and loving wife (you!) tears down the brick wall that husbands have constructed over their hearts.

It is a magnificent thing, indeed, to be the wise and godly power behind the throne who can speak and influence with kindness, goodness, and self-control!

DAY 2, PART B
Yes, Kids Are a Lot of Work
(Research That Documents Season 1 and Season 2)

Waiting in a doctor's office once, I picked up a magazine called *Outside*. In the magazine was an article on happiness. It gave a study that compared the happiness of couples with children to the happiness of those without children. The first study said that a couples' happiness diminishes when they have a child, and that each additional child lowers the happiness rating. (Our sixth child was with me when I read that. He joked about how sad we must have been when he arrived.) The article said that childless couples at this stage are happier than couples with children.

I thought about that and I understood it. In the short run, a farmer is happier in May if he is watching TV in his air-conditioned home rather than being outside in the hot sun, plowing the fields. Likewise, I am happier in the moment when I am surfing the net versus when I am pushing this stiff body to work out. But let me continue with the study in that magazine.

The next study compared couples that never had children with couples who experienced empty nest. *The couples with grown children were happier.* This is a perfect example of Season 1 and Season 2. Kids can be exhausting and can rock your world. And multiple kids doubly rock your world. But the joy of having mature grown children is quite fulfilling. (I am certainly not setting my children up on any pedestals as examples. They are normal young people with many normal struggles. Nevertheless, they are quite the delight to their father and me.) If you are currently in Season 1, I realize your children are wearing you out. You are scraping just to get through the day. Boy, do I remember those days. But friends, children are God's gift of hope to us. They are worth every ounce of your effort. Children indeed are a blessing from the Lord (Psalm 127: 3-5). In my opinion, friendship with adult children is one of the supreme blessings on this side of heaven!

Back to the farming example. Guess who is happier when the harvest has come in? The guy who has a full barn or the guy who was watching TV in the air conditioning during planting season? And guess who is happier, the person who surfed the web for hours or the person who lost fifteen pounds working out? Sowing is hard. Sowing is no fun. But reaping is a blast.

Everything worthwhile takes effort. Nothing is worth more effort than your sweet (but ornery) children. *Don't begrudge all the work they are.* Don't see children as a burden; they are your purpose. They are definitely worth it. Sow in Season 1, reap in Season 2. (Btw, Love and Logic (LoveAndLogic.com) sure makes Season 1 easier so be sure to devour their resources.)

DAY 3, PART A
The Spiritual Leadership of Your Husband...Revisited

Women are always looking for emotional closeness in their marriage. And the latest ploy of women is to bash their husbands for *not being spiritual leaders.*

Let me give you the spiritual leadership fantasy of many women. Ready? The fantasy is of a husband who gathers his wife and little chickens under his wing and with a great servant-spirit, he prays, "Oh God, may I decrease and may my family increase. May I understand how to meet my wife's every need and be a perfect father. God, help me learn to love to help with the dishes. Oh God, help me bind up all the myriad wounds and hurts of my family. Put their trials on me and protect them from any harm or discomfort. May I instead, be uncomfortable, not them. May I meet my wife's need for emotional intimacy with great fervor. Help me listen to her and compliment her so that she feels safe, adored, and treasured. May I lead my children with the utmost of gentleness and be the world's greatest dad, as well as the most fun dad in town. And now, use Your Word in my life so that I may royally bless my family. Amen."

That nailed your spiritual leadership fantasy, didn't it?

Do you know how many men I know that do that perfectly? Zero. Right, zero. Do you know what real spiritual leadership is? Real spiritual leadership is when your husband makes time to read his Bible. Spiritual leadership is when he finds time to pray. Spiritual leadership is demonstrated in a man when he is faithful, honest, hard-working, and full of integrity. Men demonstrate spiritual leadership when they coral their sexual craziness. They demonstrate their spiritual leadership when they get hold of their anger, and surrender to the portion that God has given them today—all the while peacefully and proactively seeking to improve their situation. Men who are spiritual leaders hold their little girls in their laps and throw baseballs with their sons.

That's a spiritual leader. If your husband gathers the family together to teach them the Word and pray, then that is a *bonus.* Yes, the husband is commanded to wash his wife with the Word (Ephesians 5:26), but the wife is also commanded to respond to his disobedient behavior without a word and instead, with a gentle and quiet spirit (1 Peter 3). *How well are you doing with that?* When you get your part right, then maybe you can ask your husband to lead the family in Bible study and prayer. But not until...

We humans tend to see our own goodness and other people's failings. Reverse that. Talk to the Lord in prayer about your sin and then look for virtue in your husband. This is a great picture of *extreme maturity* in a woman.

There is a nice song out now about spiritual leadership in marriage that says, *"Lead me with strong hands..."* That's a good song to convict men to do better, but honestly, *it makes women discontent.* If your husband makes a living and is faithful, be thankful. Those are the only two expectations you can have in marriage. Yes, of course you want more. So figure out the next biggest thing you want and ask for that. But you know by now, you can't ask for everything at once. Spiritual leadership is not a right that you can demand from your husband. *It's a bonus.* Give your faithful, hard-working, honest husband a break. You need to quit expecting him to be Jesus.

DAY 3, PART B
Something Husbands Like

Regularly, a group of friends and I have lunch. While two of us were waiting on a couple of the others to arrive, I asked the wise woman with me (who mentors women) what she thought were the most important principles to communicate to young wives about what is important in growing a great marriage.

She said two things that you regularly hear in Wife School. One was get rid of the emotional turmoil (she put this in her own words, of course) and two, was to make the physical intimacy part of marriage fun for him. Then, she added a new phrase that I like. She said, "Husbands want you to 'tend' to him." I like that word. Let's talk about what *tending* looks like.

Tending to a husband could be that we notice his glass is empty and we refill it. It could be that we know we will be gone for the afternoon, so we make sure there is a sandwich prepared for him in the fridge. It could be that we notice that he has had a busy week, so we make plans where he can relax and regroup, instead of scheduling an event that we want to do. Tending to your husband is nothing more than noticing him, thinking about what he is going through, demonstrating concern, and giving him *attention.*

The common projectile in marriage is for the wife to be consumed with the children/ her events/ her goals and to take the husband for granted. The normal thinking is that "he can fend for himself since I'm so busy and overloaded." But a little tending is huge to men. Bringing him a treat to eat, getting his briefcase out of the car for him, being on time when you are going places together, remembering that he likes to play golf on Saturday mornings so you don't schedule a meeting then, standing up and going over to kiss him hello when he comes home, asking him about his day (then deeply listening)…there are endless situations where we can be mindful of what attention and tending he would like.

So many women ignore these little acts of kindness after the newness wears off. Wise wives tend to their husbands until *death do them part*. They show their concern and respect through thousands of little daily gestures.

Men love their wives to tend to them and give them attention. This never changes. Never.

DAY 4
Handling Your "Disappointing Thing"

I like to go to bed early and get up early. This morning at 4:30 a.m., I was in the kitchen, starting the coffee. Morning is a happy time for me, when the rest of the world is asleep and I am getting started on my day.

The thoughts start their usual parade across the screen of my mind. "Where is the cat?" "I need to start my son's laundry." "How much time do I have to write before I have to leave today?" And slam, out of nowhere, thoughts pop up about the deep hurt in my heart that I have wrestled with for years. Just out of nowhere, thoughts of What is Missing and Disappointing (the WMDs) are right there, in the quiet of the kitchen, marching with force across my mind. It's almost as if I can feel the energy drain from my heart when these thoughts enter. It's as if someone squeezes my heart, and then harshly slaps my wrist with a ruler. The WMD thoughts were unannounced and didn't even knock. They just let themselves into the Rooms of my mind, wanting attention.

There I am, waiting for the coffee to brew, thinking about how many years Disappointing Thing has cut me.

Honestly, I realized that I see little hope for things to change in this area in the future. Just like so many times before, there I am in my jammies with Disappointing Thing, all cozy together in the kitchen at 4:30 a.m.

However, I am **not** my old self. I have now learned that when I see Disappointing Thing enter the room of my mind, he is immediately escorted right back out the door, since this is not a good time for him to visit. My response to Disappointing Thing is "You're not welcome to come and make me sad." *I immediately find another thought to think about.* I only talk about and think about Disappointing Thing when I am with God in prayer, thinking about proactive ways to fix this with someone who cares about me (or who could have answers), or when I am proactively researching answers.

What is so interesting to me is *that I have the power* to make Disappointing Thing leave. He is not in charge of which thoughts I think; I am. I am always able to make Disappointing Thing leave by intentionally thinking about something else. (In *Happy School*, this is called Moving into Another Room of My Brain.) The coffee is now ready so I go to my office (ha, my office—which is an undecorated spare bedroom) and begin my day, back with a happy heart.

Whatever your Disappointing Thing is, corral it. Quarantine it. Don't let it consume your thoughts. Decide you will only think about it in the three situations that I just stated: in prayer, when you are legitimately discussing proactive solutions with someone who cares about you (or has access to answers), or when you are proactively researching answers. Otherwise, put Disappointing Thing back in a box on a shelf in heaven.

Whether your hurt and disappointment is infertility, a lack of intimacy in the marriage, a child that has repeated struggles, loneliness, health issues, financial problems that won't resolve, relationship issues, weight trials, dreams that are not happening…address these issues in your mind *only* in the above three situations. Don't let Disappointing Thing burst in unannounced and unwanted into the sacredness of your mind. He's not welcome. He's not wanted. And you get him to leave *by thinking about something else.*

There's a whole new science about the plasticity of the brain (how the brain can change) that is truly amazing. You can change your brain by what you think about. You can change your life by what you think about. And you have control in this area.

1 Peter 5:8 says, "Be alert and of sober mind. Your enemy the devil prowls around like a roaring lion looking for someone to devour." I don't think that the random and sudden appearance of Disappointing Thing on the landscape of my mind is an accident. I think Someone very devious and very intentional is trying to keep me from joy. Don't let your Enemy suggest upsetting thoughts to you, but instead, have a strategy to fight back.

By now, I hope you have some pages in your Turquoise Journal called Recurring Problems. (In *Happy School,* we call these WMDs, What's Missing and Disappointing.) On the left side of the page, write down your problems. On the right side of the page, write "encouragement from the Lord on this issue, proactive ideas that might solve the problem, and how you are to 'frame' this issue in your mind while you work on it and wait on the Lord." After you pray through each issues, you put it on the shelf in heaven, not letting it slap you around. Instead, substitute positive thoughts for Disappointing Thing.

We have to fight discouragement, friends. We fight it in our minds, on our knees (with Scripture), and in one more place, which I will now discuss.

One more very important piece of information about fighting the hurt of Disappointing Thing is that *burdens are to be shared in life*. When we lived in Virginia, a certain lady was new to the area and went through some very hard trials in her life. Not being well-connected to a community, she shouldered the burden alone with her husband. Later, after she got connected to an intimate group of friends in her church, she again went through another painful trial. This time, she said, the burden was halved, because she was able to share the burden with others who cared about her.

There is a video that has gone viral called *This Might Be the World's Most Romantic Proposal* (you can find it on YouTube). What I loved about this video was of course, the effort of the man to propose like this. But what really made this video was the community of the couple. (Get your Kleenexes out before you watch it.)

Who is this community for you? You may need to proactively seek some new relationships because living alone stinks. We were created for community and you will never find great joy living by yourself.

Don't try to make it alone. You won't.

The Disappointing Thing in your life is probably not going to go away anytime soon. "In this world, you will have tribulation" (John 16:33). But having a strategy to battle Disappointing Thing will help you tremendously.

It took me 30 years to learn how to have a happy heart and to live above disappointing circumstances. Happy School was just written last year (and the Happy School Study Guide was just published.) Together, they have everything you need to know about overcoming discouragement. I no longer linger on the lowlands, but ride in victory with the Lord. Overcoming is your birthright as a Christian!

DAY 5, PART A
A Difficult but Necessary Discipline to Master

This morning, I got tickled as I read about our girlfriend, Eve, in Genesis 3. Did you know that Eve is ridiculously just like you and me? She is thinking about whether she should eat the apple or not and here is her reasoning (everything in parentheses I added): "When Eve saw that the fruit was good for food (pleasure, yum yum), pleasing to the eye (yes, like, pretty clothes, makeup, fixing up our house, creating beauty), and desirable for gaining wisdom (thinking that with wisdom, she could make everything turn out okay for herself and those she loved), she took some and ate it."

Right there you have Everywoman. Isn't that hilarious? This passage describes every woman I know: wanting pleasure, wanting beauty, and wanting wisdom so she can know how to make everything turn out okay for herself and those she loves. Much of a woman's natural motivation is described in *one* sentence. Scripture blows my mind.

The next sentence is even funnier: she wanted her husband to understand her. So, "she also gave some to her husband who was with her." Can you believe how identical Eve is to you and me?

What this again tells me is that this Book is *divinely written*. God has all sorts of hidden gems for you and me, if we will just open up His Treasure Box. The Bible has the power to change my heart because the Person who wrote it *created* my heart. Dr. Adrian Rogers used to say, "You read most books. This Book reads you."

Henry Ward Beecher said, "The Bible is God's chart for you to steer by, to keep you from the bottom of the sea, and to show you where the harbor is, and how to reach it without running on rocks and bars." It's hard to hear from God when you're not reading *the main method* that He gave humans to communicate with Him.

I hope you are systematically studying your Bible. Jack Hayford said, "The Bible is…as necessary to spiritual life as breath is to natural life. There is nothing more essential to our lives than the Word of God."

This Book changes you and this Book changes me, because this Book is *living!* Hebrews 4:12 says, "For the word of God is alive and active. Sharper than any double-edged sword, it penetrates even to dividing soul and spirit, joints and marrow; it judges the thoughts and attitudes of the heart." No woman can spiritually grow unless she has a huge intake of Scripture. This is non-negotiable for a Christ-follower.

I'm not a creature of routine. So I frequently change what I do for a Quiet Time. Currently, I am reading out of a Bible called *The Case for Christ Study Bible* by Lee Stroebel. But in a few weeks, that will change. (This is similar to how I switch from going to the gym, doing exercise DVD's at home, using weights at home, etc. as I get bored easily and like to mix things up.) You may be a creature of habit and that is fine. Get a plan so that you are having time every day with the Lord in His Word.

Romans 10:17 says, "Faith comes from hearing the message, and the message is heard through the word about Christ." If you are having doubts, or are struggling with letting God rule your life, maybe you are eating junk food for a spiritual diet (like some of those trashy TV shows). And on that note…

DAY 5, PART B
Are You Having Difficulty with Your Faith and Subsequently, Your Role as a Woman?

A young girl in our neighborhood who is in grade school was fighting with her brother in her front yard. I asked her what was wrong. She told me that she looked out the window of her fifth grade classroom and saw her brother playing sissy games with the girls at recess, instead of playing sports with the boys. She said her brother embarrassed her. Of course, we know that siblings care about how their siblings act, because they feel it is a reflection on them.

You and I understand this about siblings. And Jesus understood this. In John 7:5, the Bible says, "For even His own brothers did not believe in Him." In another passage in Matthew 12: 46, the Bible says, "While Jesus was still talking to the crowd, his mother and brothers stood outside, wanting to speak to him." Jesus' brothers did not believe in Him and were embarrassed by his claims.

Josepheus, the secular Jewish historian, later wrote that James, the half-brother of Jesus was stoned to death (from *The Case for Christ Study Bible* by Lee Stroebel). Think about that. A half-brother, who was earlier embarrassed by Jesus's actions, now gets himself stoned defending his brother's claims of being the Messiah.

Why did James change from being embarrassed about his half-brother to putting himself in leadership where he is stoned? What happened to James?

1 Corinthians 15 says that Jesus "appeared to James" after the resurrection. This half-brother saw Him after the resurrection. *Saw Him.* Not only is James not embarrassed anymore, he becomes the leader of the church in Jerusalem, the most hostile place toward Jesus on earth! James saw his half-brother, Jesus, risen from the dead!

Friends, the story of James reminds me, once again, that the story of Jesus *is true.* Everything in the Bible hinges on the fact that *the resurrection is true.* And since it is true, we can believe God has a plan to bless us when we live in a Biblical mode. The whole book of Proverbs is about two things: the path of the righteous leads to blessings and the path of the wicked leads to curses. God made rules and paths so that we might be blessed.

If you feel your Biblical role and life are difficult to embrace, realize that the One who created the universe created you to live *the role of a biblical woman.* There is much blessing for women when they embrace their role.

Quit fighting your role. Study it. (Titus 2, 1 Peter 3, Proverbs 31, 1 Timothy 5, etc. are good places to start.) Delight in the beauty of it. God wants you to learn this role. It is indeed a garden full of peace and blessing.

WEEK 16

Prayer

Lord,

Sometimes, I get a little weary, God, with working, cleaning, handling arguments with the kids, doing my job at church, shouldering my girlfriends' problems, and being *on* to Bump. It. Up. with my husband. It seems that I give and love and then do it all again. The workload is heavier than I want. The life I dreamed about as a little girl certainly didn't turn out like I thought it was going to.

Yes, I have some nice moments in life. I do love my husband and children. But still, there is a lot of heartache in my life. A lot of disappointment seems to come my way (and yes, I know I am supposed to be fighting that but it is so hard to fight). Help me be a woman of joy, Lord. Help me get rid of this self-pity that just doesn't seem to want to go away.

Another thing, Lord: I'm tired! Help me figure out what to let go of…and what to do so that I'm not so exhausted all the time.

I want to be close to you, God. You know that. Remind me to pray more. Help me get organized so I will have a daily time where I *get my soul happy in You*. You never designed me to figure out life by myself. Your design was that You are going to live through me and that is where the joy and power is. Help me learn this. I'm still such a child as far as my faith.

Forgive me, God, for trying to live in my own strength. Of course, that's why I've been failing. You want to fill me with the Holy Spirit and He wants to run my life. Will I ever get that?

In Jesus name,

Amen

Assignments and Group Discussion Questions

1. How could you improve your relationship with your husband's family?

2. Do you seek first to understand or seek first to explain your opinion?

3. Is Season 1 a lot of work for you? Do you ever resent your children for all the workload they represent? Do you now accept that Season 1 is sowing and Season 2 is reaping?

4. What are your thoughts about your husband and spiritual leadership? Do you accept what he gives or are you disappointed?

5. How good are you at tending or giving attention to your husband?

6. Does your Disappointing Thing slap you around a lot? If so, what are your plans to corral that beast?

7. What are you doing for a daily Quiet Time? Is this a struggle or not?

8. Do you struggle with your faith? If so, do you also struggle with your role as a woman?

WEEK 17

Flirting, Hospitality, Discouragement, Aging...and More

Contents

Day 1: Is a Little Flirting with Other Men Harmless?
Day 2: The Lost Art of Hospitality
Day 3: What is *A Life Well-Lived* for a Woman?
Day 4: Conquering Discouraging Thinking
Day 5: Losses Accumulate with Age

Chapter 17 in *Wife School* is *How You Contribute To or Diminish Your Husband's Reputation*. Yesterday, I ran into a woman while I was shopping and we exchanged stories about our sons who are friends. In between though, she softly and cleverly bashed her husband, saying how he didn't understand something and how he had wrongly responded. I know this guy, and I like him. But honestly, my respect for him dropped a few points. Be very careful how you talk about your husband. You and your husband are one, so you are really slandering yourself. Be smarter (and have more virtue) than that.

DAY 1
Is a Little Flirting with Other Men Harmless?

Nothing is more thrilling to a woman than being pursued by an attractive man. The tingle of feeling attractive and wanted in a man's presence is a gift God gave women to enjoy with their husbands. Most of you experienced this during your courtship with your husband. He desired you, pursued you, and it was exquisite. But husbands often quit pursuing wives to the same degree after marriage. They have *conquered* you and they are now moving on to conquer their work, hobbies, and other pursuits.

So here you are, with the most thrilling part of life for a woman—being desired and wanted—gone. The unenlightened and untrained husband wants to watch sports, have sex, and then get a sandwich—which is totally pathetic in most women's opinions (see Chapter 3 on the A of Acceptance in *Wife School* if you are still struggling with accepting your husband's weaknesses).

Nevertheless, we need to talk about how a woman inappropriately tries to fill the void of romance she is missing from her husband with the attention of other men. I'm not talking about adultery with other men (we all know that is wrong). I'm talking about something that might, on the surface, seem innocent: flirting. Flirting is the first step, though, that leads to adultery.

It is very easy to rationalize (when your romantic tank in your marriage is empty) that it is permissible to subsequently accept the attentions of other men. The arousal of other men toward you gives you that feeling again of being wanted and beautiful. You know what I'm talking about.

It is true that many men have failed their wives by not continuing to pursue them with affection and romance after the wedding ceremony. However (and here is the money), *his failure does not give you the right to find tingly excitement from other men.*

"I'm just being friendly" is what a woman might say, but what she is really doing is enjoying the attention and arousal of a man *who is not hers*. Friends, this is disrespectful to the *max* to your husband. I know that teaching your husband to pursue you is difficult and thus far, a big disappointment. But flirting and drawing other men to yourself is *wrong*.

One woman said to me, "I can't help it. Men just seem to notice me." I wanted to say (but didn't), "Well, sure they do, with the signals you give off the way you dress and act." Some women ridiculously think they have some sort of magic power with men. No, these women are sending out signals that they might be a little available.

I am thinking of a particular pastor's wife right now who is as beautiful as they come. But because of her regal and pure demeanor, no one tries to hit on her. That is because men react to women according to how *they dress and act*. These are the two methods women employ to tell other men they are seeking their attention. A low-cut blouse with a portion of your breast exposed is a billboard that tells men you desperately want their attention. An extremely tight, short skirt is again, telling other men that *you want them to notice you and pursue you*. Don't play innocent. You know it's true.

Knowing how to dress takes discretion and wisdom. I know the current styles are immodest and I am certainly *not* going to be legalistic, because I love fashion as much as the next woman. But the code word is *modesty*.

The more immodest a woman dresses, the more she is telling the world that she is *needy and hungry for male attention*.

Yes, look beautiful. Look stylish. But know you are sending signals when you dress like a scamp. Are you a

Proverbs 31 woman who is clothed in fine linen and purple? This woman didn't dress honky-tonk. Personally, I like a modern, edgy look, so I am not giving any rules for sure, but only the guideline of *modesty*. Maybe you have a blind spot in the modesty arena if your mother didn't teach you how to dress appropriately.

Back to the subject of flirting. Know that flirting with other men means *there's a hole in your heart that you are trying to fill* (inappropriately, I might again add). Yes, continue to work on your relationship with your husband and continue to endeavor to teach him how you would like to still be pursued. But find godly ways to fill your own needs instead of *seeking the attention of other men*.

One of the most disrespectful ways you can treat your husband is to *solicit and receive* the flirtatious attention of other men. (This is very different from receiving good-ole-fashioned, harmless friendliness from others).

What does Proverbs 31:11-12 says about a wife? *Her husband has full confidence in her...She brings him good, not harm, all the days of her life*. Flirting with other men and receiving their under-the-radar sexual attention is certainly not bringing your husband good. It is more like putting poison in his coffee. Just ask your husband how he feels about this. Ask him how he would feel if you and another man were sharing under-the-radar sexual attention. Watch him come unglued.

Instead, be a woman of virtue. Be a woman of purity. That alley-cat behavior is below you. *Decide you will pay the price* of the long-haul of teaching your husband to meet your needs. We want our husbands to come into marriage with the romance software already downloaded, but more often than not, it isn't. You have to win your husband's affection and then he will open to your influence. As you know, *then* you can teach him your needs. That's the way wise women have taught husbands their needs for centuries.

Godly women cannot find favor with God or their husbands if they are stirring up and enjoying the sexual attention of other men by flirting. Remember how rare virtuous women are? Be one of *the magnificent few*.

Back it up. Rein it in. Your husband will appreciate your *loyal behavior* beyond words. Know that it is extremely humiliating to your husband for you to stir up the feelings of another man toward yourself.

Ephesians 5:3 says, "But among you there must not be even a hint of sexual immorality...because (this is) improper for God's holy people."

God's holy people...that's you!

DAY 2
The Lost Art of Hospitality

Neil Warren Clark suggests that unmarried people write down a "Must Have" and "Can't Stand" list for what they are looking for in a future spouse. Several of my children have written these lists and have them tucked away.

A group of mature young Christian men were over one night a while back and for fun, all the guys wrote their "Must Have" and "Can't Stand" lists in my kitchen. (Some of the lists were pretty comical, as these guys were obviously cutting up. One guy wrote *straight teeth* on his Must Have list.) On a more serious note, one of the items in one of the boys' Must Have lists was "loves hospitality." I know his family-of-origin and I understood the wisdom he had learned from watching his parents offer hospitality over the years.

Michael Hyatt, former CEO of Thomas Nelson Publishing, looked for a wife who was "given to hospitality." These men know a secret. Women who are given to hospitality reveal a lot of character traits about themselves.

Hospitable women usually have a love for people and ministry whereas emotionally and spiritually immature people are repeatedly *not given* to hospitality (as they as just trying to keep their own heads above water).

Hospitable women demonstrate a servant quality because having people over is *work*. A woman given to a lifestyle of hospitality is telling us something about herself and it is this: she is a giver. In contrast, women who are lazy, self-focused, or caught up in addictions will not be able to offer hospitality to nearly the same extent as emotionally healthy women. This is not an iron-clad statement about people by any means. It is only a pattern that I have noticed over the years and this is only my opinion. For certain, though, hospitality does take a certain amount of "having it together" to pull off regularly.

Now from the vantage point of Season 2, I realize that hospitality is something that successful and healthy families do. Families are like ponds. Without fresh water, they become stagnant, moldy, and full of disease. Hospitality is a way to keep the fresh life of other people streaming through your home. Let me give you multiple reasons that I think hospitality is so beneficial to you and your family.

With hospitality, your children will be exposed to multiple godly thinkers, not just you. Another reason that hospitality is so valuable is that your children learn and improve their social skills when they are around other mature people. I remember reading how Greg Harris, a guru in the homeschooling movement in the 90's, said he repeatedly had godly people at his table, influencing his children all the time.

Another benefit of hospitality is that the marriage can get boring without the new input of other people. You must have friends in the marriage and hang out with others or boredom can set in.

Having people over is a fabulous way to demonstrate a servant's heart to your children. Your children will watch and learn as you invite "the least of these" and "the hurting" over and minister to them. There are three types of people in the world: those ahead of you spiritually, those like you, and those behind you. All three types of people are helpful to have over.

Hospitality is an amazing anecdote for loneliness. Also, having people in your home is a wonderful way to get to know people on a deeper level. Meeting others at a restaurant is great, but there is something special about meeting in homes.

Some of you are already good at this naturally. To those of you who are not, I'm not suggesting you start having large groups of people in your home all the time. I'm only saying that hospitality is an interesting concept God gave the wise woman to bless her! Yes, *bless her*!

This is not another brick for your already-too-full backpack. I know many of you are just trying to get a good night's sleep and I'm not talking to you. However, this is one of God's methods to bless your family with interesting people. It is one of God's ways of having various people in your home with different opinions so you don't get stuck in a narrow, judgmental mindset. It is, as I said, an opportunity for your children to see servanthood modeled, to learn social skills, and to hear other godly people talk besides you. *A lifestyle of hospitality blesses others, but mostly, it blesses you.*

Isn't it interesting that the overseer in 1 Tim 3 must be hospitable? Being hospitable says so much about a family. People with dark secrets and recurring sin patterns aren't given to hospitality. There is a certain transparency in a family if they have regular hospitality. It's a lost art and we as Christians must bring it back. Our homes are to share. Our lives are to share. This is where the wise woman realizes that God's ways are always meant to bless her and her family, rather than to give her one more thing to do.

I am certainly not the role model in this area. My friends Kendall, Karen, Michelle, and Leslie are, though.

Their homes are repeatedly open to others. Actually, I just stand back and gasp as I watch them minister through hospitality. What beauty these women bring to their families and communities.

One more observation and again, this is not Scripture, but only my opinion: For me (and only me) there has been a direct correlation with my hospitality during the years and my walk with the Lord. I know, that sounds crazy, but it's true. During the times that I was struggling with my walk with the Lord, those are the times my doors were closed. I'm not saying this is true for anyone else, but the correlation in my life is striking.

If your mother was hospitable, seeking to serve others through her home, there's a good chance you watched this and caught it. But to the rest of us, we might need to put on our learning caps and do as the Lord said over and over again in Haggai, "Give careful thought to this."

The problem with hospitality is, of course, how much time, energy, and money it takes. You will have to figure this out for yourself. Having people over also takes forethought, planning, and as I said before, work. Only a woman with margins can be hospitable.

1 Peter 4:9 says, "Show hospitality to one another without grumbling." Romans 12:13 says, "Contribute to the needs of the saints and seek to show hospitality." Titus 1:8 says, "… (an overseer) must be hospitable, a lover of good, self-controlled, upright, holy, and disciplined." The verses go on and on (see the next section on *A Life Well-Lived*).

I used to read those verses on hospitality and think, "Dang, more to do, more to do." Now I read those verses and say, "Wow, that's so like You, God, giving us commands that *bless* us!"

Something to consider…something to consider.

DAY 3
What Is *A Life Well-Lived* for a Woman?

If you search the internet for *A Life Well-Lived*, you will get thousands of people's opinions about what that phrase means. Some of the myriad of examples on the internet were "laughing often, following your dreams, spending your time the way you want, taking care of the earth and its animals," and on and on.

In Bible times, Paul was trying to help the church decide which widows should receive help from the church. Paul gives what I call the "1 Tim 5 List." I have found this list to be remarkable during the years, as it is a beautiful list of activities that signify a woman has had *A Life Well-Lived*.

You might notice that a nice bank account, a good figure, and trips to Hawaii are *not* on the list. I am not saying those things are bad at all; they simply are not on the list.

So let's look at the 1 Tim 5 List and see how Paul thought a woman should have lived in order to receive help from the church in her older years. 1 Timothy 5: 9-10 says that a widow cannot be put on the list to receive help *unless* she is over 60, "has been faithful to her husband, and is well known for her good deeds, such as bringing up children, showing hospitality, washing the feet of the Lord's people, helping those in trouble and devoting herself to all kinds of good deeds."

Catch your breath. That was a power-packed list, wasn't it? Let's look at each item in that list and see what it might say to us.

The first item in the 1 Tim 5 List is that she was faithful to her husband (see Day 1 of this lesson about flirting). The behavior of a woman towards her husband stands as the up front and center tenet to being a godly woman. Being a good wife is exorbitantly valuable in God's eyes, as we have discussed over and over again. It is virtuous and honorable work to be a godly wife. Don't ever forget how important this job is to the Lord. If you honor your husband in a godly manner, you demonstrate to the world how a believer should treat the Lord.

I really like the little phrase that Paul adds next. He says that this widow is well known for her good deeds and then comes the phrase, "such as." I like the phrase "such as." In other words, there are many kinds of "good deeds" and Paul is listing some that he thinks are important, but this is not an exclusive list. Don't you love the freedom here?

Let's get back to the suggestions that Paul thinks are important in the 1 Tim 5 List. I love the first item in the "such as" list. It speaks of the magnificent and meaningful job of *mothering*! "Bringing up children" is the first good deed. I'm so glad that the thing that captures my heart— my children—is also what God has proclaimed a good deed. Children. What a lovely word. Is there a word that is more beautiful, besides the word *Jesus* than *children*? The word rings with love, care, and nurturing. How I love my children and how you love yours. God gave us this intense love for them and it is a beautiful, godly attribute. Godly mothers love their children and want to rear them for the Lord.

The next item Paul lists is *showing hospitality*. (See Day 2 in this lesson). God has given us homes and He wants us to invite others in. I have noticed that women who love hospitality often make efforts to have pretty dishes and care about their curtains and sofas. The Proverbs 31 woman made coverings for her bed. She invested care in her home so that her family could live in peace and beauty and so she could extend the warmth of her home to others. She is not trying to show off, but to nurture and minister. I know this premise can get bent out of shape by women but there is a connection with godly women and a lovely home, a home of cleanliness, order, and beauty. This desire in your heart is God-given. You are right to want to have a welcoming home that nurtures the spirits, souls, and bodies of others. God loves the Christian home!

My goodness, have you noticed how much of Proverbs 31 talks about the food and the furnishings of the home? Did you know it is of the Lord to spend some time and money on making your home attractive? Clean it up, simplify, get rid of the piles and the mess. Your home is an important place. This is where God wants us to have ministry, in our homes! Fix yours up a little bit and then open it up.

The next item on Paul's list of gems is *washing the feet of the Lord's people*. In John 15, Jesus washed his disciples' feet. The obvious implication in this verse is to *humbly assist others*. There is no end to this list. Discover your gifts and give them away to others.

The next phrase in this wisdom-loaded passage is that the 1 Tim 5 woman was *helping those in trouble*. Now, that's something to think about. How much do you like to help those in trouble? Usually, it means there is a wear and tear on you when you help others in trouble as you will be expected to either give time or money, two of your most precious commodities. I love it that Paul doesn't tell us exactly what helping those in trouble looks like. He knows that we will figure this out. I love the freedom here, that we can minister through our gifts to help those in trouble.

The last phrase that Paul lists in order for the 1 Tim 5 widow to make the cut to be put on the assistance list is the knock-out punch. This little phrase should describe our daily life. When other people talked about this 1 Tim 5 woman, they didn't say, "She's the best dressed woman I know." "Her jewelry is exquisite." "Have you ever seen anyone with such gorgeous hair?" What they said about her was that *she was devoting herself to all kinds of good deeds*. This woman *was a giver, not a taker*. She had a lifestyle of being *useful and helpful*. When I run into a woman who is older and still obsessed about what restaurant she is going to, what cruise she just took, or where the designer jewelry show is being held, I know I am dealing with a woman who would *not* make the cut.

Dedie is a woman in her sixties at my church who just got back from a missionary trip to China. I talked to her daughter recently, who told me how *she hoped to be like her mother* when she got older. On Sunday, I saw Dedie in the kitchen at church, serving lunch. My hunch is that Dedie would make the cut.

Yes, it's alright to buy cream to get rid of your wrinkles and yes, you can take nice trips. But is *your very inmost being* about being a godly woman who devotes herself to all kinds of good deeds?

The natural downhill slope is to become more selfish and more self-absorbed as you age. But God's Word can change you. God's Spirit can change you. You can become a woman who could make the cut on Paul's list. Now is the time to think about what *A Life Well-Lived* looks like, and make adjustments to move in that direction.

DAY 4
Conquering Discouraging Thinking

As you know, school doesn't teach you the most important lessons in life. You don't learn how to have rich relationships, you don't learn about health, no one teaches you the proper use of finances nor do they teach you to discover and use your gifts—to name a few important subjects in life. You certainly don't learn how to think properly about the obstacles and disappointments in life. I didn't know there was a way to *think* until a few years ago and it truly changed my life.

I am not talking about when a person is born again, and they receive a new nature in Christ. That rebirth transforms *your spirit.* We will discuss that aspect in regards to being discouraged in a moment. Right now however, I'm talking about a skill that *saved or unsaved people* can learn as it is *mental*. This skill is *to monitor the thoughts that enter our minds.* Instead of letting negative thoughts meander around our brains unchecked, we are to control and choose which thoughts we decide are allowed to hang around awhile.

God has given Christ-followers a list of what to think about in Philippians 4:8. The thoughts that are profitable to think about are the ones that are "true… honorable… just… pure… lovely… commendable… excellent… or worthy of praise." We are not to think about what is "awful, terrible, horrible, upsetting, sinful, or disappointing" all the time.

An example might help. This last weekend something happened to one of my children that if it had happened eight years ago, I would have fallen through the floor. (One nice thing about having six kids is that no one ever knows which child I'm talking about.) I mean honestly, eight years ago, I would have become unglued if this same situation would have happened. But since I have learned Philippians 4:8 thinking, I was able to sail through, think proactively, and not dive down into emotional hysteria.

There are several aspects to Philippians 4:8 thinking which we will now discuss.

The first thought to immediately think when you are presented with bad news is, "Somehow, God will use this for good in my life and in the lives of those I love, even though I can't see it right now." That kind of thinking—that there is a glad surprise around the river bend—will immediately pull you up and out a bit. We extract this truth from Jeremiah 29:11 and Romans 8:28. The ugliness of your current circumstance will try to tell you how bad this situation is. Having these sentences written in your Turquoise Journal are helpful to have when unwanted situations arrive.

Another thought that is helpful to think is that "although this seems horrible right now, other *people have had hard things* like this before and *they recover* and conquer the situation. Just because this seems horrible/ terrible/ crummy-to-the-max at the moment, we will get through this because God can shift things. God gives His children the ability to rise and press forward. We do not have to stay in ditches. Yes, this is an unwanted circumstance, but *how I think about something determines my emotions.*" (Remember the alley/park examples? Week 2, Day 1). If I can believe/think that God is for me, that God can see the whole picture, *that I am* not *helpless*, but instead, I am actually very resourceful with God's creativity pumping through my mind, *then* I can hugely corral my emotions in a positive direction.

Another example of what to say to yourself when faced with unwanted circumstances is a sentence like, "At least it is not X or Y" (think of something worse). This thinking enables you to access your gratefulness buttons and be glad for what this *wasn't* (it can always be worse).

In contrast, if I let my weak mind tumble down into "how terrible, how awful, I'll never recover from this situation, we'll never be able to fix this," not only will my emotions go bonk, my creativity for problem solving will be hindered.

For example, let's say something tremendously severe happens to you, such as your daughter gets pregnant out of wedlock. That's a very harsh situation to happen to a Christian family. The embarrassment, the questions about whether the kids should get married, decisions about who rears the baby, etc. are *huge*. That trial is heart-breaking for Christian families.

If that trial happens (God forbid), the first thing to do is to fight all the millions of downer thoughts that would come pressing into your mind. Try to replace them with Philippians 4:8 thoughts. Examples would be "God is going to eventually use this situation to bless our family." "Other Christian families have gone through this and it didn't undo them." "This won't change how people who love me view me." "God has a plan to bless this baby." "God has a plan to use this in the life of my daughter." "We have the resourcefulness to find out how other people who have had this trial have coped…" and on and on. If you fall into "This is awful, this is terrible, how will I take this?" you will not only be terribly upset, but you can't minister to others, because you need ministering to. In these situations, you need to rise above circumstances, be the voice of reason, the voice of hope, the voice of sanity, the voice of overcoming (not the voice of *poor-pitiful-me* and *how-will-I-make-it?*)

Proverbs 31:25 says "She is clothed with strength and dignity." You can't portray strength and dignity if you are belly-aching in a ditch because your weak mind is out-of-control with negative thoughts. You have to believe God is going to use this hard circumstance for good and go forth in that faith. You have to control your mind and not let those negative, *how-horrible-this-is* thoughts parade across the screen of your brain.

We are to "gird up the loins of our mind" (1 Peter 1:13). Loins were the long, flowing parts of robes that people wore in Biblical times. If they needed to walk fast or work, they would gird up the loins of their garments so the flowing, cumbersome loins wouldn't get in the way. We are to gird up the loins of our mind, not letting the flowing, cumbersome thoughts get in the way. Your negative, *woe-is-me-this-is-terrible* thoughts need to be girded up. They are not helpful; they are damaging. Kick them out of your mind by intentionally thinking about something else. Refuse to let non-Philippians 4:8 thoughts rest in your mind.

This Philippians 4:8 thinking has been life-altering to me. Just a few minutes ago, I was getting chicken off the bone for soup tonight and rather randomly, I thought about how I had *failed in a significant area*. The thought tiptoed in and wanted a seat in my brain's living room. "No-sir-ee," I said, "I'm not going to go down that discouraging path" and I got busy thinking about something else. We are not helpless with our emotions and mental health! Your thoughts are powerful but you can battle your non-Philippians 4:8 thoughts.

The angst from this weekend's blow has already subsided to some extent. But actually, I feel like I usually do in the morning. No despair. Not down and out. In fact, I have joy this morning. Hope. Faith. "For I know the plans I have for you, plans to prosper you and give you a hope and a future." I choose to believe that God gave us this trial as an eventual blessing and to do us good.

Memorize Jeremiah 29:11. Believe it. God is for you. There is a glad surprise around the river bend.

Learning to think like this not only allows you to enjoy the internal landscape of your brain more, it makes you a much more delightful wife and mother. The woman is the heart of her home and if she is a Philippians 4:8 thinker, that means she is watering her family with positive thoughts, affecting how the others in the home think.

A young man was here this weekend, thinking life was terrible. "This situation is not terrible and horrible," I reminded him, "only highly inconvenient." We have to help young people learn to think right, too.

Use your Turquoise Journal to list the benefits of trials and unwanted circumstances. Frame the trial in a positive light. Don't give any room to negative, pessimistic, down-and-out thinking. Be a woman who is clothed with strength and dignity and controls her thoughts, not a weak-willed, whiny alley cat. Be mentally strong and simultaneously, be ridiculously soft in your heart. (Now that's a combo in a woman that I admire!)

I was a complete loser in this area for the longest time, but God has given me "beauty for ashes" (Isaiah 61:3). He can do that for you, too.

I repeatedly harp on your mental health and exhort you to be a "happy, grateful, person-in-a-good-mood" because it is imperative if you want to be a delightful spouse (and as I've said, for you to enjoy you). Grouchy, negative, upset, depressed, unhappy women drain the life out of everyone (and what a bummer to live with yourself). You will have many difficult and unwanted circumstances during your life. Since that is the norm, why do you kick and scream when it happens? Instead, learn to calmly say to yourself (I actually have sentences like these written down in my journals), "Oh, here's a trial. Yes, this is highly unwanted, but I know these things happen. I will face it, walk through it, pray over it, research it, get counsel for it, and then, I will not let it dominate my thinking. I will put it on the shelf in heaven where I know God is using it for my good, even though I can't see it right now. Yes, I will proactively seek solutions. However, I will not let this disappointment turn into discouragement. Life includes disappointment, but that is not synonymous with *discouragement.* Discouragement comes from repeatedly *thinking* about disappointment. Heaven will be free from disappointments, but life on earth will have an abundance of them. Therefore, I will learn to live above my trials by controlling my thoughts (focusing on what is good and guarding against thinking about what is missing and disappointing)."

You do not have to be "a wave of the sea, blown and tossed by the wind" (James 1:6). This is a perfect description of what unguarded, negative, non-Philippians 4:8 thoughts do to your brain.

Let's discuss the spiritual aspect of discouragement. This morning, I read Ephesians 6:10-20 about spiritual warfare. Verse 12 says, "For our struggle is not against flesh and blood, but against the rulers, against the authorities, against the powers of this dark world and against the spiritual forces of evil in the heavenly realms." Friends, you have an Enemy, seeking to destroy and devour you. Don't try to fight him in your own strength. In the presence of the Lord, say to Satan, "Satan, get thee behind me. I don't come against you in my own strength, but in the name of the Lord Jesus Christ, be gone!" (That's not praying to the devil. Dr. Rogers used to say it was like saying scat to a cat.) Spiritual warfare is real and alive. Pray a hedge of protection around your children, begging

God to protect them from evil. Pray that the peace of God that surpasses understanding (Phil. 4:7) is downloaded to you from God. You have access to this peace as well as access to His phenomenal guidance (Is. 30:21).

We are body, soul (mental), and spirit. Let's quickly talk about the physical side of discouragement. A woman who repeatedly eats a lot of sugar and refined carbs throws off her hormones. The women in my *Skinny School* groups say they have recovered their sanity by ditching sugar and unhealthy starches. We are mental-spiritual-physical beings and we must repeatedly address all three areas. You know how easy it is to be a coward when you are exhausted.

Discouragement is not something you have to accept and live with. Yes, you have to accept and live with your *disappointing* circumstances, but not with *discouragement*. The difference in the life of a woman with a happy heart over the years (versus one who is not) is like a bank account where $1000 is deposited weekly for ten years versus one where $1 is deposited weekly for the same time. I admit that for years, I often struggled with discouragement before God opened up this truth and told me that I could conquer it with His help.

This morning, my seventeen year old and I were talking as he walked out the door to school and he said something that could have been interrupted as abrasive. But because my heart was full and happy, I laughed and said, "Well, good-bye, Affirming and Encouraging Son." He laughed and then went on to explain how "he was like me in this area and that it really wasn't so bad if you look at it like this, blah, blah". He hadn't meant to be abrasive. I just had not understood him. So we laughed and shared a moment. What if my heart had been down when he said that? What if I was offended and started harshly correcting him instead of the light-hearted path? Girls, there are no/none/zero excuses if you are a Debbie-Downer. Slice off her head!

Go back and reread all the lessons on a happy heart, contentment, laughing at the days to come, etc. until you figure out how to get a heart that sings and rejoices in the portion you were given, knowing that *you call on a God who listens, a God who cares, a God who moves in response to prayer*. Fix your mind, fix your prayer life, and you'll fix your discouragement.

*Years *after* I wrote the above article, I wrote the book, *Happy School*. It is my favorite of all my books as the principles changed my life so drastically. As I've said before, after you are through with this study, I hope you will take 9 weeks and go through *Happy School* and the *Happy School Study Guide*. I have methodically broken down the journey for you from a chronically discouraged heart to a happy heart.

DAY 5
Losses Accumulate with Age

One thing I've noticed about aging women is that if they are not walking closely with Jesus, some harsh characteristics inevitably appear. For example, I just got off the phone with a man about an event in which he and I are both on the publicity committee. He is very polite, competent, and honest. We were discussing the pros and cons of certain aspects of the event. As he was giving his opinion, in the background I could hear the harsh, shrill voice of his wife, correcting him, giving him non-negotiable advice, all with a recalcitrant, angry tone. He kept talking in a calm manner, incorporating what she said.

I was very uncomfortable as I listened to the obvious tension and emotional turmoil in his wife. I've known this woman from afar for many years and it seems that as she has aged, she is more self-absorbed—and less self-aware. If women don't constantly apply the principles in 1 Peter 3, Titus 2, and Proverbs 31, *this is sadly the natural downhill slide.* As the losses accumulate for aging women, they can become more opinionated, less gracious, and more contentious. We should be *more* loving, walk closer with Jesus, be more concerned with other people than ever, and more willing to be a poured out drink offering. I know this is hard for aging women because they lose so much of the power and influence that the culture gives them for their youth and beauty.

If you are aging and find yourself getting easily annoyed, telling people off, foregoing graciousness, or becoming cynical, then it's time for you to spend some time with Jesus in confession and repentance. Jesus said He didn't come to be served, but to serve and give His life as a ransom. As we walk with Jesus, we should be more foregoing, more accepting, more forgiving, more gracious, more generous, and more compassionate.

We certainly should be more foregoing, patient, and forgiving of our husbands. As they age, they will slow down and inevitably, need more grace from us.

Charm is deceitful and beauty fades, but a woman who fears the Lord is to be praised. A woman who fears the Lord will get more beautiful in her spirit as she ages.

Prayer

Today's prayer is from Habakkuk 3:17-19. I thought it was perfect to go along with Day 4 on *Conquering Discouraging Thinking*.

>Dear Lord,
>
>Even though the fig trees have no blossoms,
>and there are no grapes on the vines;
>Even though the olive crop fails,
>and the fields lie empty and barren;
>Even though the flocks die in the fields,
>and the cattle barns are empty,
>YET I will rejoice in the Lord!
>I will be joyful in the God of my salvation!
>The Sovereign Lord is my strength!
>He makes me as surefooted as a deer,
>able to tread upon the heights.
>
>God, continue to teach me how to be as surefooted as a deer, so that I can tread upon the heights in the midst of unwanted circumstances. Help me to remember that You are my strength! Christ in me! Alone, I fail; with You, I soar.
>
>In Jesus's name,
>
>Amen

Assignments and Group Discussion Questions

1. Have you ever considered flirting as "crossing the line" before? What are your thoughts about this subject?

2. Have you felt like hospitality was a burden before? Do you see now that it is something God gave us to bless us?

3. When you think of *A Life Well-Lived*, what do you think of? What did Paul's teaching say to you?

4. How are you doing with your mental health? Do you have a happy heart? Or are you given repeatedly to discouragement? What is God trying to say to you?

WEEK 18

Giving Your Input, a Happy Heart, A Test...and More

Contents

Day 1: Two of the Most Important Wife Skills

Day 2, Part A: How to Give Your Husband Your Input

Day 2, Part B: When You Are Grieved by Your Husband's Lack of Spirituality

Day 3: The Advanced Wife Skill of Communicating Contentment

Day 4: More on a Happy Heart

Day 5: Are You a Marriage Champion Yet? A Test to See

Chapter 18 in *Wife School* is *When Your Husband Doesn't Reciprocate or Try to Meet Your Needs.* You will be reminded that contradicting, correcting, and negatively teasing your husband upsets him. These *foxes in the vineyard* may unknowingly be *under your radar*. Little things count in marriage.

DAY 1
Two of the Most Important Wife Skills

There are numerous wife skills that we have learned in our study together, but I want to again re-emphasize what is the Big Kahuna and what is the Big Cheese. Even women who have been studying this material for years admit they continue to wrestle with doing/giving these two skills/concepts to their husbands.

The first of the two most important wife skills/concepts to master is *to quit trying to fix, change, or lead your husband.* Of course, you can give your input to him and *Wife School* discusses how to appropriately do this multiple times. But being in commander-mode is a wife's natural propensity and this tendency *absolutely slays* a husband's affection toward his wife. Men do not like being bossed around.

I realize that your husband's weakness set drives you bonkers, so therefore you try to fix, change, and lead him. How interesting it is to note, however, that a woman's weakness set *doesn't drive her husband bonkers* (as long as there is not too much emotional turmoil and he's getting enough sex.) Did you get that? Husbands are not the primary ones who try to change and fix us; *we are the ones* who want to change and fix them. (Reread chapter 2 in *Wife School* on Acceptance for more review.)

Guess where this struggle comes from? "Your desire will be for your husband, and he will rule over you." That's right, your desire to *change, fix, and lead your husband* has been going on since Genesis 3. This trait of contentiousness has been in the female DNA since the Garden.

Even with you becoming the new and improved Wife of the World, your husband will still have his weakness set until the day he dies. If you don't deal with this issue of *accepting his weakness set,* you will communicate disapproval to him. And friend, communicating disapproval to your husband is Trouble with a capital T. *Men do not feel affection* toward women who communicate disapproval towards them.

I absolutely love the way Scripture nails it when it discusses our greatest struggle of contentiousness as early as Genesis 3. But then, just as remarkable, the antidote to our struggle is given in 1 Peter 3: "…your inner self, the unfading beauty of a gentle and quiet spirit, which is of great worth in God's sight."

The antidote for fixing, changing, and leading your husband is to instead, have a gentle and quiet spirit. There is only one way to get a gentle and quiet spirit and honestly, it's not very glamorous. It is found by asking yourself the biggest question of any woman's life: "Who will rule my life? Who will sit on the throne of my heart and rule?" That is the billion dollar question for any woman. You can learn charm, good sentences to say to your husband during conflict, and all sorts of wonderful strategy to help him understand you, but *until your heart is surrendered to the One who created it,* you will not have a gentle and quiet spirit. And without a gentle and quiet spirit, you will attempt to fix, correct, and lead your husband. This boxing match between you and your husband will continue until either the day one spouse dies or until *you get your commander-personality in check.*

Realize that every day, your tendency to fix, change, and lead your husband will surface. This one action of yours—slaying your contentious spirit—will do more to change and improve your marriage than anything else, uh, well, except skill/concept number two, which we will now discuss.

Here comes number two. Maybe you should go get a cup of coffee first. Then, take a deep breath before you jump into this next tank of cold water.

Women, the number two skill/concept we have to learn is to understand the *enormity* of a man's sex drive. Actually, there is so much science available now that documents the huge discrepancy between a man's desire and a woman's that this is no longer an issue that women have to take on faith from their mothers. (Again, I remind you, this is only true in 80% of marriages. Reread chapter 32 in *Wife School* if your marriage is in the 20%). Understanding and accepting men's voracious appetites for sex is difficult because it's like telling you that although you need to sleep 8 hours a night, this other person needs to sleep 16 hours a day. No, that's not even a good analogy, because the numbers are much larger than just *double*. The numbers are as large as "men want sex 37 times more than women." I can't even think of anything that is an analogy where something else is up to 37 times more. I mean, *it's a crazy difference*. It's not your experience and you don't have this appetite. It's very difficult for women to accept something they don't feel and don't see. It's like saying there is a new color in the rainbow, sloom, and you can't see it or experience it. That's what it's like for women to understand this appetite of men for sex. We can't see or feel it. So our tendency is to dismiss it, or at the least, minimize it.

If you reread chapter 9 in *Wife School*, you'll be reminded how to navigate this discrepancy in sexual appetites. Again, you'll see that the first step in sex is not *arousal* but *willingness*. You'll also be reminded how we give our husbands a drink of lemonade when they are thirsty because we love them. This whole paradigm stands on the premise that we meet a need in our husband because that's what love looks like. We figure out how to make our husbands happy because as Proverbs 31 women, we "bring them good, not harm, all the days of our life" (Proverbs 31:12).

Let me remind you once again that you, the wife, are the only legitimate sex that your husband is allowed. That's right, just you, babe.

And guess what else I've recently learned? Sex is incredibly *good* for men. And I mean lots of sex. Just explore this on the internet and see as the studies abound. Forbes.com on NBCnews.com said "that by having sex three or more times a week, men reduced their risk of heart attack or stroke by half." By half! What may seem like an inconvenience and burden to you is *lifeblood* to your husband. When women learn about men and their sexual appetites, and then make huge allowances to satisfy men in this area in the marriage, men get happy.

As you now know, when husbands get happy in the marriage, they turn to you, open to you, and allow you to *influence* them. There, my young chickadee, is where *you* become satisfied in the marriage. As I mentioned earlier, researcher John Gottman found that husbands who accept their wives' influence are four times *less likely* to divorce or have an unhappy marriage.

There are umpteen-and-one skills to learn to become a Marriage Champion. But rules number one and two cannot be overlooked.

DAY 2, PART A
How to Give Your Husband Your Input

I wish I had known the skill of how to give my input to my husband years ago. Learning this skill is actually easy and has hugely changed how my husband *receives* my input. I used to tell my husband, "I think you should do X." Men don't like that. They feel you are telling them what to do. Now I say, "I want to give you an idea that you may or may not like. It is only a suggestion. I want to give it to you as input, so that you can consider it when you make your decision." La la la, much, much better.

Some other sentences I say before I drop suggestions are, "This is only a suggestion and an idea. It may not work, but here's the idea." Then he feels the freedom to take it or reject it. Another sentence you can say is, "I'm only brainstorming with what I'm going to tell you. These ideas may not work at all. But maybe this idea will help you think of the right one." Fingertip-offer your opinion like that. Not, "Do this, Bozo, because your way is ridiculous." (That's how our husbands hear our commands.)

Do you see the quantum difference? In my old style, there was a pressure to do what I recommended. In the new-and-improved-me, I am only giving input and possible suggestions. It is obvious to my husband that he is still in control of making the final decision. Men can take input all day long as long as they know they are the final decision makers.

Honestly, I must use a version of the *input* paragraph five times a week. Yes, really, I do. I help my husband with the marketing of his business so it is especially tricky when I give suggestions about his work. He does *not* want me telling him what to do, but he appreciates my input when it is offered as *take it or leave it*.

I have written this before but it is important so I will repeat it again: Once you give your husband your advice, suggestions, input, remember, they are now *his*. Later, you don't say, "Wow, I'm so glad I thought of that. I'm a pretty savvy cookie." No, it's now *his idea* if he takes it. You were created to be a help-meet so don't get all bent out of shape when you don't get the credit. (Reread Chapter 24, *When Your Husband Doesn't Appreciate You* in *Wife School* for more review.)

DAY 2, PART B
When You Are Grieved by Your Husband's Lack of Spirituality

Many women ruminate over their grief that their husband is not more spiritual. He doesn't desire the Word or prayer as much as the wife would like. Possibly, the husband has some sin habits that aggravate the wife. For sure, the husband doesn't lead the family as he should. What's a wife to do?

Before we get started, let's examine how well you're doing spiritually as a wife. I will give you the Philippians 2 Test and you rate yourself on each of these. Score yourself 1-10, with 10 being "Yes, I am excellent at this." Ready? Write your answers in the blanks below.

1. Phil 2:3a "Do nothing out of selfish ambition or vain conceit." Score: _____
2. Phil. 2:3b "Rather, in humility value others above yourselves." Score: _____
3. Phil. 2:4 "… not looking to your own interests but each of you to the interests of others." Score: _____
4. Phil. 2:7 We are to have the mindset of Christ, such as, "by taking the very nature of a servant." Score: _____
5. Phil. 2:14 "Do everything without grumbling or arguing." Score: _____
6. Phil. 2:21 "For everyone looks out for their own interests, not those of Jesus Christ." Score: _____

How did you do on the test? I imagine you were pierced to the heart, just like I was. We are sinners, friends, in need of fresh mercy every morning (Lamentations 3). We keep forgetting that. We live *far below* where we are called to live. And we keep forgetting that our husbands are merely human, too. What often happens in marriage is that wives blame husbands for not being more *spiritual*. Honestly, we need to look in the mirror.

We want our husbands to be Jesus and lead us. But contrarily, the Scripture says if our husbands are disobedient to the Word, then we are to "call them up" with our gentle and quiet spirits (1 Peter 3), not with emotional turmoil and a lecture.

Here are some Scriptural truths to think about when your husband sins or fails:

When a woman was caught in adultery, Jesus said, "Let any one of you who is without sin be the first to throw a stone at her" (John 8:7).

Jesus' advice to his disciples when they wanted to judge others was, "…first take the plank out of your eye, and then you will see clearly to remove the speck from your brother's eye" (Luke 6:42).

Paul's advice to the church in Rome was to "…Accept one another, then, just as Christ accepted you" (Romans 15:7).

It is possible that you have been given to your husband to "draw him up", though not by your words, but by your *heart*. This is what *influence* is all about. Focus on your heart and work on that. Live purely. This lifestyle will call him up.

Be grateful for what your husband brings to the marriage instead of focusing on What is Missing and Disappointing (the WMDs). This incessant thing we do as women where we repeatedly attempt to change our husbands is insane. *Change yourself.* I'm pretty sure that the items in the Phil 2 Test are enough to keep you busy for a while (and maybe off your husband's back.)

Of course, there's a time to speak the truth in love. But most women err on the side of too much judging, correcting, and criticizing. Hopefully, not you, my Proverbs 31 friend.

DAY 3
The Advanced Wife Skill of Communicating Contentment

A man wants a happy wife. Not only does he enjoy her delightful spirit, but it also tells him he's doing a good job as a husband. Get your heart happy in the Lord and then out of the blue, unexpected, text or tell your husband how happy you are *living life with him.*

For example, when one woman was out-of-town and away from her husband, she texted him, "When I woke up, I looked over to see if you were awake. Then I realized you weren't there. I'm so glad you are there most mornings. How happy I am with our life and how I love being married to you."

When women text these emotional things to their husbands, they expect the husband to text back, "And you are the queen of the world." But often they text back, "Thanks." Please don't get offended. Your husband recorded your gift in his mind. He doesn't know you'd like a mushy text back but you have 30-40 years to teach him, right?

Again, do not be offended at your husband's lack of emotional/romantic words and gestures. This need you have is not on his radar yet. As you know, it's hard to teach kids to pick up their rooms, to not use their sleeve to wipe their noses, and to say thank you. But it can be done and your husband can learn that *you have needs for expressions of affection.* Just be patient, be patient some more, stay in the game, not slamming him, but filling him with the 8 A's. When you see a glimmer of a behavior that you like, praise it once and then praise it again.

You should be starting to get the male psyche by now. You are beginning to understand how to coax this tiger. Tell him and show him often, in a million different ways, "I'm happy being married to you."

DAY 4
More on a Happy Heart

I know I pound this topic, but a happy heart is imperative in order to delight your husband.

Another aspect to learn in order to have a happy heart is that you must learn to frame things in the best light in your mind. This morning I texted a person to invite them to dinner. They texted back, "I'll have to let you know later." Just being honest, I was a little offended. (Hey, just because I'm the teacher doesn't mean I have this stuff mastered)! I thought to myself, "Well, they want to keep their options open and see if something better comes up." See how negative that was? I had no idea why this person needed to let me know later. Maybe they already had plans and super-want to be with me for dinner (haha) and they are going to see how they can rearrange their schedule so they can come.

Now *that* is Philippians 4:8 thinking, framing things in the best light. (The exception for this is if a woman is single and a guy sends messages to her like that. He is saying, "I'm Just Not That into You" so she should take off and bat her eyes at someone else.)

To continue, you have one of two habits. One is that you tend to think the worst. Or two, you automatically reframe things for the best. Actually, either ditch can be a problem, but if you have to err, err on the side of reframing the situation for the best. I'm not encouraging you to live pie-in-the-sky with your eyes closed to reality. I am trying to tell you that you have so much control over your thoughts, and therefore, your subsequent emotions. Sometimes we have to face the truth of a bad situation, I agree. But there is facing the situation with hope…or despair. You can always choose the thoughts you let into your brain.

Viktor Frankl was in a concentration camp in Germany during World War II. Later, he wrote an excellent book called *Man's Search for Meaning.* Even with the atrocities and horrors of Auschwitz, some people still chose to share their bread. Frankl wrote, "The last of human freedoms – is the ability to choose one's attitude in a given set of circumstances." (If you are struggling with self-pity, just search the internet for images of the concentration camps at Auschwitz. You will quickly blast out of your self-pity.)

Years ago I heard the phrase, "Bloom where you are planted." When I heard that, I thought, "Impossible. No one could bloom here with the heaviness of what I have." Friends, I was ridiculously wrong! We can be a sunrise in the lives of others, no matter where we are planted. At that time, I was eaten up with self-pity. I didn't know how to think at that point in my life. I let Mr. Disappointing Thing rule the landscape of my mind, walking in whenever he wanted and staying as long as he decided. No longer! He has been booted to the alley.

It will be an amazing day when you take responsibility for having a happy heart, not blaming anyone else. The day when you decide to bloom where you are planted, your life will change. This is not accomplished by looking at how others give to and love you, but by looking at how you *give to and love others.* God says that His grace is sufficient. I'm pretty sure that verse covers both you and me.

Just to be super clear here, I am not talking about *true grief and sadness.* Of course, those are normal human reactions to deep tragedy. But friends! We get all wadded up over not being invited, not given enough attention, or by being overlooked when the high treatment is passed out. It is time to lay down our self-pity.

DAY 5
Are You a Marriage Champion Yet? A Test to See.

This is week 18 out of 22. Four more weeks of lessons coming down the pipe. How are you doing in *Wife School*? Today we are going to have a little test. If you score 6 out of 6, then you are already a Marriage Champion. I will pick one of our past lessons, *Asking Your Husband for What You Want*, and we'll see how you do.

Here we go:

1. Before you ask your husband for what you want in your marriage, what two major premises/situations should you first be rocking?
2. Before you ask your husband for what you want in your marriage, what strategy do you apply to the list of all the things you want?
3. When you ask your husband for what you want in your marriage, what is your demeanor? And what about the timing?
4. When you ask your husband for what you want and he balks, what do you say?
5. If your husband continues to not give you what you want in the marriage, how do you respond in your mind?
6. If your husband gives you what you want, how do you respond?

Okay, here are the answers. Score yourself. Give yourself one point for every question you answered right.

1. Before you ask your husband for anything, you should get the emotional turmoil out of your life (chop off her head, remember?) and you should be daily rocking the 8 A's, especially the 7th A of Affection which is sex.
2. Before you ask your husband for what you want in your marriage, you should rank everything you want and only ask for the top one (or two at most) things, knowing you are on the 50-year-plan and will eventually be able to ask for all you want. Asking him for a lot at once overwhelms him.
3. When you ask your husband for something in your marriage, your demeanor should be sweet and soft, not commander-mode of "you better do this, Buddy, or else." Also, you should select a good time, not when he is upset or tired.
4. When your husband balks at what you want, you sweetly say, "I try to meet all of your needs. I try to not ask for very much, only my very top things. I want you to give this to me just because you love me." Then, you drop it. You don't continue to argue your case. You repeat, "I want you to give this to me just because you love me." Note: This would be very manipulative if you are *not* seeking to meet your husband's needs with your whole heart. I am assuming you are.
5. If your husband does not give you what you want the first time you ask, you realize it may take 1-50 times of asking. Teaching husbands what you want is like teaching someone Chinese. Don't resent this. This is a law of marriage, just like gravity is a law of physics.
6. If your husband gives you what you want, you praise him to the moon and back at least two times, and preferably more. Your happiness is very satisfying to your husband. He feels like a good husband according to your happiness in the marriage.

How did you do, *Wife School* student? Anybody get 6 out of 6?

One More Thought

I recently met with a woman who told me about multiple trials she was facing. Honestly, they were pretty significant in my opinion. However, she then told me that she had a heart full of gratefulness, that she continually "guarded her thoughts" and focused *on the good in her life*, not on the WMDs (What's Missing and Disappointing).

Gratefulness is indeed *the key* to happiness. Friends, this is beautiful. Are you doing that? Are you living above your circumstances because you focus on all the many benefits and blessings that you have? Or are you still wallowing around in self-pity? My prayer is that your life will be grafted into the Vine and His sap will flow generously through you (John 15) teaching you to become an extremely grateful and happy person.

Prayer

Dear God,

I come into Your gates with thanksgiving and enter Your courts with praise. Today, I thank You for my eyesight and that I can therefore see the sweet faces of my children. I thank You for legs that can walk and enable me to do my daily tasks for my family. Thank You that I have healthy food nearby to buy for my family as well as good hospitals if I need them.

I thank You for indoor plumbing, heat, and air conditioning. I thank you for soft beds, comfortable house shoes, apples, white jeans, and flip-flops. I thank you for friends to laugh with, family that shows up when I need help, a husband who is kind, faithful, and employed, and children that rise up and praise You.

I thank You for a mind that can read a recipe, figure out how to use an iPhone, and can read your Word. I thank you for sunshine, clean air, and a free hour to lie in the sun.

Thank you, God, for books, for blogs, and for the internet. Thank You for daughters that radiate goodness, for sons that understand the call to provide and protect, and for healthy parents.

Thank You for roses, for swimming pools, and for strawberries.

Thank You for the ability to enjoy life. Thank you for the peace that comes from being forgiven. Thank You for the comfort of Your presence and the gift of Your guidance. Thank You for this one chance at life. May I honor You with my entire being during my short stay on planet Earth.

And when hard things come, which they will as surely as the fact that I will soon need another breath, may You give me the grace to believe that You're in control, that You will do me good through the situation, and that You can find a way to bless those I love, even though I can't see any of that. May I remember that when the winds blow and the storms beat down that You created the winds and the storms and can stop them whenever You choose.

In Jesus name,

Amen

Assignments and Group Discussion Questions

1. In the article in Day 1, *Two of the Most Important Wife Skills*, how are you doing?

2. How are you doing at giving your husband your input?

3. Are you able to get hold of your emotions when you and your husband have conflict?

4. Are you grieved at your husband's lack of spirituality? How did you do on the Phil. 2 test?

5. Do you often tell your husband how happy you are just to be married to him?

6. How would you rate your happy heart? Great? Moderate? In need of an overhaul?

7. How did you do on the Marriage Champion Test?

WEEK 19

Conflict, a Bossy Husband, Disappointment in Others...and More

Contents

Day 1: Celebrating Your Husband's Victories with Him
Day 2: Getting Hold of Your Emotions When You Have Conflict
Day 3: What to Do When Your Husband is Bossy and Inconsiderate of Your Opinion, Part 1
Day 4: What to Do When Your Husband is Bossy and Inconsiderate of Your Opinion, Part 2
Day 5: Cynicism and the Continual Disappointment in Others

Chapter 19 in *Wife School* is *What to Do When the In-laws Are a Problem*. This is one of the top struggles that couples face in marriage. For more review on in-laws, see Week 7, Day 5 and also, Week 16, Day 1 in this study guide.

DAY 1
Celebrating Your Husband's Victories with Him

We have discussed how you need to show up with empathy when your husband has a trial or failure (see Week 3, Day 2). Today we will also discuss how you need to show up in a magnificent way when your husband has a victory. There is one main person a husband longs to celebrate his achievements with, and that's you, his sweet and encouraging wife!

When your husband has a victory, either small or large, you don't just say, "Well done. Good job. So, what time is the game on?" No, instead, you ask him *all* about it, wanting as many details as possible (he will love this). You are excited and happy for him, as well as proud of him. Don't assume he knows this. Tell him. How we all *long* for someone to be proud of us.

Say something like, "I can't believe you were chosen with so much other competition!" Later you might say, "Your persistent work ethic really paid off. I am bursting open because I am so proud of you!" Possibly, you could bring it up in front of his parents (he especially likes this), the kids (always, always), and if appropriate (and not too braggy), your friends. (FYI: Praising your husband in front of friends is tricky. Friends get annoyed with very much of this. Spread your bragging around about your husband, and not very much with any one person. Strangers are great, ha ha. Your husband will love it all.)

Remember, you are the main person he wants to be excited for him. As I said, we all desire our spouses be excited with us about our wins and achievements. But also remember, we have *double standards* in celebrating victories. We celebrate victories to the max with others and yet, we try to have no expectations that others will do that for us. We endeavor to get our affirmation from the Lord. Anything anyone else gives us is a *bonus*.

Celebrating your husband's victories in spades is guaranteed to delight him.

DAY 2
Getting Hold of Your Emotions When You Have Conflict

The most common problem I see with wives is that they speak to their husbands with *emotional turmoil* or with *disrespect.* This tenet of *Wife School* is so important to your husband's affection for you (and for him to open to your influence) that I am addressing it again.

Recently, David and I had a unique situation/problem that we needed to address. We had talked about it and then talked about it again. I told him that I had given this circumstance a lot of thought again and wanted to give him some new ideas on how to handle the situation. So, I presented my new suggestions/ideas to him.

At first, David shot my ideas down. He didn't like them at all. I sat there, looking at him, thinking, "Oh, dear. Here's another hard marriage conflict to navigate." Wring, wring hands. But I didn't let any disappointment show.

Instead, I said, "What about x?" and I offered an additional idea.

Again, he didn't like it. With much restraint, I hid my large disappointment. No emotional escalation, although I was definitely feeling it.

Honestly, I wanted to say some rather rough things here. It would be easy to be sarcastic, snide, or unpleasant because after all, I had given this situation a lot of thought. However, I know that "death and life are in the power of the tongue" so thankfully, *this time, I held mine.*

Back to the story. After a long silence, David said, "Here's what I think we should do" and began to tell me.

This was almost comical. I was so shocked because *his suggestion was so dang generous*. I thought he was going to completely shoot down all my suggestions, but instead, he *improved* them.

What if I had unloaded on him? What if I had expressed great disappointment for his lack of excitement at my ideas? (Believe me, I have done this wrong too many times to count.) Wives, we have to get control of our emotional reactions. There are often presents with big bows right around the river bend!

What is amazing about this story is that the end result is exceedingly, abundantly over what I had ever hoped for in the beginning. In fact, it took me a little while to believe this was happening. I kept thinking he was going to withdraw the suggestion, saying, "Oh, I didn't understand you at first. No, that's not what I meant. I take it back."

But he did mean it. He was being crazily generous.

There were a few places, as I said, at the beginning of our conversation, when the thought came to my mind, "Oh dear, he's acting out of his weakness set. This is bad. This is not good at all." But I didn't let those thoughts spill out and I didn't give any hint that I was thinking negative things. I corralled those monkeys. And look what happened! Look what I would have missed if I had let those wild monkeys out of their cages. Holding your tongue when the urge to be unpleasant arises is one of the *most phenomenal* relational skills you will ever develop.

This turned into a fabulous marriage moment in which David was extremely generous to me with his decision and I was able to tell him how loved and cared for I felt. As I've said before, husbands love it when you are satisfied and happy in the marriage because it tells them they are good husbands and they like feeling that they are good in their roles.

You will have conflict in your marriage. That is the norm. What is *not* the norm is to hold your tongue, to speak respectfully, to ask your husband's opinion, to continue to negotiate without negative emotion, to let the matter rest and come back to it without snide remarks, and then to gush it big with praise and admiration when your husband gives you something. This is not rocket science. *This is baseline behavior for wise women.*

The conflict will *never* be over between the two of you. You and your husband will wrestle with different opinions/perspectives until one of you is in the dirt. Learn to have healthy conflict, one that is coupled with great self-control.

A wise woman builds her home with self-control of her tongue. You cannot be an amazing wife until you get hold of that snake.

I was at a shower yesterday and two of the sweetest, most godly young wives told me how their husbands said some ridiculous stuff and yet, they (the wives) didn't react. They both talked about how the husband did this and did that, and still they didn't react. They spoke of the trials their husbands had and how they tried to be a source of comfort to him, instead of a mother fixing them. What is so interesting about these young wise wives is that their husbands *adore* them. These young women are women of prayer, of goodness, and who love the Lord. They have learned that is it not necessary to confront every one of the husband's crazy ideas and suggestions *at the moment*. They have learned great self-control, great reverence for their husbands, and are happy, sweet wives who hugely deposit the 8 A's. Their husbands are normal husbands but these are *not* normal wives. All is lost in *Wife School* if you do not get control over your *emotional hysteria, contentiousness, and unpleasant words.*

This next paragraph may sound like it is a little out of place, but actually, I feel this is an important concept to mention right here since we are discussing emotional escalation. Many women in my *Skinny School* groups have said that they recovered their sanity by getting excess sugar and refined carbs out of their life. We are spiritual/mental/physical beings. You know what a wet noodle you are when you are physically exhausted. Similarly, when you are eating excess sugar and refined carbs, you are jacking up your hormones and that messes up your emotions. Women who were easily set off before they got off sugar have said over and over that they have gained a calm by ditching sugar and refined carbs. This is a FYI to those of you still eating junk. In *Skinny School*, we call that food Trash Food. Remember, even though it tastes great for 20 seconds, it messes up your hormones, your blood work, your emotions, and your hip size. It affects your children's behavior, too. Learn to eat food that God created, not the man-made trash that harms our bodies and makes you an emotional wreck. (Reread Week 11, Day 5 if you want to review more on health.)

DAY 3
What to Do When Your Husband is Bossy and Inconsiderate of Your Opinion, Part 1

Husbands fall into two ditches as far as leadership. We have repeatedly discussed the passive leader, in which he sits back and you fill in the space with your opinions, ideas, and actions. Today we will discuss the other ditch, when husbands want to run the show exclusively without your input and without considering your desires and opinions.

The Scripture is repeatedly crystal clear in that the husband is the head of the family. (1 Corinthians 11:9, Genesis 2:18, Ephesians 5:22, Colossians 3:18, etc.) In the military, it is understood that you salute and obey the officer in a higher position, but actually you are saluting the uniform, not necessarily the man. As we know, often the man with less authority is smarter, wiser, etc. Many people like to use this analogy for marriage.

However, a marriage is not a military organization. The woman is a help-meet. She is "bone of his bones and flesh of his flesh" (Genesis 2:23). This is not a master-slave relationship, but two people "joined to become one flesh" in order that together they might mirror Christ and His bride, the Church. Yes, the wife is to submit, but if you have carefully studied Scripture, you know that the Church appeals (prays) all the time to her authority, Jesus. Jesus was a servant-leader, not a harsh dictator. He did not come to be served, but to serve others.

Some of you are married to men that *misunderstand* the role of leader. They think that their role gives them power to make decisions *alone*, instead of using their power to serve. These men can be very inconsiderate to their wives at times.

This is one of the hardest situations in marriage because you are faced with a man who thinks he is the center of the wheel, and that he has a spoke called work, a spoke called ministry, a spoke called wife, and a spoke called kids. He sees all of these spokes as extensions of himself and thinks he is the center and most important part of the wheel. Instead of his true calling to "empty himself and take the form of a servant" (Philippians 2), he becomes a *boss* and is inconsiderate of the desires of his wife.

If you have been with me for these 19 weeks, you know that I believe women should be under the authority of their husbands. But what I want to be very clear about is *Wife School* is *not* a doormat approach with a "whatever-you-say-dear" mentality. You are a gift from God *to help your husband think* and to help your husband navigate life.

Just a little rabbit chasing here: Scripture does teach that a wife is to learn in silence (1 Timothy 2:11) but that is only in the church meeting. I personally think we women talk too much in church meetings. I think it dishonors a man for his wife to be a big mouth and always give her opinion in a church setting. Instead, encourage your husband to give his opinion at church, and then admire it. You are a very smart woman, so give your opinion other places besides a church meeting. Business, school, and community are *not* the same as church. I am not trying to give hard, legalistic rules. Just know that when you are gathered in a church setting and your husband is present, it is wise to not talk too much and to let your husband be the primary speaker for your family.

(Getting back on track…) A woman is definitely allowed to appeal her husband's opinions (see the book of Esther) and discuss matters with him. She is God's gift to him to help him be successful and he needs her input. But her words must always be bathed in humility, respectfulness, and self-control.

To be continued tomorrow…

DAY 4
What to Do When Your Husband is Bossy and Inconsiderate of Your Opinion, Part 2

To continue…

Luke 18:1-8 is the parable of the persistent widow and the judge. It is one of my favorite passages on marriage. Yes, marriage. The woman is humble, respectful, and has self-control, but she is *persistent*. "Grant me…" she implores. Wives, you are allowed to ask your husband for good things, even things with which he disagrees (be sure you have God's go-ahead). When he says no, and you feel God wants this, you have to submit for now, but you can continue to appeal.

How tricky this whole subject of appealing is. Knowing when it is time to lay down the appeals and to let your husband make the final decision is one that you must find in prayer. We are to submit as well as we are allowed to appeal. I wish I could give you an easy formula but *walk in the Spirit* is the best advice I can give you.

When husbands pull the "I'm-in-charge" card and make big decisions without consulting you, or are reluctant to receive your input about family matters, you can respectfully, with humility and great self-control, say "Honey, I know you are the head of this family and you have the final decision. I want you to know that I respect the position you have. However, I was given to you by God as a helper. That is not only a sex partner and a housekeeper, but someone who helps you *think*. I am not trying to control you, but I do want to give you my input and opinion. I want you to consider it. Yes, I am the weaker vessel, but that is physically. I am not weaker mentally. I want to have my opinion considered and feel heard."

Now, if you have a bossy husband, know that he will *balk* at this. He will give you reasons why he's exclusively in charge and you are to *follow*. He will challenge your right to give input. This is the hardest kind of man to reach. You must maintain a calm, forgiving, loving, patient outlook when trying to beseech him to listen to and consider your input.

Know that this is definitely a difficult thing to do. Teaching bossy husbands to slow down and listen to your input can be very energy-draining work. Always reassure your husband that you know he is the ultimate decision maker and that your input is from a heart that ultimately wants to make him successful and happy. (If you are really rocking the 8 A's, he already knows this, and is softening to your influence.)

Do not be discouraged if you have to have this soft conversation 50 to 100 times. If you are truly loving and giving, your husband will eventually soften. *Never* go into Commander-mode or speak with disrespect or emotional turmoil, because if you do, *all your good work is wasted*. He will think, "She's a crazy. I don't have to listen to her." If you can unemotionally appeal, talk sanely and calmly, not get upset when he doesn't immediately receive your words, and persevere, these men can be softened and taught over the years to consider your input.

What a long road this is. You cannot let yourself get discouraged. Bossy husbands are difficult to win. Bossy husbands think that because they are the man, they can make decisions without your input. But that is not what Scripture teaches. It teaches that husbands are to…

1. give their wives' desires equal weight ("husbands ought to love their wives as their own bodies." Ephesians 5:28)
2. demonstrate self-sacrifice for their wife ("Husbands, love your wives, just as Christ loved the church and gave himself up for her" Ephesians 5:25)

and

3. be considerate of the wife's views and mindset ("husbands, live with your wives in an understanding way, showing honor to the woman as the weaker vessel" 1 Peter 3:7).

Be prepared for a long journey to address this untrained and erroneous mindset of a bossy husband. Forgive him. Accept him. But stay in the struggle to explain to him the true, Biblical model.

There are many things you can say to your husband when he balks about receiving your input. One thing is, "I'm bone of your bones. I'm created to make you successful and I want to do so. But I also want you to live with me in an understanding way. I want you to give me honor as 1 Peter 3:7 says, and listen to me. I want to make you happy, but I also know that God gave me to you *to help you think*."

If you have the emotional turmoil out of your house and are making huge deposits into your husband's tank with the 8 A's, he will eventually turn to you and open to your influence.

If he is disrespectful, you will have to confront it later, not when it happens. Everyone is too stirred up. (Reread Chapter 14 in *Wife School* about being mistreated). Remember that when you discuss his inconsiderateness with him, you always start with, "One of my top goals in life is to make you happy and when I feel *hurt* like I do now, that is difficult for me to do." Always frame how you feel as being hurt, *not angry*. Dear wife! Death and life are in the power of the tongue! "A word fitly spoken is like apples of gold in settings of silver" (Proverbs 25:11).

I'd like to address something else that will definitely help your husband see your viewpoint, and that is your ability to admit when you are wrong. If you see you are wrong and he is right about something, be humble and tell him. Say, "I see that you were correct and I was wrong. I really appreciate your wisdom in that and how it protected me." You aren't weak when you say that! You demonstrate your maturity and humility by admitting you were wrong! *You gain his influence by being able to admit you are wrong.* (Few people can do this because they have too much pride.) You also model for him how to "admit when he is wrong." He thinks to himself, "Wow. She can admit when she is wrong. That is impressive. I can listen to her input because she is demonstrating how mature she is."

God may have given you a bossy husband, but with patience, kindness, forgiveness, and perseverance, bossy husbands can be reasoned with and taught to consider your input.

DAY 5
Cynicism and the Continual Disappointment in Others

An easy thing for humans to do as they age is to become cynical. Cynical means "distrusting of the motives of others." The longer you live, the more opportunities you'll have to be mistreated, to be disappointed in how others give to and love you, and to see that mankind is deeply sinful and broken, especially in that most humans basically mainly care about themselves. The deep brokenness of the world continues to find you.

Meeting with women is one of my favorite things to do. Probably, the most common issue is that they are having issues with another person, such as a husband, a child, a relative, a friend, or a co-worker. People don't get counseling because of the evil in the world, *but* because of the evil and mistreatment by others toward them in their lives. No one has ever sat down in my living room with me and said, "I'm overwhelmed by the conditions in the Middle East. Can we talk about it?"

Being mistreated by others is nothing new. I think about the original twelve apostles, and how they were horrifically mistreated. Beaten, whipped, stoned…. you name it, they suffered from it. All the apostles but the Apostle John were martyred for their faith. But at the end of their lives, they still lived with great joy, love, and purpose. How is it that you and I become cynical with the weaknesses and disappointments of others, but the apostles—who were much more mistreated than we've ever even thought about—remained as ones who contributed, gave, and loved?

It's an interesting question and one I'd like to discuss.

You and I are not great at forgiving. That's where it all starts. People sin against us *all the time* and we don't empty their accounts. We allow accumulations in their accounts of offenses. And because we are not steeped in the Word (distracted by consumerism and social media, mostly), we forget that we are to forgive 70 times 7.

The apostles knew that Jesus was raised from the dead. They knew that "ease of life and pleasure" were not their goals, but pleasing their Commanding Officer. They saw Him resurrected. They knew it was true. They didn't waste time or energy thinking about being takers, about "who wasn't loving them or giving to them enough." They were intentional, knowing that when Jesus invades a soul, it is new life, and changes the person astronomically.

As far as when other Christians were self-centered, selfish, and sinned against them (remember the lists who deserted Paul and tried to harm him?), they forgave. They focused on their mission which was to tell everyone about the resurrection and that new life could be found in Jesus. They were intentional with their mission, not letting the naysayers drag them down.

Becoming cynical says a lot about how you don't believe that Jesus rose from the dead. It says that you are letting the schemes of Satan enter your life. Forgive and open your heart to the world again. Jesus did rise from the grave and He is going to come back and you will stand before Him and give an account. Just like the servant who was forgiven a billion dollar debt and couldn't release his fellow servant from a debt of a few dollars, we refuse to forgive others when we've been forgiven so much.

I struggle with this, just like you. It's a conscious decision to hand over my resentment to the Lord. But it frees my soul *again*. I can focus on my mission, which is to love God and love others—not sit in my room and stew over how others disappoint me.

You and I know this, and yes, we should be past this, but that's why Jesus taught extensively about forgiveness. Humans are dumb sheep as far as learning these kinds of spiritual lessons. Take those two or three people who continually disappoint or hurt you, or who cheated you and mistreated you, and forgive them. God only uses clean vessels to do His work, and resentment clogs up pipes more than anything I know.

One More Thought

Addictions are predictable (though unhealthy) sources of pleasure and self-soothing. That's where alcohol, Trash Food, gambling, drugs, and porn get their power, as they meet those two needs of the human heart. Wives! Why can't *you* be a predictable source of *pleasure and self-soothing* to your husband? This is what healthy human bonding looks like! Talk about opening your husband's influence to you! The idea of being a source of pleasure and self-soothing to your husband is one that I think King Lemuel's mom had in mind when she said that a virtuous wife "brings him good, not harm, all the days of his life." Of course, implied in that verse is also integrity, diligence, goodness, godliness, and humility (and much more). But men need reliable sources of pleasure and self-soothing…so let that be *you*!

Prayer

God,

How easy it is to sometimes get discouraged with life. Trials abound everywhere, and there is a strong current pulling me to focus my mind on all that is difficult. I'm pretty sure this is the Enemy who would love to devour me.

To fight discouragement, You have repeatedly told Your children to be thankful as that is the *secret weapon* to being happy. Help me focus my mind on the abundance You have given me. Help me see that with You, all things are possible. Although my situation may look impossible, You can open the eyes of the blind, heal lepers, and raise the dead. I refuse to be hopeless about my marriage but hopeful.

Restore me so that I may run the race marked out for me and finish well. Pull the veil from my eyes, and let me see that the resentment that I want to hold onto is injurious to me and distasteful to You.

In Jesus name,

Amen

Assignments and Group Discussion Questions

1. How good are you at celebrating your husband's victories?

2. Are you able to get hold of your emotions when you and your husband have conflict?

3. Do you have a husband who is bossy and inconsiderate of your opinions? What was helpful to you in this section? Explain.

4. Have you become cynical? Do you hold on to any resentment toward anyone?

WEEK 20

A Happy Heart, Alcohol, Parenting...and More

Contents

Day 1: A Relationship Skill that Grows a Happy Heart
Day 2: Drinking Alcohol
Day 3: Important Parenting Concept #1
Day 4: Important Parenting Concept #2
Day 5: Handling Your Husband's Sin Nature

DAY 1
A Relationship Skill that Grows a Happy Heart

Of course, most of the questions I receive from *Wife School* students are on the subject of marriage. But a close second is the amount of questions I receive about the struggle of having a happy heart. Struggling with worry and discouragement and learning to replace it with gratefulness and contentment is one of the biggest learning curves in any woman's life. Today we will discuss another relationship skill related to your mental/emotional health and that is the concept of *not being easily offended.*

A few days ago I was corrected by someone I admire. I remember thinking, "What? Really? You think I'm bad at that?" I stewed around a bit, thinking how actually, this was a weakness in *them,* not me. I thought, "I don't do that wrong. Actually, you have a big problem with that instead."

Then I called David and gave him my sob story of how this person wrongly accused me of X. I stomped around in my pride, telling him how I had been falsely accused. Why, this was unfair of them to say. This was not true. I am not guilty of this, I said. He let me huff and puff.

Finally, however, I heard the Holy Spirit whisper, "Don't be offended. Be humble. Take correction." Friend, this will never be easy to do!

Remember, addicts are easily offended. They say to themselves, "No one treats me right. No one shows up for me. No one understands or appreciates me. Poor me!" Addicts have huge self-pity issues ("I have it so hard"), they have grandiosity ("I need to be treated like a big shot and have high treatment"), and they are easily offended ("Wow, that person is a jerk for saying/doing that").

The gulf between the treatment we want and the perceived treatment we get (which is where we become offended) is painful. That's why addicts need to medicate with a mood changer (porn, food, gambling, alcohol, etc.). The real antidote is *humility*! Humility is not needing to be treated like a big shot because you know your calling is to serve, not to be served. Humility is *not* being offended because we are to focus on how we give and love, not on how we're given to and loved. Humility tells us our calling is to do good to those who mistreat us. We are to act like…ta-dah…JESUS!!

I have mentioned before that when offenses from others come your way, you have two options with which to react. You can be a brick wall and let the offense hit hard. (See my first reaction above. Embarrassing.) This is the norm. Or you can choose a mature response and be steam, letting the offense pass through. Yes, you notice the offense, but you let it pass through. *This is one of the most helpful relationship skills you will ever learn.* You need it for navigating life with your husband, your adult children, your friends, your mother-in-law, your daughter-in-law, the people at work, the people at your child's school, your neighbors, the people at church, etc. Learn to *not* be offended. Bury the weaknesses of others in the cemetery in your back yard.

I do this much better than I used to, but I am still not where I need to be. Opportunities abound for me to be steam (haha, abound) and opportunities abound for you, too. It takes a lot of humility to say to yourself, "Maybe I am right. Nevertheless, I am going to let it go and I am going to forgive them." Be steam. Be humble. Receive correction. Let it go.

This relationship skill of "not being offended" is essential if you want a happy heart. People who are always offended don't experience the emotional freedom that comes with *overlooking*. Only the most emotionally mature can overlook the offenses of others. OLAT, remember? (OverLook A Transgression) "The discretion of a man delays his anger; and it is his glory to overlook a transgression" (Proverbs 19: 11).

Here's one more tip for the advanced learner: When you feel unjustly criticized, look for the *smidgeon of truth in the accusation*. There is usually one there. Ask God what He wants you to hear.

Here is an example: Since my husband and one of my sons have an auto-immune disease, often they cannot eat the food that is served when we go to events. Therefore, I frequently volunteer to bring extra food for them. This morning, this annoyed an upcoming hostess (who is a relative). When I asked if I could bring some extra food, she insinuated that this was "indeed rude" but that "I could do it." I thought about that and at first, was extremely annoyed at her lack of consideration for my husband and son. I was upset that she didn't want her beautiful dinner party to get messed up with my Tupperware of extra food. But after thinking about it, I realized she had gone to a great deal of effort to have her beautiful party and I (truthfully) wasn't concerned about the beauty of her party at all, merely the health of my husband and son. *Not being concerned about her* was the *hard true part* that God wanted me to hear. I was only looking out for my interests: my husband and son.

Honestly, I need to be a witness to her. I need to demonstrate care for her agenda, even though I repeatedly don't agree with it. Here's where the double standards come in again: God wants me to forgive her for not considering my agenda, but not be offended that she does *not* consider my agenda. Friend, this is only possible with the Spirit of Christ. Loving difficult people is one of the hardest jobs on the planet.

Learning not to be offended will definitely make you easier to live with. *But this will also allow you to enjoy your own internal landscape more.* You live minute by minute with yourself. Learn to live in such a way that you can *enjoy yourself.* You have one single, short life on earth. Learn to live it with a robustly happy heart.

DAY 2
Drinking Alcohol

To begin this section, let me say that Christian women are in no way exempt from having alcohol problems. No one sets out saying that they are going to become an alcoholic or have alcohol issues. It is a gradual thing, like a canoe that is in water with soft undercurrents and is soon on the other side of the river. Alcohol, like sugar and drugs, can immediately change your mood, and therefore, it is commonly used to change how one feels.

It's difficult to argue that Jesus turned water into some form of intoxicating wine. Yes, maybe those beverages weren't as strong as they are now, but they did contain alcohol. This is proven by John 2:10 which says, "Everyone brings out the choice wine first and then the cheaper wine after the guests have had too much to drink." Unquestionably, Jesus turned water into (some form of) intoxicating drink.

The problem with alcohol is, of course, when people drink *too much*. The Bible does not tell us how much wine one can drink but it does give a principle that I think is helpful for Christians who choose to drink. It is this: "Do not get drunk on wine…Instead, be filled with the Spirit" (Ephesians 5:18). It's very clear that we are *not* to get drunk. Getting drunk is crossing the line. But what is drunk? Where exactly is that line? I think the Scripture tells us. If you are drinking so much that you cannot simultaneously be filled with the Spirit, then it is too much.

If you go to OpenBible.info and click on the Topical Bible tab, you can search for *Drinking Alcohol* and find 80 verses on drinking alcohol. This is a good Bible study if you or someone you know is having trouble with alcohol.

The government has set standards for how much alcohol can be in your blood if you are driving. Different health organizations have given different standards on how much alcohol one can consume without it impairing your health. Most health websites say that women can handle one five-ounce glass of wine a day and it not impact their health in a negative way. But some health experts insist that only three glasses of wine a week are allowed for optimum health. Scripturally, we don't have exact rules or limits on how much you can drink except "don't get drunk" and "don't cause your brother to fall." "It is better not to eat meat or drink wine or to do anything else that will cause your brother or sister to fall" (Romans 14:21).

Again, I am not going to give specific rules, but I want to give you a strong warning on the dangers of alcohol. Besides the terrible consequences that obviously result from driving while intoxicated, alcohol can ruin your marriage if you drink too much. Alcohol decreases your self-control and loosens your tongue. It is probable that you will say harmful things that you will later regret.

Christians are adamant about their position on alcohol on both sides of the fence. Martin Luther's wife brewed her own beer. C.S. Lewis drank. However, Charles Spurgeon said, "Next to the preaching of the Gospel, the most necessary thing to be done in England is to induce our people to become abstainers." Whatever your conviction is, just know that if you are having trouble with alcohol, it is time to "throw off the sin that so easily entangles" (Hebrews 12:1-2).

Friends, excess alcohol ruins homes. Be very careful with your alcohol. Do not let alcohol master you.

DAY 3
Important Parenting Concept #1

There are two main concepts about parenting that I want to discuss in this section and the next. The first principle in parenting to understand is that it is imperative for couples to have *harmony* in the marriage or else the children suffer.

You will certainly have conflict in your marriage and you will most likely have conflict in regards to parenting. This is why I beseech couples to go to as many Christian parenting seminars, listen to as many DVD's, etc. as they can. The more teaching you hear together, the more you will be on the same page. Being on the same page in parenting is crucial because parents need to provide a united front. Find the style the two of you can best agree on. In the end, you will still have conflict in your marriage about parenting and about life in general. How you respond to that conflict is incredibly important in parenting.

Children learn how to submit to and follow God *by watching their mothers submit to and follow their father*. Children naturally rebel; that's in their DNA. They must have *a model in which to see submission* such as when they see their mothers rightly respond to their father. *Resisting your husband's leadership is incredibly unwise if you want your children to follow Christ*. Your husband will *not* be a perfect leader. But when you can still respond with honor and respect, your children will learn how to respond with honor and respect to the Lord when things don't go their way. Yes, of course, you can give your husband your thoughts and input. Of course, you can respectfully appeal. But your husband is the head of your home, and if you resist his leadership, you will eventually see children who resist the leadership of the Lord.

David and I have struggled in agreeing on several areas in our marriage and we probably struggled with the area of parenting more than any other. We didn't struggle much when the kids were little, but more when they became teenagers. If I could do one thing over in my marriage, it would be to not have had such an *independent spirit* during a few years of my marriage. I would have been more submissive to David's leadership.

The very best gift you can give your children is to love the Lord with all your heart. Secondly, the best gift you can give them is to honor, respect, and submit to their dad. Resentment, annoyance, and disrespect towards your husband is a terrible environment for your kids. Don't underestimate the importance of how you treat your husband as far as the impact it will have on rearing your kids. As I've said many times, kids see how the Believer submits to the Lord as they watch Mom submit to Dad. And kids see how the Lord provides and protects as they watch Dad take care of Mom. Marriage could not be more important in parenting!

You have been given an incredible power to influence. But remember, there are negative consequences to your children if you have a contentious spirit. Harmony in the marriage is ultimately obtained by a wife not resisting the leadership of her husband. Your willingness to ultimately submit to your husband's leadership could not be more important.

Yes, go to parenting seminars. Yes, order Love and Logic DVD's and get the yelling out of your house. But in the end, children watch the marriage and learn about submitting to God from how their mothers submit to their fathers.

See more in Day 4.

DAY 4
Important Parenting Concept #2

The second important concept I want to discuss as far as parenting is if you want to have a general idea how your children are going to turn out, remember that apples fall from apple trees. Oranges don't fall from apple trees. Bananas don't fall from apple trees. Like begets like.

When our kids were little, I read almost every parenting book I could on kids. I decided if I could get enough *knowledge,* then I could produce awesome kids. I soaked up books such as Ferber's *How To Solve Your Child's Sleep Problem.* I lived by Ezzo's materials on Baby management and Toddler management. Later, I thought if I home-schooled, I could control their environment and they would all love Jesus and be perfect little soldiers for Him.

Friends, none of this was bad. *However,* whether you homeschool or not, whether you have Santa Claus or not, whether you go to church on Wednesday nights or not, whether you count to three or demand first-time obedience, whether you spank or have time-out, whether you do any of a million other random things, the bottom line is your kids will generally turn out *like you and your husband.*

If you love and serve others with a pure heart, your children will. If you are critical and judgmental, they will be too. If you love the Word, they will. If you struggle with the love of money or sexual lusts, so will they. If you love missions, they will. If you love the poor, they will. If you are hospitable, they will be. If you tell lies, they will lie too. If you cheat, they will cheat. If you slander others, they will. If you are sarcastic, they will be, too. If you are depressed, then they will struggle with depression. If honoring Jesus Christ is the most important thing in your life, then honoring Him will probably be the most important thing in your children's lives, too. This is not an exact science, of course, but it has much general truth.

Let me tell you what messes up your home, friend. One word. SIN. That's right, one little word. It shows itself in anger, selfishness, underhanded business deals, racial prejudice, prescription drug addiction, rebellion to authority, ungratefulness, judging others, a harsh tongue, no concern for the least of these, loving money, and a million other different scenarios.

Yes, read all the parenting books and go to all the conferences. I've counseled you to do this numerous times. But the very best parenting advice is to surrender your life to the Lord, submit to your husband, die to self, read your Bible, prayer earnestly, and get involved with other believers in community. That's the real parenting advice because children *learn what they see lived.*

Research has shown that the number one predictor of whether children follow their childhood faith is *if they are close to a warm and nurturing father.* Many of you have husbands who are not very relational, and when the kids get to be teenagers and more difficult, your husband will retreat. Instead of bashing him for his lack of fatherly involvement, tell him the good things the children say about him. Tell the children good things the father says about them. Suggest outings where the father has one-on-one time with each child. Don't begrudge this work. You are the wife and you are the relational one. You are the one who is called to build your house. Massage the relationships with your teens and your husband. As I've said before, when there is tension in the marriage, the wife tries to pull the children to herself to hurt her husband. This is the most selfish thing you could ever do to your children! They need a close relationship with Dad!

One other piece of parenting advice is necessary. In the secular atheism worldview, your children will be confronted with the teaching of evolution. It is imperative that you learn apologetics and teach your children these truths. Otherwise, they will be confronted with the (false!) New Atheist thinking (like Sam Harris, Christopher Hitchens, Richard Dawkins, etc.) and will not have answers to deal with these fallacious teachings. There are many, many good books. I like *Cold Case Christianity* by J. Warner Wallace, as well as *Man, Myth, Messiah,* by Rice Brooks. Also, my favorite resource is an amazing DVD called *Evolution's Achilles Heel* to help you understand the *impossibility* of evolution. Many young people are leaving the church as they have not been trained in apologetics. Don't let this happen to your children.

To summarize, nothing is more important to you on earth than your precious children. God has such awesome instructions for us in His Word. We best not ignore the instruction.

DAY 5
Handling Your Husband's Sin Nature

Wives, we are fixers. We want our nests to be clean, beautiful, and tidy. The first element we observe that needs tidying up is *the husband.* We think our husbands don't lead like they should, they don't desire God like we wish they would, and they don't do a hundred other behaviors that we classify as *things good Christian men should do.*

But shock-a-roo. Did you know that you have been given power from the Lord to help your husband grow in his relationship with Him? That's right. God wants to use you to reach your husband. No, it is not a Bible study to take him through. It is not a course at your church.

Peter, who was in the inner circle of the disciples and walked with Jesus while He was on earth, has given wives a strategy. You don't have to read a million books or go to counseling to figure this out. In one paragraph, Peter tells wives—whose husbands are disobedient to Scripture—what to do. Are you ready for the game plan?

Peter says when your husband sees "the purity and reverence of your life," your husband will be "won over without words" (1 Peter 3). God's plan is not that you tell your husband to change, it's that you change yourself! That's how God uses wives to pull their husbands to Himself. It's the *influence* wives have over their husbands when wives' lives are full of *purity and reverence*. Swim around in that thought for a while. God wants you to confess and repent of anything that is not pure. (What are you doing, saying, or *thinking* that you shouldn't be?)

God wants you to live with *reverence*. My definition of reverence is "respect on speed." God gave wives a blueprint to deal with husbands whose hearts are not turned to Him!

The funny part is next. Peter knows and addresses the two methods that women employ to try to change their husbands. The first approach, as I mentioned in the prior paragraph, is *words*. This is the number one choice by all women (you already know this, right?)

Choice number two is that women try to win influence *with their beauty*! Yes, beauty does captivate men's hearts. Women know that and therefore, they care a great deal about beauty. Peter takes it a step further and talks about true beauty. He defines this beauty as "the inner self, the unfading beauty of a gentle and quiet spirit." Thank goodness there is one kind of beauty that doesn't fade, because even the Elizabeth Taylors of the world have beauty that fades. Peter then takes this a step further, and gives advice on how the holy women of the past used to make themselves beautiful. Oh dear, here it is *again*. Take a deep breath. *They were submissive to their husbands.*

I wish I could tell you that after twenty or thirty years, you will be completely in sync with your husband and will never have to worry about resisting his leadership again. Last night (!) as we were falling asleep, my husband let me know that he didn't like the way I handled a situation with a child. I told him why I was right and we went to sleep. This morning, while I was having my quiet time, the Lord nudged me. "You are resisting the leadership of your husband." I admit, I hate these moments. Hate. Hate. Hate. So when my husband got up, I had to go and say those horrible words I hate to say: "I was wrong. Will you please forgive me?" Those words will never be easy for me to say. Submitting to my husband's leadership will never be easy. But I know it is the path of blessing. I know it is God's plan for the home to thrive.

After watching marriages and families for thirty years, I can promise you that until you get this principle of submission right, your family will never flourish. You can be gorgeous, witty, hospitable, and able to do it all with your hands tied behind your back. But until you lay down this clamoring to be in charge, until you lay down your anger and your strong will, you will never be the beautiful woman that God desires. God created women to be help-meets and yes, our husbands need us to help them *think*. But ultimately, your husband is the head of your home, and your insistence on doing things your way will harm your marriage and definitely, your children (as they learn how to follow Christ as they see you follow your husband).

I don't understand it completely, but something happens in the heavenlies when a wife has a gentle and quiet spirit and can learn to submit to the leadership of her husband. A wife's gentle and quiet spirit *plows a husband's heart to soften it* so God can work in it. This is God's plan for reaching stubborn men. I know you'd rather give him a lecture but that is not the divine method. Believe me, I've been looking for another method for 30 years and there's not one.

Friends, I didn't write the rules; I am only the herald. This is the only path of blessing for women. Don't neglect this pot of gold. The world thinks this is ridiculous hogwash. But in fact, it is the most fabulous piece of advice that any woman could ever hear. God created the family. God created marriage. We are richly blessed if we hear His still small voice and obey.

One More Thought

Friend, as you and I fight the struggles of life (and there are many), remember that the best weapon you have is prayer. Prayer is where God shows you your sin. Prayer is where chains are broken. Prayer was how Jesus talked to His Father to hear His will and it is how we are to talk to our Father and hear His marching orders. You will have many trials in life and prayer is how we conquer.

Become a woman of prayer. Schedule your prayer like you schedule your exercise or your family's meals. Be a woman who lets the Spirit of God cleanse you in prayer. How impossible it is to be the woman God wants you to be without prayer.

Prayer

Dear God,

As I linger in Your presence this morning, I feel the pressure of You telling me about some thoughts and actions in me that You don't like. Honestly, this guilt is an unpleasant feeling. Your Holy Spirit is pressing in on me, God.

The person I present to the world is vastly different from the person that You and I know lives in the secret places in my heart.

So, for the zillionth time, Lord, I come to the cross with my wretchedness in my backpack. What do I do with this heavy burden?

You tell me to lay down my backpack of sin. Just lay it down. You paid for that ugliness, therefore I don't have to. I get to lay it down and get a free bath for my soul.

Your Word says, "as far as the east is from the west, so far has He removed our transgressions from us" (Psalm 103:12). You are handing out forgiveness. It's almost hard to accept because it seems unfair, that I get to walk away free and not pay for the filth and junk buried in my heart.

Actually, there is a price. There is a condition. And that condition is that I become Your bond slave. "For as many as are led by the Spirit of God, they are the sons of God" (Romans 8:14). I now have an obligation to follow and obey You. Yes, I get to be free of my backpack of sin, but getting freedom from my sin comes with a condition. *Repentance is part of the condition.* I don't get to believe, be cleansed from my sin, and then *hold on* to my sin. Repentance is *turning from the sin* that Your Spirit has highlighted in my conscience.

Lord Jesus, I turn. I know the "sin that so easily entangles" and I repent. I lay down the sin. There are doctors that can help cure illness; there are teachers that can help us learn; and there are brilliant people who can help us think about government and social issues. But there is only One that can forgive sin, and He is not a man. It is You, the Creator of all. I believe. Therefore, I will repent and lay down this sin that You have asked me to give to You.

"If we confess our sins, He is faithful and just and will forgive us our sins and purify us from all unrighteousness" (1 John 1:9).

In Jesus name,

Amen

Assignments and Group Discussion Questions

1. How do you handle correction? Have you basically overcome self-pity or are you still struggling? Are you easily offended by others?

2. What are your thoughts on alcohol? Do you think this area could possibly be a stumbling block for you?

3. How did you react to the idea that your children will basically submit to the Lord by watching you submit to your husband?

4. Since apples fall from apple trees, what character trait do you need to change so that your children will not "be like that"?

5. Are you a "blamer" or instead, someone who takes responsibility for how things turn out?

6. What are your thoughts about the idea that you are God's instrument to woo your husband toward Him with your gentle and quiet spirit? What are your thoughts on submission?

WEEK 21

Ex-wives, Bad Circumstances, Discontentment...and More

Contents

Day 1: Thoughts on Ex-Wives and Stepchildren
Day 2: When Your Husband's Ideas Are No-So-Great
Day 3: When You Don't Like Your Circumstances
Day 4: For Those of You with a Non-Cinderella Disposition
Day 5: If You Are Still Often Getting Upset with Your Husband

Chapter 21 in *Wife School* is entitled *How to Be Attractive to Your Husband*. What a struggle this area is for most of us, either that we pay too much attention to it, or not enough.

DAY 1
Thoughts on Ex-Wives and Stepchildren

Even if you don't have to deal with ex-wives and stepchildren, please read this section as it applies to people who are difficult for you to love. Also, this is not a biblical treatise on divorce and re-marriage. Please read John Piper (desiringGod.org) or someone of his caliber to learn about remarriage. This is merely advice for wives who are already now married to someone who was previously married with children.

I run into marriages all the time where wives are involved with ex-wives and children from their husband's first marriage. I want to lay down a few foundational truths for any of you that are married to a man with an ex-wife or children from another marriage. Beware: icy water ahead.

Life is messy, as you know, and ex-wives and stepchildren are about as messy as it gets.

Repeatedly, women complain to me about ex-wives and stepchildren. The chorus is shockingly the same and it is this: "They are trouble and I'd rather not deal with them." I get that. I understand that. That is the natural way to feel.

But friend, you are *not* to be normal. You have been jerked out of darkness into His marvelous light. You are a child of the King and now you are expected to think and act like heavenly royalty.

Following are a few anchors as far as how to think about ex-wives and stepchildren.

One foundational truth is that your husband loves the stepchildren as much as he loves your own children. It is horrible (!) for you to treat your kids better than his kids. I heard of a couple—a woman married to a man with kids from a previous marriage—that *don't include* the children of his first marriage when the new couple goes on vacation. Of course, you'd rather not take the kids from your husband's first marriage. They belong to another woman and you just want your sweet blood kids to go. But look at the situation from the perspective of the kids from the first marriage. They think, "Dad is going on vacation and I'm not invited. He loves his new family more." Friend, that is plain mean and selfish of you to not consider those children. You married the whole man and his kids from his first marriage are now to be treated like yours. You must love them, help them, care for them, and include them. I know a teenage girl who was devastated because her dad and new wife took the "new kids" to the beach. How she wish she had been invited. The pain that this young girl felt burned a deep hole in her.

Again, when you marry a man, you marry his past. If his past includes children, then you are to treat them as yours as far as being kind to them. The children from the first marriage didn't ask to come from a broken home. You, as a Christ-follower, must understand that those children are due your love and acceptance. They need access to their dad and you are the gatekeeper. You know that. You know that what you say affects your husband. You know that you control a lot of your husband's relationship with his first set of kids. Men don't like to go against the wishes of the person from whom they are counting on to get sex!

I understand the first wife might be a psycho (she is always accused of that, for sure). However, Jesus said, "But I say to you who hear, love your enemies, do good to those who hate you" Luke 6:27. (See also Matthew 5:44 and Romans 12:14, 19-21 on how to respond to *your enemies*.)

Another woman (woman A) told me her husband was still dealing with the grief and pain of his divorce and prior marriage. He is also experiencing difficulty with the children of that first marriage. The new wife (woman A) told him, "You should be over this by now! Why don't you just go to our hunting cabin until you figure it out!" Wives, when you marry a man, again, you marry the whole package. If he needs healing, then you are to help him find healing. Just because you are sick of something doesn't mean beans. You are crucified with Christ and now, it's about how you can represent Christ to others, not about you being comfortable all the time.

Yes, you might have to set boundaries with a crazy ex-wife, but there is never a place for yelling, slander, malice, rudeness, or meanness. You always deal with everyone by *returning a blessing*. That is what you signed up for when you said Jesus was Lord in your life. I know it's hard. I know it's next to impossible to love those who mistreat you. But that's why we are grafted into the Vine, so that God's sap, the Holy Spirit, runs in our souls. That's why we linger in prayer, so that His will can be downloaded to us. This is merely *the Christian life*.

So, figure out how to bless the children of his first marriage. They are from his loins and they are equal with your darlings. The children have been wounded and now, even though that was not your fault, you are part of the solution.

I am sorry this is such hard information. Let God change your heart. Let God break the anger and resentment you have toward his first family. Don't be normal. Be Christ-like.

DAY 2
When Your Husband's Ideas are Not-So-Great

A husband calls his wife. "Honey," he says. "I have a *great* idea!"

The wife is excited. A great idea? That is wonderful. What could it be? I hope it's something I like.

Then the husband begins. "I was thinking about x, and y, and z. Then I thought we could a, then b, and then c. What do you think?"

The wife is speechless. It's not that it is a *terrible* idea, but it certainly needs to be tweaked. Why, he had forgotten the most important things: M, N, O, and P!

Wives, we have to remember that it is our nature to want to improve *everything*. Even though his idea is good, women always want to *tweak it a little more*. This is how we are. Most wives respond with, "Well, maybe, but I really think the best way to do it is M, N, O, and P."

Guess how a husband hears that? "She's certainly a Debbie Downer. It always has to be her idea. It always has to be her way. I tried to come up with a good idea, and as usual, she shot it down. The women at the office don't treat me like that. When I have an idea there, they think I'm brilliant."

What's a wife to do when her husband gives her a not-so-great idea? Seriously, I'm asking you. You're in week 21. What would you tell someone to do?

The answer is you praise what is good about his idea and then *you let it rest*. Unless this is a very important issue at stake, *let him do as he wants*. You don't get unlimited appeals. If you fuss about the way the yard is mowed and if you fuss about how he wears the same shirt to breakfast every Saturday morning, you are using up your appeal points. If you can let things go, let them go.

But sometimes, you need to give him your input. However, the point at which he gives you the initial idea is *not* the time to tell him how you could improve on it. You praise everything you can about the idea. Examples might be, "I love how you're investing your time thinking about matters like this that affect our family. That means so much to me." Or, "You are the right person to think of that, as you model it with your life. I love being married to that sort of person!" Or, "I can't tell you how much this means to me that you are concerned about our family and you are working to solve problems. How wonderful to have a husband like that!"

Do you see that Death and Life are in the power of the tongue? The wise woman builds her house with the self-control of her tongue because she knows Death and Life are there.

Later, if absolutely necessary, you might have to say, "I was so excited about your idea. Again, thank you for thinking about our family's issues. I'm not sure if this is something you want to add or not, but it's something I've been thinking, and I just want to give it to you to stir in your pot so you'll have this idea when you're making final decisions."

Most men can receive input like that. They hear your praise, they hear your respect, and then they hear your input that is fingertip dropped. There was no Commander-mode going on, did you notice?

Yes, this is advanced *Wife School* and this is definitely an art that you will learn by practice. But men's egos are always on their shoulders, ready to get knocked off at a moment's notice. Don't knock your husband's ego off and let it crash to the floor. No, hold it tenderly, cradle it, kiss it, massage it, and put it back gently on his shoulder. Did you know men *adore* women who treat them like this? Do you know men are ravenous for women like this? You can learn to be the *Wife of the World* in your husband's mind, but it takes a lot of care and effort to treat a man like this. But men ridiculously appreciate it. Men absolutely cherish these wives.

Take the time and do the extras to take care of your husband's ego when he gives you a not-so-great idea. It means the world to him.

Remember, you're on a fifty year plan. You get to say everything you want; just not all at once.

DAY 3
When You Don't Like Your Circumstances

Back in my self-pity days when I was blaming others for my hardships, I read this sentence: "If you want to know what you've been sowing, look around and *see what you are currently reaping.*" This was a hard, unwanted, and unpleasant truth. I was faced with accepting that my circumstances (my reaping) were largely because of my sowing! Dang! I hated that. It's so much easier to just blame someone else.

One of the *most important days of your life* is the day you quit blaming others for your unpleasant circumstances and take responsibility for your life. When you look at what you're now reaping and accept responsibility that it was *you* who sowed and that's why you're reaping such-and-such, then you can begin to change things.

We blame, blame, blame. When I hear a woman start blaming, I know I am listening to someone who still hasn't gotten out of the self-pity ditch. We blame our childhood (our parents), we blame our husbands (for not leading or loving better), we blame our churches and pastors (for not giving us the teaching we need), we blame our kids (for being difficult), we blame our friends (for not being more loyal or supportive), we blame our finances (on the economy), we blame our health (on our genes versus our junk eating and refusal to exercise), and on and on. Friend, stop it. Today say, "I am fully responsible for my life. I will lean hard on the Lord and I will get my necessary food from Him." (Man shall not live on bread alone, but on every word that comes from the mouth of God Matthew 4:4). It's you and the Lord. That's it. He's your portion (Lamentations 3:24). He is enough. ("My grace is sufficient for you" 2 Corinthians 12:9). Get your needs met in the Lord and get full in Him. Then sow extravagantly from your overflow.

One marker of emotional maturity is to take responsibility for your life and to bloom where you are planted. Do that. Quit blaming. Your mess is most likely *your fault*. Take it like a grown-up. Change how you sow and you'll eventually change how you reap.

The story of the Prodigal Son illustrates this principle perfectly. The younger brother sees himself in a pigpen, hungry, lonely, and a loser. He realizes he has been sowing to the wind. He realizes (here's the money) it is *his* fault. He devises a pro-active plan to apologize and turn his life around. If you're in a pigpen, apologize (confess, repent, etc.) and make a proactive plan to turn your life around. No human is coming on a white horse to rescue you.

I know this is not a perfect truth. Car accidents happen. Robbers and muggers sin against us. However, the sowing and reaping law still stands largely true. Accepting that your current circumstances are mainly because of your sowing takes a lot of humility. Transitioning from a *blamer* to a *responsibility-taker* can change your life.

When women begin to take responsibility for the harmony of the marriage and take responsibility for the beauty of the home (instead of blaming her husband for his lack of contribution), I see miracles abound. One woman who was in one of my groups many years ago initially came to the group and said, "My husband is such a pig. I tell him that, too." In fact, this husband disgusted her in many ways. Now, 25 years later, she is the epitome of service, kindness, encouragement, and submission. Their grown children have turned out terrific. She decided to quit blaming her husband and to take responsibility for the marriage by serving and loving her husband. A few years ago, her husband said to me: "My wife used to be madder than a hornet. Now she purrs like a kitten." Then he proceeded to tell me how he adored her.

A wise woman builds her house by learning not to blame others for her unpleasant circumstances. She takes responsibility for changing things and for changing herself.

Quit blaming your husband. So many wives say, "If he loved me better, then I would be happy." Hogwash. Get your tank full of the Lord. Nuns don't have husbands and they are some of the happiest people on the face of the earth. This is about expectations, don't you see? Nuns don't expect anything from husbands so they take responsibility for every aspect of their life. Get rid of expectations from your husband (except a living and faithfulness) and take responsibility for your happiness and good mood. Quit blaming anyone or anything at all. Your mood and happy heart is all about your thoughts and nothing else. I am a failure if I don't teach you the huge, colossal, ginormous truth of the importance of taking responsibility for your own happy heart. God feeds the birds, but doesn't put the worms in the nest. Get your mind right. Control your thoughts. You can't be a delightful mother or wife or friend or anything until you do. Be an energy giver. Be a sunrise in the lives of others. Just as Peter Lord said, get your heart happy in the Lord *as your first order of business every day.*

Nothing replaces a happy heart in a woman. Walk with the Lord and learn to be a happy song in the secret places of your heart. No self-pity. No woe-is-me. No whining. Zilch. None. Zero.

DAY 4
For Those of You with a Non-Cinderella Disposition

One thing we love about Cinderella is her lovely disposition. Even living with the tyrannical step-mother and step-sisters, Cinderella had a gentle and quiet spirit. Our Disney princess never allowed any annoyance, anger, or self-pity to appear on her flawless animated face.

That is why Cinderella is a fairy tale. Real women have emotions and moods that are very un-Cinderella-like. You have them; I have them. We need help with them.

Almost every day I talk to a woman who is emotionally distraught (sometimes, it's me). Just as men desire sexual release, women want *emotional release*. Remember, most men don't get as much sexual release as they would like. Of course, you know what is coming next: most women don't get as much *emotional release* as they would like.

It is easy for women to think, "Men need to zip it up and get control of themselves" as far as corralling their sexual natures. In fact, we're often weary with their abundant desire and lack of self-control. But alas, men feel the same way about our emotional natures.

Yesterday I met with a girl who had a miscarriage. Nothing is more painful for a woman than to be infertile for years, conceive, and then miscarry. My heart went out to her. Now her marriage is having issues. It's so classic. This woman is even *more* in need of emotional release and at the same time, her neediness is annoying her husband. If only we could understand how our spouses feel! This young wife was mad at her husband for not being there for her during this traumatic time and simultaneously, he felt pulled on because she couldn't talk about anything else.

Another precious girl was talking to me in church and her husband came up. She turned to him and said, "I am sharing my prayer requests with Julie." The husband laughed and said, "Well, she'd better get a legal pad." It was harmless, but still, the husband was communicating that her emotional nature was extensive.

Men often don't understand our desire to have emotional release. What can we do? Try to answer before you read on. It's week 21. You should have some pretty good ideas.

First, we give husbands a break for not understanding us. They come into the marriage untrained and it is our job to gently, over time, teach them how we feel and what we want. We are not mad at his mother (she tried!) but realize that God gave the wife the ability to break down the shield that is over a man's heart. We accept the responsibility that it is the wife that is responsible for this training.

Second, we use—ta-dah— word pictures! They are amazing and forceful (this is how Jesus taught!). Explaining to a man that your desire for emotional release is *comparable to his desire for sexual release* will open up his closed mind. Analogies are powerful things, friends. (For review with word pictures, reread chapter 13 in *Wife School, How to Explain Anything to Your Husband*).

Third, we accept that men can't see the color Pateen in the rainbow. Therefore we know it will take 50 to 100 times to explain this to them. We submit to perseverance without anger.

Fourth, we use other acceptable means to handle our emotional turmoil. Physical exercise is remarkable. Talking and praying with friends is healing and releasing. Music is powerful to help release emotional tension. For a double whammy, combine two of those: walk with friends, walk with great music, or walk and pray. Legitimate means to help us with our emotional release *abound.*

I was in a mild funk yesterday morning but got myself to the gym. I cranked up a Christian station that I love on Pandora and thirty heart-pounding minutes later, I left with 75% less turmoil.

Women, you will have emotional drama. Yes, I know you want your husband to absorb your emotional turmoil, but get a hold of yourself. Husbands do not like absorbing too much emotional turmoil and therefore, you have to corral your craziness.

If you struggle with being easily upset, then it is imperative for you to keep yourself in a straight and narrow lane. By that, I mean regular sleep, healthy (non-sugary, non-refined) food, daily exercise, a huge intake of

Scripture, much prayer, time to debrief and connect with other Christ-following women, reading and adding to your Turquoise Journal lists, and reading inspirational literature. You are not powerless. God has given you *many avenues* to help you control your high-strung emotional nature.

One more tip: Make a list of all the people that you would not want to trade places with, i.e., people who have it worse than you. For example, I saw a precious woman in the gym that I know has a serious disease; I had dinner with a woman who is addicted to prescription drugs; I chatted with a woman whose needy husband would be extremely difficult to live with. I am not saying that you are happy these people have problems. Of course, pray for them. But I am saying that their hard circumstances should make you grateful you don't have to deal with *those* problems. This list can make you grateful very fast. Abundant gratefulness is the *key* to happiness.

To summarize, you are responsible for growing a heart that is filled with the Lord and that thinks Philippians 4:8 thoughts. I have seen God change even the whiniest, most critical, headstrong women (like me!) so I'm pretty sure He can change you.

DAY 5
If You Are Still Often Getting Upset with Your Husband

It's pretty normal to get upset with your husband. We women have a ridiculously high standard for what we want and expect from our husbands. Even something small, such as a husband with bad breath, can send us into Crazytown.

One woman recently told me that her husband was complaining to her that their sex life was not exciting enough. Another woman told me that her husband was still not healed from his first marriage which was twenty years ago. A third woman told me that her husband just doesn't understand her and the kids. The list of reasons that women are upset with their husbands goes on and on.

When you hear yourself say, "Wow, that annoys me about him," just remember that it is *a plague and curse of women* to be annoyed with their husbands and their imperfections. Somehow, someway, most men are usually able to overlook our weaknesses (as long as there's not too much emotional turmoil and there is enough sex). But their weaknesses hit us right between the eyes.

It's the plight of women to be unsatisfied with her husband. Contentiousness is in our DNA. I keep writing about it because until we see this in ourselves, we will keep thinking that *our husbands are losers* and their dispositions are the problem instead of seeing that *we are the ones* who are hard to live with.

Men have a crazy problem with their sex drive but we have a crazy problem with our contentiousness *which causes our constant disappointment with our husbands.* Examples of women being disappointed are when your husband doesn't understand your love for your family of origin, when your husband doesn't praise or appreciate you, when your husband complains about your provisions (such as the food), when your husband does not pour enough into the family, or when your husband perks up for sex but then is a bump on a log the rest of the time. Yes, all of these things upset us, but this is *normal marriage*. Your husband has many areas you want to change and that upsets you. Yes, you get to address one thing at a time, but slowly, slowly, slowly.

I've been asking my husband for something for about three years. Not three months, not three weeks, but three years. This week, he came to me and told me that God has given him a plan for the thing I've been asking for! But right on the heels of my husband giving me such a great gift, he did a couple of small things that I didn't like and *I got annoyed*. I thought to myself, I'm like every woman in that it's *never quite enough*. I want perfection from him. That's the contentiousness in my sin nature. Prayer is the only answer for this.

David and I are normal in that we still confront issues in which we disagree. At dinner in a restaurant last night, he gave me his perspective on something in our family and I disagreed. On the way home though, I said, "I want you to know that I realize that ultimately, you will make the final decision in this area and *I will not fight you on it*. I appreciate you listening to my input, though." After watching the destruction of many marriages because the wife insists on *leading instead of following*, I am still learning to hand my husband the scepter. Knowing that it is God's will for your husband to be the head of the home will help your family more than most anything.

Here's one tip to help you when your contentiousness rises up or when his BSA (behavior/speech/attitude) upsets you. Ready? Remember the 2 day rule? (Week 15, Day 5). If you can be quiet, pray over it for 2 days, get some rest, pray again, the heavens will open up and you will have a better handle on how to talk to him. "Death and life are in the power of the tongue" so hold yours until you can get God's perspective. This action alone changes marriages.

I know your husband has weaknesses. I know he is a sinner. He's breathing, isn't he? You have weaknesses, too. (Have you ever deeply thought about what your husband has to endure because of *your* weakness set?) If you can see that *this thinking* (that your husband never measures up) is normal for women—and if you can lay down your contentious, condescending, critical spirit—then your marriage and home will skyrocket in harmony. It is not his weakness set that is as much the problem as it is *your contentiousness*.

I've been living and breathing *Wife School* principles for around 35 years. I still mess up. I still want perfection from my husband. I still have to stay in prayer, in the Word, and have community with godly, prayerful women so I can get back on the narrow path. The sin nature will always live in us while we are on earth.

I remember reading once that life can never be solved or conquered, it can only be managed. The same is true for marriage. It will never be easy, smooth, and perfect. We learn to understand marriage, learn skills for managing it, and then work on the real problem: our contentious, rebellious hearts.

Proverbs 21:9 and Proverbs 25:24 are identical: "Better to live on a corner of the roof than share a house with a quarrelsome wife." Proverbs 21:19 *also* restates this thought, too: "Better to live in a desert than with a quarrelsome and nagging wife."

Okay, Solomon. *Message received.*

One More Thought

There are so many pleasures in life: the pleasure of seeing, the pleasure of hearing, the pleasure of smelling, the pleasure of laughter, the pleasure of thinking, of enjoying people we love, of sunlight, of a walk, of a great conversation, of a hot bath, an apple, an interesting book, a nap, a good cup of coffee, your baby's face…so many joys abound. Find places of joy and savor them. God has dropped many pleasures and delights into your lap. Enjoy them and be thankful. Focus on all you do have, *not on what you don't have.*

Prayer

God,

There are so many weaknesses and sins in my life. But at the foundation of all my sins is the sin of *neglect* in praying and in spending time with You in Your Word.

If I neglect Your word, how can I know what You want me to do? If I neglect prayer, I won't be convicted of sin. If I neglect these disciplines, I won't understand how You want me to think and act.

Trying to live spiritually without Your Word and prayer is analogous to trying to live physically without food and water. You, the Creator of the Universe, have given me an opportunity to know You. How ridiculous to try to live life well and not schedule precious time where I can linger.

So many of my problems are from my lack of discipline in spending time with You. My worry and fretting is because I don't allow You to give me the Peace that passes understanding. My annoyance and discouragement are because I don't allow You to give me Your perspective on how trials have silver linings. My influence with others is limited—and even negative—because I am filled with myself instead of You.

Help me form the daily habit of spending time getting to know Your Word and time listening to Your still small voice. May this habit be as important to me as my daily food.

In Jesus name,

Amen.

Assignments and Group Discussion Questions

1. If you are married to a man who has an ex-wife or children from a prior marriage, what were your thoughts about this section?

2. How well do you handle your husband's not-so-great ideas?

3. Do you take personal responsibility for your life or are you a blamer?

4. Would you say you are a woman with a non-Cinderella-deposition?

5. Do you still regularly and easily get upset with your husband? How has your thinking been changed toward your husband in the last six months?

WEEK 22

Loneliness, Church, Impact on Children...and More

Contents

Day 1: Struggling with Loneliness
Day 2: A Very Important Sentence to Frequently Say to Your Husband
Day 3: The Importance of Church in Your Family
Day 4: The Impact You Have on Your Children and Grandchildren
Day 5: Spend Time to Learn and Grow

After 22 weeks of *Wife School,* you are now a Marriage Champion. You have paid the price to study, practice, and then try again after failure (right?) Now your husband has turned toward you with an openness that you could never have even imagined (not perfect, but hugely improved).

I want to warn you though that the *normal inclination* of women is to *revert to their former selves*. The best way to cement any new thinking is to *teach it.* After you have gone through the lessons the first time, gather a few women and take them through the material for a second run. Your depth of understanding will increase exponentially. With marriage being the *single most important* relationship in your life, and with good relationships *predicting the majority of your happiness,* why would you not?

DAY 1
Struggling With Loneliness

For years, I have been fascinated by the craving women have for intimacy. Because women do not get enough intimacy, they subsequently feel lonely. Women long to be known in the deepest part of their beings and then, to be loved. It was years before I understood this craving women had, and even longer for me to recognize it in myself. We will discuss several legitimate sources of obtaining intimacy in this section which will hopefully be helpful to those of you who struggle with loneliness.

The number one place where women want intimacy is from (no surprise) her husband. And honestly, deep closeness and friendship in a marriage is extremely satisfying. But this often takes years to grow. I cannot tell you how often I hear, "My husband doesn't get me" or "I don't feel loved by or cared for by my husband." You are now working on growing your intimacy with your husband. But as we've said a hundred times, this takes time. The magic word is persevere. Some husbands can be taught to listen deeply early in the marriage and some husbands learn over years. However, I have never seen a husband who was given the 8 A's, who was hugely respected, and who was patiently taught "what the wife wanted and needed" who didn't eventually get it. I'm sure there are some, but I have never seen them.

The second source of intimacy in which most women draw is from the women in her family. For example, two of my best friends each have multiple sisters, multiple adult daughters, multiple sisters-in-law, and great relationships with their mother. Another friend, Mindy, told me how her mother was her best friend, and her eyes got moist as she explained how her sweet mother is now waiting on her in heaven. If you have women in your family with whom you are close, then rejoice, because this is a gift from God to help meet your intimacy needs. I have noticed that often, these women have less of a need to pull on their husbands because so many of their needs are met by other women in their family.

A side note: A few women have brothers that help fulfill their intimacy needs, but this is not nearly as common as female family members. Also, a very few women (very few, haha) claim their mother-in-law is a source of intimacy.

Another and not-surprising source of intimacy is of course, close friends. How refreshing to take off your mask and let it tumble out, just like it feels! Friends are one of the best gifts on earth. Treat yours well. Bury the mistakes of your friends in the cemetery in your back yard and focus on how you love and give to your friends, not on how you're loved and given to.

Another source of intimacy can be from an older woman who agrees to mentor you. These older women are often happy to listen to you and care for you. And actually, you can receive intimacy by mentoring a younger woman. Anyone who is "younger than you and behind you" (college? high school?) is a great person to pour into. You will be surprised how satisfying giving to a younger woman is and how many of your intimacy needs are met in these relationships.

But even with all of those great sources of intimacy mentioned above, God never planned for any of us to get all our intimacy needs met. Instead, He wants to be the Friend that sticks closer than a brother (Proverbs 18:24). We are fully known by Him and accepted in the Beloved. We are to get our most important intimacy needs met in our relationship with God! Then when we are full of that relationship, we are able to be givers, not primarily takers, in our relationships with people. Isaiah 41:10 says, "Fear not, for I am with you; be not dismayed, for I am your God; I will strengthen you, I will help you, I will uphold you with my righteous right hand." Once you find deep intimacy with God, you will quit needing so much intimacy from humans. (You will still need huge doses, but bathtub portions, not swimming pool portions.)

Go to openbible.info and click on Topical Bible tab. Then enter *loneliness* in the search bar for a fantastic list of Bible verses on loneliness and the incredible promises that God has for us.

My husband is my closest human friend and I'm sure that is either true for you or your goal. But know that a woman's friendships are *incredibly helpful and necessary* to keep the husband from having to carry the intimacy load *all by himself*.

Loneliness is a serious condition. If you are struggling with relationships, friendships, and intimacy, just know that you reap what you sow. If you want to know what you've been sowing, look around at what you are *currently reaping*. If you listen well, if you are deeply interested in others, if you are loyal, trustworthy, dependable, generous, sensitive, and honest, you will find deep satisfaction in relationships. Again, failure in the past does not predict failure in the future because humans can change. It is hard to admit that maybe your problems with friendships are your own fault. But actually, *taking the blame* is a great place to get turned around. Start where you are and build some deep relationships by focusing on *how you give and love*, not on how you're given to and loved.

DAY 2
A Very Important Sentence to Frequently Say to Your Husband

In 1970, a movie came out that everyone talked about. It was *Love Story* with Ali MacGraw and Ryan O'Neal (I was in the ninth grade and most of you weren't born). There's a line from this movie that became famous and was engraved on posters, coffee cups, etc. This line, said by Ali MacGraw as she was sobbing on the steps was, "Love means never having to say you're sorry."

Excuse me, Ladies, but that is cow manure. Love is saying you are sorry all the time! Not only should you say you are sorry, you should say, "I was *wrong*. Will you please *forgive* me?"

I don't know about you, but I can't stand it when someone says to me, "I'm sorry about that…but…" and then they go on to tell me why they were not really wrong.

No one likes to be wrong. Saying I'm sorry is very difficult. But a really good sentence to add is, "Will you please forgive me?" It's ridiculously hard to say, I agree. But it forces the other person to decide if they are truly going to forgive you or not. I can barely squeak it out but I am always glad I did. Relationships are dirty and stinky, and they need the cleansing waters of asking each other for forgiveness.

Do you need to ask your husband for forgiveness for something? Get caught up. Don't let there be anything between you for which you have never sought his forgiveness.

Last night I said a mean thing to one of my sons. Yes, mean. And I didn't even think about it until I had my quiet time this morning and the Holy Spirit pricked (kicked) me. What's worse about this situation is that the thing I criticized him over upset me so much *because it is something I struggle with*! (You spot it, you got it.) When I asked forgiveness this morning from this son, do you think he said, "Sure, Mom, it's fine"? Heavens, no. He went on to tell me how bad it was, blah, blah, blah. I had to keep eating mud, saying, "Yes, you're right. That was wrong of me."

Friends, humble yourself and go to everyone you have offended (start with your husband and children) and ask forgiveness for your mean, critical, judgmental, insensitive, arrogant, and rude remarks. It's not fun. But doing relationships well means a lot of non-fun things. As you know, life includes a lot of non-fun things.

Maybe you need to ask your husband for forgiveness for not considering his opinion in the past, for making decisions without consulting him, or for not being sensitive to his leadership. Wherever you have sinned against him, ask for forgiveness.

When you mess up again (which, of course, you will), ask again. Keep a clean slate with all of your close relationships.

This is huge stuff, ladies. Asking for forgiveness may be the just the thing you need to do to un-block some clog from the past.

DAY 3
The Importance of Church in Your Family

Today I want to discuss the importance of the Church and her influence on your marriage and family. I do not pretend that this is a spiritual treatise on the doctrine of the universal Church. These thoughts are simply to enrich your thinking in the area of the church's importance to your marriage and to your family.

Of course it is easy to see why many people are burnt out on church. I believe the problem is in expectations. You have probably heard the quote, "The church is not a museum of saints; it's a hospital for sinners." If you realize that you are a porcupine, that every other church member is a porcupine, *and we are all going to prick each other*, then we can begin to quit being offended so easily and instead, forgive each other.

The Church is God's idea and although it is far from perfect, it is the best we have. Don't give up on church. Instead of looking at the leaders and the members and seeing what is wrong with them, decide to be a sunrise in the lives of others at your church. Decide that you will be a woman of prayer, a woman under authority to her husband, a woman of hospitality, a women who refuses to engage in slander, and a woman who is eager to serve with her gifts. The church will never be rid of the lukewarm, the devious, and the chronic complainers. But *you* can be rid of that. You can show up every Sunday morning and look for what's right, for how you can contribute, and come with a heart that is grateful for the good that is there.

In *Wife School*, we've learned to list the good in our husbands and overlook his weaknesses. We need to do that to our churches. If you look for weaknesses in your church, you will find them. If you look for strengths, then that is what you will find.

Prayerfully, find a Bible-based church where you and your husband can follow the pastor and put down a stake. Be ready for problems because they *will* come. If you determine that your attitude is "How do I give and love" versus "What is here for me?", then blessings will appear everywhere at your church. 1 Peter 4:10 says, "Each of you should use whatever gift you have received to serve others, as faithful stewards of God's grace in its various forms."

Who is the most important person to a man? It's his bride. The Church is the bride of Christ. God loves the church. And He wants us to meet regularly with other Christ-followers ("not giving up meeting together, as some are in the habit of doing, but encouraging one another" Hebrews 10:25). Not being involved in church is not really an option if you follow Christ. God's will is that we are to be actively involved with other believers, meeting together for encouragement and prayer.

I know there will be things at your church you don't like. Overlook things you disagree with, if you can. At my church, there has been a lot of discussion as to whether Sunday School should be age-segregated or if Sunday School should include all seasons of life in each class. It is fine to have an opinion, but if the pastor and the elders want to try something new, let them. Most issues are not a hill to die on. Save your barking for extremes, like moral violations. Come to encourage, not complain.

If you are struggling with your church, maybe you could write a list of things you like and appreciate about your church in your Turquoise Journal and bathe your mind with that. I have found that most of us find whatever we are looking for. Lists of positive attributes about your church will greatly grow your affection for it.

Don't give up on the church, no matter how hard it gets. It is God's idea and it is a path of blessing. The Church is the lone voice, crying in the wilderness of what is True North. It is a solo voice in the world, pointing to the only path of eternal life. Only there will you find those that have also been called out of darkness. Make church a priority for your family.

Church will never be perfect. But with a renewed mindset of how you can contribute (versus focusing on what is annoying you), church will be one of the greatest blessings to your marriage and family. *Community* is absolutely necessary to grow a healthy marriage and family, and church is the divine choice for community.

Just because you've had failure in the past in the area of church doesn't mean *you will have failure in the future.* Shake yourself off, talk to the Lord and your husband about church, and jump in again.

"Love the brotherhood of believers" (1 Peter 2:12).

DAY 4
The Impact You Have on Your Children and Grandchildren

A couple weeks ago I had the opportunity to spend time with a family of three generations. There were two grandmothers (80's and 90's), the next generation (in their 50's-60's), and then the third generation (in their 30's and 20's—no fourth generation yet). I've been around these people for years in social settings where we have had small chit chat. But because of the nature of this celebratory event, the family was giving speeches and telling stories about the family's past. Witnessing this family interact was fascinating to me. Repeatedly, the center of their stories was "what the Lord was doing." Not just one person, but the entire family's perspective was "how God was moving in our lives during such-and-such." It was "the Lord" did this, and then "the Lord" did that. The 30-year-old's were thanking the 90-year-old's for living for Christ and for leaving a godly example.

Every family has a flavor, much like strawberry or blueberry, only the flavor is based on "what is most important to us." For example, what is most important to this family is *the Lord* and under that, *family*. If you were there listening to their stories, you would hear the third most important element to these people's lives, which was *church*. These are not rich, influential people. They are ordinary people. But I doubt God thinks they are ordinary.

What you truly value will show up in your kids. You pass down what you value, like you pass down your green eyes. If what you truly value is how you look and what kind of house you live in, then most likely, that value will be in your children. If you value being famous, being first, being the best, being rich, being the best on the team, then your children will most likely value that too. I just want you to realize that *you cannot live outside the rules of sowing and reaping.* Whatever is in your heart, you will give to the next generation. If you value grandparents, then your children will. If you value prayer, your children will. If you value looking ten years younger, then your children will. If you value the praise of man, so will your kids. Many people think that they can keep their pet sins deep in their heart and no one will know. *Friend, God is NOT mocked.* You will reap what you sow. You cannot keep a heart that secretly despises the success of others and then hope your children will be humble and loving.

Our hearts are the problem. *We are rebellious, pleasure-loving, ego-crazy human beings that don't want to be told what to do.* This is a plea to become disciplined in three of the safeguards that God has given us to fight our sinful nature: (1) soaking in the Word (the gold nuggets are buried, you have to dig to find them), (2) becoming addicted to prayer (confession is where the Spirit of God changes us), and (3) finding a way to become immersed in community in the Church (not church attendance, but deep relationships where you pray for, rejoice with, and share burdens with one another). The Enemy prowls around and seeks to devour you. Have safeguards as protective mechanisms from your fleshly desires.

One more comment that is incredibly important concerning who you will become and who your children will become: You will never outgrow the spiritual maturity of the people you have coffee with. If you choose to hang around people who focus on restaurants, their tennis game, and exotic vacations (instead of growing in Christ, loving and serving others, and finding ways to contribute), you will never grow into the fullness of Christ. We become like the people we hang around. You will never live outside this truth.

Wife, there is a tendency to drift away (Hebrews 2:1-4). Christians don't jump from loving the Lord with all their hearts to apostasy and heinous sin. *They drift there.* Put anchors and safeguards firmly in your life so it doesn't happen to you.

DAY 5
Spend Time to Learn and Grow

There are so many resources to help you think biblically. The main issue is, *when* will you listen to sermons and podcasts? When will you read? Your time is already maxed out, I understand.

Two young men I incredibly admire, Stephen and Trent, both told me that they use their exercise time at the gym to listen to sermons and podcasts. When I heard this, I had already been working out for years, but listening to music. When they told me their habit, I switched to their habit. That was over a year ago, and I cannot tell you what I've learned in the last year! I've been studying apologetics for the last two years, and in the last year, I've listened to hours of talks, debates, lectures, etc. about the evidence for the existence of God, the (fallacious) arguments of the New Atheists, the reliability of the New Testament documents, the scientific evidence for a young earth, and on and on and on.

Pick something productive you want to know about, and listen to podcasts while walking, working out, driving, or even cooking. Don't waste your precious short time on earth with trash TV and movies. How can you be an ambassador if you aren't knowledgeable? (If you have teens, there is especially no time to waste. When they leave your home, the atheist worldview will descend upon them with fervor. Prepare them.)

One of my favorite resources is TheBibleProject.com. It is a masterfully done website with free animated videos to help you understand the Bible.

Another wonderful resource is the Bible commentary at EnduringWord.com. I use this website almost every time I study the Bible. David Guzik, the author, sites classic commentators (like Spurgeon) as he discusses Bible passages.

If you go to YouTube.com, you can search for lectures on the evidence for God, on the evidence disputing evolution, etc. and for sermons galore. Don't fill your mind with junk. Redeem the time. "All people are like grass, and all their glory is like the flowers of the field; the grass withers and the flowers fall, but the word of the Lord endures forever" (1 Peter 1: 24-25). Use your time wisely, and fill it with God's truth.

Prayer

Dear Father,

We live lives of anxiety. Our prayerlessness causes us much grief. Please give us the faith to understand the verse, "If you, then, though you are evil, know how to give good gifts to your children, how much more will your Father in heaven give good gifts to those who ask him." (Matthew 7:11)

May we spend enough time in prayer that our anxious hearts no longer condemn us. May we hear Your voice and be assured that indeed, we are forgiven. Remind us that not only will You give us good gifts, but that You are exceedingly, abundantly able to perform beyond what we ask or think (Ephesians 3:20). May we know that death has been swallowed up in victory and we no longer have to fear. Teach us, O God, to rest in You.

In Jesus name,

Amen

Assignments and Group Discussion Questions

1. Do you struggle with loneliness? What are your best sources of intimacy?

2. How are you at saying you are wrong and in asking for forgiveness?

3. Is church an important aspect of your marriage? Do you have a giver or taker mentality about your church? Are you a complainer or an encourager?

4. What is the flavor of your family? What is most important to you and your husband?

Epilogue

Your huge problem is my huge problem, and that is our tendency to go our own way, to do what we want, instead seeking the face of God. This morning as I read Psalm 33 in my devotional time, I was reminded that "He gathers the waters of the seas into jars" (v. 7) and that "No king is saved by the size of his army" (v. 16). We must seek the One who is powerful and who is in control.

You will always want to rule your husband, but as you know, that is not your assignment. Your assignment is to be a godly influencer, with a gentle and quiet spirit (1 Peter 3). The wise woman builds her house, and she does it with God's methods. *Lecturing and scolding have never made a man want to do anything but hide.*

When you get pushed into a corner in your marriage and don't know what to do, there is one verse that will help guide you. It is Proverbs 31:12: "She brings him good, not harm, all the days of her life." Look to God and ask Him how to bring your husband good. "Indeed, He who watches over Israel will neither slumber nor sleep." Bring your husband goodness, as God is watching.

Blessings to you and the generations that come from you,

Julie Gordon
April 2021

I love hearing from readers. You can write me at JulieNGordon2012@gmail.com

TURQUOISE JOURNAL LISTS

LIST 1
Strengths, Gifts, and Qualities I Admire in My Husband

LIST 2
Things Other Husbands Do Wrong

LIST 3
Unmet Expectations I Have of My Husband

I recommend you use code in this list so that other people can't read it if they find this study guide. After you write this list in code, I suggest you offer it to the Lord. We can legitimately expect a living (which is food and clothing) and faithfulness from our husbands. Please give up other expectations at this time. In time, you will learn to ask for what you need and want.

LIST 4
Nice Things My Husband Says or Does

LIST 5
Things My Husband Might Find Difficult to Accept in Me

Wife School Study Guide

LIST 6
100 Things I Appreciate about My Husband

1.
2.
3.
4.
5.
6.
7.
8.
9.
10.
11.
12.
13.
14.
15.
16.
17.
18.
19.

20.
21.
22.
23.
24.
25.
26.
27.
28.
29.
30.
31.
32.
33.
34.
35.
36.
37.
38.
39.
40.

Wife School Study Guide

41.
42.
43.
44.
45.
46.
47.
48.
49.
50.
51.
52.
53.
54.
55.
56.
57.
58.
59.
60.
61.

TURQUOISE JOURNAL LISTS

62.
63.
64.
65.
66.
67.
68.
69.
70.
71.
72.
73.
74.
75.
76.
77.
78.
79.
80.
81.
82.

83.

84.

85.

86.

87.

88.

89.

90.

91.

92.

93.

94.

95.

96.

97.

98.

99.

100.

LIST 7
Activities My Husband and I Might Enjoy Together

LIST 8
My 8 Top Concerns/When to Use My Appeal Coupons

1.
2.
3.
4.
5.
6.
7.
8.

You can write Julie at JulieNGordon2012@gmail.com.
She loves to hear from readers!

NOTES

NOTES

NOTES

NOTES

Made in the USA
Monee, IL
11 March 2024

54843312R00155